THE LIBERATION OF THE NAZI CONCENTRATION CAMPS 1945

For sale by the Superintendent of Documents, U.S. Government Printing Office
Washington, D.C. 20402

THE LIBERATION OF THE NAZI CONCENTRATION CAMPS 1945

EYEWITNESS ACCOUNTS OF THE LIBERATORS

EDITED BY
BREWSTER CHAMBERLIN
MARCIA FELDMAN

WITH AN INTRODUCTION BY
ROBERT H. ABZUG

UNITED STATES HOLOCAUST
MEMORIAL COUNCIL
WASHINGTON, D.C. 1987

Printed in the
United States of America
by the
Government Printing Office,
Washington, D.C.
for the
United States
Holocaust Memorial Council
Washington, D.C.

Library of Congress
Card Catalog
No. LC 86-050178
ISBN 0-9616518-0-6

CONTENTS

NOTE: Photographs appear between pages 116 and 117.

FOREWORD

In 1980 the United States Congress voted unanimously to establish the United States Holocaust Memorial Council and charged it with the task of planning and providing appropriate ways to remember and commemorate the victims of the Holocaust and the millions of others who were murdered by the Nazis.

The President of the United States appointed the esteemed author, Professor Elie Wiesel, to serve as Chairman of this Council and lead it in fulfilling its mandate.

One of the first tasks the Council undertook was to establish the historic veracity of the atrocities committed by the Nazis and their collaborators. To accomplish this most effectively, the Council decided to record the eyewitness accounts of those who were the first to encounter Hitler's factories of death—the liberators of the concentration camps.

As Chairman of the Committee on International Relations for the United States Holocaust Memorial Council, I was assigned the tasks of organizing and coordinating the first International Liberators Conference in Washington, D.C.

In October 1981, combatants from 14 nations, who at the time of the Second World War had joined forces to put an end to Nazi tyranny, gathered in Washington for a unique reunion. They came from various parts of the world and they represented governments of different political philosophies. They were citizens of nations who often opposed one another; but, regardless of this fact, all those who gathered had one common denominator: they all were members of military units that first crashed the gates of the Nazi concentration camps.

They came to Washington upon the invitation of the State Department and through the initiative of the United States Holocaust Memorial Council to give personal testimony. They came to bear witness.

For two days, eyewitness after eyewitness recounted the horrible sights they discovered as they entered the concentration camps. All of them continually and repeatedly recounted stories of horror and brutality that stagger the imagination. All of them testified—American officers and soldiers, Russian generals, Polish combatants, Canadian doctors and nurses, Danes, Yugoslavs, Czechs, and officers of the Jewish Brigade—all recalled those first few moments. Many of them broke down as they bore witness.

They were battle-weary veterans of fierce military campaigns—the Normandy Invasion, the Battle of the Bulge, Stalingrad, and Kursk—soldiers who were hardened in battle and thought they had seen everything, and were beyond shock. Then they entered man's worst Hell.

Some had quietly told friends and relatives what they saw there. They always searched for words to describe their impressions. Others, knowing the difficulty of the task, kept the witness in silence, refusing to speak the unspeakable, unable to convey what they saw.

In the audience and among the participants were those they had met once before—the survivors whom they liberated—who now joined them in testifying to what they had experienced and to what liberation meant to them.

In this volume the United States Holocaust Memorial Council has gathered those eyewitness accounts and testimonies. In doing so, we continue to serve truth and memory and continue to bear witness both for the sake of the dead and for the sake of the living. We present these testimonies and accounts for future generations as a contribution to historical knowledge and understanding.

It is a rare, historic privilege that we bring their testimony to you.

Miles Lerman
Conference Coordinator
Chairman, Committee on International Relations

PREFACE

The great majority of the participants in the International Liberators Conference are not trained historians or scholars in other academic disciplines; they depended for the most part upon their memories of events 40 or so years earlier. These memories remained fresh in their minds for understandable reasons.

Thus, with few exceptions, this volume is not intended to be a work of academic scholarship. Rather the testimonies are a way of bearing witness by those who found themselves variously involved in the horrors of the Holocaust and the physical, if not emotional or mental, release of the liberation.

The value of these testimonies lies both in the information they contain and the first-hand accounts they provide. There is no substitute for such immediacy in describing the "climate" or "feeling" of a historical period.

Whenever possible, the editors checked statements to ensure factual accuracy. Discrepancies with the historical record as well as validation of questions asked by the participants are indicated in the Notes. Items and persons not identified in the text or in the Notes are usually included in the Glossary of Terms, Names, and Camps printed at the end of the volume.

Given the extensive number of non-English words and phrases in the text, the editors decided not to italicize them in order to keep the pages as aesthetically "clean" as possible and not unduly distract the reader.

These papers are not strictly speaking verbatim transcriptions of the presentations at the Conference. The editors have made adjustments in the text where the requirements of syntax and clarity called for them. However, every attempt has been made to retain the spontaneity of the spoken word. Where the emotional and psychic impact of statements depend upon ungrammatical constructions, these have also been retained.

The editors apologize in advance for any misspelling of people's names. It was not always possible to find more than a phonetic spelling from the tape recordings of the proceedings.

Wherever possible the editors checked the transcription of the tapes against notes or texts provided by the speaker at the time of the conference. Where the spoken presentation departed from the prepared text, in those few cases where such a text existed, the editors integrated the two with a view toward preserving the spontaneity of the former and the detail of the latter.

The editors request the understanding of those participants who did not see their texts for review prior to publication in this volume. The editors have made the greatest effort to be true to both the spirit and the letter of the often highly emotional and moving presentations.

It is important to note that the opinions expressed by individuals in this volume do not necessarily reflect the opinions and policies of the United States Holocaust Memorial Council or the Government of the United States of America.

The editors are grateful for the scholarly assistance of Alan E. Steinweiss who prepared the Notes at the end of each chapter and the Glossary of Terms, Names, and Camps at the end of the book.

Finally, the editors would like to thank the following people for their assistance in preparing this book for publication: Terry Anderson, Rusty Austin, Dr. David Blumenthal, Wanda Cowans, Marian S. Craig, Lawrence Karr, Fay Kaufman Levy, Shirley Sirota Rosenberg, Angelene Terry, and Roberta J. Wasserman.

Marcia Feldman
Brewster Chamberlin

INTRODUCTION

BY ROBERT H. ABZUG

Even amidst the ceremonial richness of its opening session—a serenade from the US army band, a colorful flag posting for foreign delegations, and personal greetings from Secretary of State Haig—the International Liberators Conference rooted itself in a harrowing and wondrous juxtaposition of past and present. "Little did I dream in the dark days when my people were being annihilated," confessed Miles Lerman as he opened the gathering he had organized, "that some day I would stand in the assembly hall of the State Department of the United States of America, the symbol of freedom and hope, and fulfill the most fervent wish of those who perished—a wish to be remembered." The Nazis had murdered 35 members of Lerman's family at Belzec. He escaped and fought as a partisan in the forests of Poland. Returning home in triumph atop a Russian tank, Lerman discovered that his town's 16,000 Jews were gone. He and 11 other survivors searched in vain for those who would never come home. Close to 40 years later, Lerman and other Holocaust survivors had joined with their liberators to remember.

Elie Wiesel, renowned writer and Chairman of the United States Holocaust Memorial Council that sponsored the conference, welcomed the liberators by recalling his first encounter with them. Liberated at Buchenwald after having seen his family murdered at Auschwitz, Wiesel was at that moment of freedom a physical and mental ghost of his former self, a barely moving body squeezed between others on a bare shelf. "We were strangers to one another," he told them. "We might as well have descended from different planets." Perhaps only those who were there knew the full truth of Wiesel's remark. Who else could imagine that these well-dressed and healthy individuals who sat together, who in the next two days would talk and eat and drink with each other as equal citizens of the world, had met once before as liberators and survivors, touching each other across a chasm of incomprehension, at the end of human history's most awful and senseless tragedy?

Say the word "liberation" and images come to mind of cheering crowds, uncorked champagne, soldiers smiling and waving and kissing pretty girls in endless parades—the zany celebrations of Paris, Rome, and countless villages across Europe. At Buchenwald, Dachau, Bergen-Belsen, and scores of other camps, recall instead the newsreels and photographs of grim-faced Allied soldiers surrounded by the last victims of the Holocaust: piles of corpses, dazed and gaunt skeletons of human beings, naked or barely clothed in the shreds of striped uniforms, but alive; barracks packed with the dead and dying, truly inhabitants of another world. Imagine the putrid odor of feces and rotting flesh, the silence of crushed lives, the bracing and then numbing confrontation with hells undreamt of by Dante. Some did cheer. Wiesel remembered the celebrating survivors, "pathetic in their futile attempts to touch you, to smile at you, to reassure you, to console you, and most of all to carry you in triumph on their frail shoulders." As one journalist at the conference described the applause of those at Mauthausen, "their hands were so emaciated, so much without flesh, that it sounded to me like seals clapping." Others, many others, were too weak to move.

"We might as well have descended from different planets," Wiesel told the assembled liberators and survivors, "and yet a link was created between us." Most of all, that link was a commitment to memory and truth, to reminding the world by personal witness that Auschwitz, Dachau, Buchenwald, and the other camps of the Holocaust universe once existed. For the survivors this had been a duty from the outset, a solemn pledge to those who had died and to those who would be born. As for the liberators, most had buried their memories; few of their friends or family wanted to hear about the horrors. They returned to the United States, Canada, Britain, France, Poland, the Soviet Union, and other lands to take up the everydayisms of civilian life. Only as the full dimensions of Nazi genocide emerged and as their own lives deepened with age did they come to understand the extraordinary significance of what they had witnessed. Who would tell this story when they were gone? Who else but the liberators and survivors could record as witnesses the tragedy of the Holocaust?

What these Allied soldiers had seen were the final scenes of a drama that had been unfolding for 12 years and which in the end took the lives of five to six million Jews, over 600,000 Gypsies, and another five million souls: Slavs and other peoples conscripted for slave labor, political opponents, and homosexuals or other so-called asocials deemed unfit to live. It had begun in 1933, when Adolf Hitler and his Nazi Party came to power promising to restore unity, prosperity, and national pride to a strife-ridden and morose Germany in the midst of severe economic depression.

The Nazis kept their promises, but at a terrible cost. They instituted totalitarian rule where there had been democracy, and envisioned a New Order based on "Aryan" racial superiority and rabid anti-Semitism. Some observers inside and outside of Germany thought Jew-baiting and murderous treatment of political enemies would subside once the Nazis consolidated their power. Such was not to be the case. By 1938, the new government had demeaned Jews with racial laws, stripped them of most of their legal rights and much of their property, and banned them from virtually every profession. What had once been a proud and prospering Jewish community became a badgered and broken ghost; thousands had emigrated and thousands more were attempting to leave. In November 1938 came what seemed the final blow—a night of vicious attacks on Jews, their homes, businesses, and synagogues. Kristallnacht convinced even the most naively optimistic Jews that Germany was no place to live. By this time, however, the western democracies had severely restricted immigration; most Jews still in Germany by 1939 were trapped.

Nor were Jews the Nazis' only racial target. Soon after Hitler's takeover, German anthropologists, supposedly engaging in legitimate scholarship, began to collect data on the Gypsies of Germany. They attempted to locate each and every member of this loosely connected group, keeping careful records for later use. Gypsies, traditionally a nomadic people and long the object of fear and derision, had no place in a racially pure Germany.

Political opposition within Germany, however, experienced the most immediate and violent attacks. From the day the Nazis took power, German Communists, Socialists, and others who defied the regime were killed, tortured, and imprisoned, many of them in a new kind of institution for Germany: the concentration camp. The Nazis created Dachau and numerous other camps in 1933 to house victims of political roundups, subjecting them to hard labor, torture, and "reeducation." By the late 30s, the government had expanded some of the old camps and built new facilities as part of a permanent system of concentration camps throughout the country, all under the administrative control of the SS, Heinrich Himmler's elite corps.

Dachau (near Munich), Buchenwald (near Weimar), Sachsenhausen (near Berlin), Flossenbürg (near the town of Floss in the eastern Bavarian Woods), Ravensbrück (near Berlin), and Mauthausen (near Linz, Austria)—these were the prewar concentration camps. At each locale, prisoners not only endured marginal living conditions and torture, but also something relatively new. The SS had discovered the profits possible in using their wards as slave labor, usually in construction, roadbuilding, or the quarrying of stone. Indeed, the SS built Flossenbürg and Mauthausen specifically to work quarries. Meanwhile, after the Austrian Anschluss and again after Kristallnacht, thousands of Jews were incarcerated in Buchenwald and Dachau. They and a growing Gypsy population in the camps signaled an important shift in the use of concentration and labor camps for "racial" enemies of the Reich.

The German invasion of Poland on September 1, 1939, which started World War II, opened vast new opportunities for the persecution of Jews and the exploitation of slaves. Poland was the center of traditional Jewish life in Europe. As Hitler's troops pushed brutally through Polish towns and cities, Jews became special targets. SS squads killed thousands of Jews in random actions and conscripted thousands more for slave labor battalions. Soon the Nazis also implemented a far-reaching scheme of deportation, removing Poles and Jews from provinces earmarked for racially pure Germans. The deportees were sent to the so-called General Government of southern Poland. Racial planners in Berlin ordered that Jews be concentrated in "ghettos" in principal towns and cities—Lodz, Warsaw, and others. The ghettos were crammed with a stream of new arrivals, sealed off from the non-Jewish community, and exploited for labor. Overcrowded and undersupplied with food, fuel, and other necessities, the ghettos became nightmares of hunger, disease, and death.

Ghettoization, extraordinarily cruel in its own right, turned out to be a crucial step on the road to still more ghastly actions taken in conjunction with the invasion of the Soviet Union. Hitler made it clear that not only should this be a Vernichtungskrieg against Russia, a war of annihilation, but that special efforts must be made to slaughter Jews. In the Spring of 1941, then, Nazi rhetoric calling for the extermination of the Jews became an awful reality. Separate armed squads, the Einsatzgruppen, accompanied the invasion army and had as their sole mission the murder of Jews, Gypsies, and political unreliables. In the end these special units slaughtered at least 1.4 million Jews and thousands of others. Those Jews who escaped death were ghettoized or exploited in slave labor camps along with Polish and Russian civilians and Russian prisoners of war.

Thus even before the name "Final Solution" (Endlösung) had been attached to the policy, the mass murder of European Jewry had begun. Yet the Nazis were not satisfied with the methods found to implement the destruction of the Jews. Ghettos had become administrative burdens for Berlin. Men in the special action units drank too much and in other ways suffered from their work. And such open methods of slaughter often caused problems with non-Jews in the area. Himmler and the SS searched for new ways of extermination. They tried mobile killing vans, which piped engine exhaust into the truck's sealed load section filled with human beings. A few of these units began to be used in the East in middle-to-late 1941. At Chelmno, in western Poland, SS personnel built a small but efficient killing center using a set of stationary vans. This simple and secret arrangement accounted for the murder of at least 340,000 persons, most of them Jews. Less than a dozen of those sent to Chelmno escaped death.

Meanwhile engineers and technicians competed to find more sophisticated methods of mass execution. They developed gas chambers with far greater capacity than vans, and adapted the pesticide Zyklon-B for "cleaner" and more efficient killing of human beings. With new technologies came new facilities. The killing center at Belzec opened in March 1942 with permanent gas chambers, though still using carbon monoxide. At this facility the SS murdered as many as 600,000 individuals. In May came Sobibor, whose gas claimed the lives of about a quarter of a million people. In July the Nazis constructed Treblinka, where they killed close to a million people, mostly Jews, in little more than a year. Also in 1942, Majdanek, just outside of Lublin, which had originally been constructed to house Soviet prisoners of war and various civilian prisoners, was converted into a killing center. The SS added Zyklon-B gas chambers to the existing facilities. Altogether about a quarter of a million persons perished at Majdanek.

Of all the extermination centers, however, none was more important than Auschwitz. Like Majdanek, the original camp at Auschwitz had been for slave labor and prisoners of war. Toward the end of 1941, however, the camp began to be fitted with gas chambers. By the following year and until its evacuation in January 1945, Auschwitz was the center of the Holocaust universe, where over four million persons met their death: Jews, Poles, Gypsies, and myriad others. Auschwitz was not just one camp, but a complex of sites used for various purposes. Buna, Monowitz, and the original Auschwitz camp provided slave labor for construction and industry. At Birkenau, the product was death.

Such mass murder was part of a developing grand scheme. In July 1941, Hermann Göring had ordered Reinhard Heydrich, a chief architect of SS policy toward the Jews, to create an "overall plan...for the execution of the intended final solution of the Jewish question." Heydrich, Eichmann, and a small group of various other SS and governmental officials met on January 20, 1942, to discuss the details of such a plan. This so-called Wannsee Conference, named for its location in the suburbs of Berlin, plotted the fate of Europe's 11 million Jews. They would be deported to the East, the able-bodied for hard labor and the rest for extermination. Thus, in 1942, the Nazis commenced roundups of Jews from all of occupied Europe. In the midst of a total war, when every conceivable resource should have been mustered for military use, the Nazi leadership diverted the manpower, transportation, and fuel necessary to pursue their mission of racial purification. They emptied the ghettos in the East and destroyed almost every Jewish community on the continent. Jews resisted when they could—in the ghettos, in the forests, and even in the camps. However, without support from the outside world, such revolts could not slow the pace of the slaughter. In the end between five and six million Jews perished.

This commitment to genocide also inspired the Nazis to harden their as-yet ambivalent policy toward Gypsies. They, too, were condemned to death as a people, murdered by special action units or deported to death and slave labor camps. In all, the Nazis killed over 600,000 of the more than two million Gypsies of Nazi-occupied Europe. These figures may even understate the losses of a people whose history and fate are just beginning to be understood.*

Even as the SS was creating a vast machinery for exterminating Jews and Gypsies, it was building a parallel system of camps for the massive use of slave labor. Millions of civilian conscripts from the conquered nations toiled in war industries and construction projects. Administered from offices in the major camps, hundreds of subcamps and temporary "Kommandos" exploited the subject peoples of the Reich. Food, clothing, ammunition, roads, motor vehicles, chemicals, and even the new V-1 and V-2 rockets—these were the products of slave labor. Living conditions for slaves varied from marginal to horrendous. Prisoner lore had it that Dachau and Buchenwald were the "mildest" and Mauthausen the cruelest (largely because of work in the quarry) of the camps; but disease, poor and insufficient food, overwork, and random torture were endemic to the entire system. Slave labor looked good only in the shadow of the gas chamber.

The Nazis had hoped to keep conditions in the camps, and most especially the killing centers, hidden from the German public and from the rest of the world. That is one reason why they chose relatively isolated regions of Poland in which to locate the death camps. No wonder also, then, as the fortunes of war turned in 1943 and the Red Army threatened from the East, the Nazis evacuated prisoners and destroyed what evidence they could. Chelmno, Sobibor, Belzec, and Treblinka were all leveled and, to the greatest de-

*I am indebted to Professor Ian Hancock of the University of Texas at Austin for these latest estimates of Gypsy losses and population.

gree possible, the camp sites restored to their former bucolic innocence. The Germans also formed special "Death Brigades" to reopen mass graves and destroy all traces of bodies.

Still, the Holocaust kingdom was too massive and time too short to destroy everything. As the Russians entered Poland, they encountered eerie relics of slaughter. At Majdanek they found abandoned gas chambers, crematoria, and mass graves. One structure at the camp offered silent but especially chilling testimony—a warehouse bursting with over 800,000 shoes of all varieties, salvaged by the Nazis from the feet of their victims. In January 1945, the Soviets overran Auschwitz; only 5,000 sick prisoners remained, the rest having been marched West in the brutal cold of winter.

Ironically, the Auschwitz death march and other evacuations of prisoners, undertaken in part to remove human evidence of the death camp system, ultimately helped create the scenes at the liberations of camps in Germany that convinced the world of Nazi genocide. Thousands of evacuees died miserable deaths on the journey, but thousands more, including many carrying typhus and other diseases, were almost literally dumped in makeshift compounds at Buchenwald, Dachau, and other camps that previously had maintained marginal order and sanitation. Especially in the first months of 1945, camp populations within Germany swelled; epidemic disease broke out; food and potable water supplies dwindled and in some cases were cut off. Even when communities near camps had food surpluses and medicine, rarely if ever were they used to aid prisoners. Worse still, the SS began to lead prisoners on death marches as American and British forces approached from the West. There were evacuations to nowhere, ones that usually ended in mass slaughter on the road or suffocation in freight cars. In some cases, SS units burned alive slave laborers in their barracks or in warehouses.

Nor was there time to hide these acts of madness or the anarchy of the camps. As British and American armies drove deep into Germany, they began to encounter refugees on the road, small work Kommandos, and other as yet undecipherable hints of what was to come. Then, on April 4, members of the American Fourth Armored Division overran Ohrdruf, a subcamp of Buchenwald. Once inside the gate, GIs confronted a group of fleshless corpses, each with a bullet hole through the back of its skull. A survivor then led the Americans to a shed, inside of which were stacked a pile of stiff yellowed corpses. These were the first stops on a seemingly unending tour of horrors. The dead, hidden or in the open, littered aimlessly on the ground or neatly stacked; dazed survivors with what one GI described as eyes that were "nothing but dark holes in their skull and face;" a few healthier prisoners who had the energy to weep for joy and to embrace their liberators; torture instruments; and a massive pyre of logs and bodies at the edge of the camp, the blackened forms of bodies still recognizable.

Generals Eisenhower, Bradley, and Patton visited Ohrdruf a week after its liberation. The camp had been left as found so that visitors could see for themselves what they might not otherwise believe. "The smell of death overwhelmed us even before we passed through the stockade," wrote Bradley five years later. "More than 3,200 naked, emaciated bodies had been flung into shallow graves. Others lay in the streets where they had fallen." Patton almost immediately became physically ill and slipped behind a barracks to vomit. Bradley and Eisenhower doggedly submitted themselves to the full tour, and left the camp angry and shaken. Ike ordered all soldiers in the area not in combat to see Ohrdruf. "We are told that the American soldier does not know what he is fighting for," he declared at the time. "Now, at least, he will know what he is fighting *against*." Soon after he also cabled London and Washington, urging both governments to send officials and newsmen to become unimpeachable witnesses to the atrocities.

Ohrdruf was a small operation. By the time the journalists and officials arrived in the war zone, it had been overshadowed by other discoveries: At Buchenwald, for instance, the crematorium and piles of dead waiting to be burned; ghastly momentoes of shrunken heads and lampshades of human skin found in SS offices and living quarters; and most of all, the "Kleines Lager," a makeshift quarter for thousands of dead and dying evacuees. At Bergen-Belsen, British soldiers took over what once had been a small compound for ransomable Jewish prisoners; evacuees from the East had transformed it into a morass of 60,000 or more prisoners, deprived of food or water and under siege by typhus. People were dying at the rate of 500 a day. The dead were so numerous—in the tens of thousands—that the liberators had to bulldoze the corpses into mass graves. At Dachau, American soldiers confronted 40 open railroad cars filled with corpses. It was as if fate had arranged these and similar scenes at countless camps and atrocity sites. The Nazis, so concerned with covering up their crimes in the East, had actually transported a remnant of the doomed to the West, just in time to create a ghastly representation of mass death for victorious American and British soldiers to discover. Journalists, photographers, and newsreel cameramen conveyed the news to the rest of the world on front pages and at local movie theaters.

The graphic record created at the liberations in April and May 1945, in fact, became something of a turning point in western culture's recognition of humankind's capacity for evil. Although the press had reported many of the basic facts of Nazi genocide as early as 1942 and covered such news as the Russian discoveries at Majdanek and Auschwitz, an air of abstraction, disbelief, and even doubt surrounded the stories. Whether due to suspicion that the news of millions murdered was simply wartime propaganda or to difficulty in literally imagining the extermination of entire peoples, the "Final Solution" and the camp system became only a partial reality in the minds of most until the liberations. Even for those who had fully believed wartime stories and had worked on behalf of rescue and relief efforts, the grim pictures from Dachau, Buchenwald, and Belsen portrayed an evil far beyond what they had been capable of imagining. These scenes did not, of course, depict the specific reality of the death camps. However, the unimaginable degradation of human beings evident at the camps in the Spring of 1945 brought all that seemed unbelievable about an Auschwitz or a Treblinka into the realm of possibility.

It was both to honor the participants and to rekindle the vivid sense of the Holocaust engendered by the liberations themselves that the United States Holocaust Memorial Council sponsored the International Liberators Conference in 1981. Held at the State Department building in Washington, D.C., between October 26 and 28, the conference brought together persons from the United States, Belgium, Canada, Czechoslovakia, Denmark, France, Great Britain, Israel, the Netherlands, New Zealand, Norway, Poland, Yugoslavia, and the Soviet Union. Liberators, survivors, resistance fighters—all came to share memories of the Holocaust. Many recorded their stories at length through oral interviews conducted by the Center for Holocaust Studies (New York) and the Witness to the Holocaust Project (Emory University, Atlanta). However, at the heart of the conference lay the presentations and panel discussions whose papers make up this volume.

There is no way to sum up the richness of the testimony recorded here, except perhaps to emphasize the variety of the participants and the extraordinary range of experience described. At one conclave, listening to and socializing with one another, were eyewitnesses from virtually every angle of vision except that of the Nazis themselves. Among the liberators came not only Americans, Englishmen, Canadians, and Frenchmen who saw the camps in the West, but Poles and Russians who liberated the death camps in Poland. There were also two veterans of the Jewish Brigade of British Palestine, whose work with survivors and freedom fighting lasted well beyond 1945. The survivors in attendance had experienced the entire range of Nazi brutality: from slave labor to death camps, from the Polish invasion of 1939 to the horrific scenes of April and May 1945. Members of anti-Nazi resistance groups included non-Jews from Denmark, the Netherlands, Yugoslavia, Poland, and France. They stood side-by-side with Jewish partisans from the forests of Russia and Poland, ghetto fighters from Warsaw, and some who had even participated in rebellions at the death camps themselves. Finally, participants in postwar war crimes prosecutions and historians of the Holocaust brought their own special knowledge to bear.

Moments of eloquence and wonder highlighted the conference from the very first session. Dr. Leon Bass, a black educator from Philadelphia, recalled what it meant to face the ultimate possibilities of racism at Buchenwald while serving in a segregated US army unit. George Blackburn of Canada searched for words to describe how different liberating Westerbork camp was from freeing various towns and villages along the way. Instead of loud cheers, there were whimpers. "My deepest memory," he related, "will always be of these dozens and dozens of skinny arms attempting to touch us." They wanted to know that what was happening was real. Dr. Michal Chilczuk of Poland seemed to relive the moment when a man at Sachsenhausen, too sick and emaciated to respond, moved his body slightly as if to greet his liberator. "And I took his hand," Chilczuk said. "Just now I can see this man with his hand in my hand."

The smaller panels brought their own special moments. At the War Correspondents Panel, Fred W. Friendly, former head of CBS News and now professor of journalism at Columbia, simply played a tape of Edward R. Murrow's radio report from the scene at Buchenwald. For 19 minutes the audience listened with rapt attention, and when the tape ended there was silence. At the Chaplains session, the Reverend George B. Wood described his encounter with the transit camp of Woebbelin, at which the Nazis allowed thousands to starve. He told how he organized the burial of the victims in the nearby town of Ludwigslust, apportioning one grave marker with a Star of David for every three crosses so as to properly honor victims who otherwise had been stripped of all identity. And he read from a letter he had written at the time, describing the service and his sermon to the German townspeople.

The drama of the liberators' testimony lay in their desperate attempts to understand and bring human order to the anarchy and horror of the camps, to find language sufficient to describe the confusion they felt. Those who lived and acted under Nazi rule or in the Holocaust universe itself hoped to convey to those in attendance the difficult and sometimes indescribable world in which they had functioned. The Resistance Panel featured a variety of such perspectives. Panelists from France, the Netherlands, and Yugoslavia outlined the activities and sacrifices of underground movements as they attempted to aid Jews. Frode Jakobsen noted that Danish resistance, while effective, did not enlist widespread loyalty among the populace until the Nazis attempted to deport the Jewish population. Then, in an effort that involved active resistance fighters and common citizens alike, virtually all Danish Jews were spirited out of the country to neutral Sweden.

The broad, straightforward accounts of the non-Jewish resistance contrasted sharply with the testimony of Jewish partisans and ghetto fighters. Here the stories were more personal. Samuel Gruber, for instance, first had to escape from a labor camp near Lublin; only then could he help form a partisan unit. Gruber reminded the audience that his case was not unique, that Jews resisted despite enormous odds. Benjamin Meed, a veteran of the Warsaw Ghetto uprising, highlighted the impossible choices facing Jews in Warsaw and other ghettos. For instance, should those inclined to resistance escape to the forest to fight, or should they stay in the ghetto to protect their families and others more vulnerable? Most of all, he attempted to paint a picture of the conditions of everyday life in the ghetto, and the heroism it took merely to maintain bare existence. And yet, simple survival was not the goal. "I remember seeing the streets of the ghetto," he noted, "the little display carts laden with books, emaciated Jews hovering over them...I can still see my neighbors standing in the doorways of our houses watching for the approaching Germans or policeman while, in our basement, teachers—I was among them—held secret classes for young children." This, too, constituted resistance.

Certainly some of the most striking moments of the conference came as survivors conveyed the many powerful and sometimes conflicting emotions that were the legacy of liberation. Esther Cohen vivified what freedom meant by recalling the "best place I have ever lived in," a small room with two cots and a bathroom down the hall that was her first home in New York. Anthony van Velsen, who as a member of the Sonderkommando at Birkenau's gas chambers literally watched hundreds of thousands of persons die, emphasized the tortured minds of survivors. His own dark appraisal was that many had only been physically liberated; inside they remained prisoners of memory. Benjamin Meed, echoing van Velsen's remarks, declared he was "still in the Warsaw Ghetto." Perhaps Hadassah Rosensaft, freed at Bergen-Belsen, best summed up the awful realization of liberation. "We had lost our families, our homes," she said. "We had no place to go, nobody to hug, nobody who was waiting for us anywhere. We had been liberated from death and the fear of death, but we were not free from the fear of life."

Another extraordinary panel took up the question of armed uprisings in the ghettos and camps. Participants included Vladka Meed, who with her husband participated in the Warsaw Ghetto uprising; Alexander Donat, who also took part in the Warsaw fighting; Richard Glazer, who helped engineer the revolt at Treblinka death camp; Esther Raab, who took part in the uprising at Sobibor extermination camp; and Leon Wells, who escaped from one of the Death Brigade units formed to obliterate the grave sites of Nazi victims. Each told his or her story in a different way, but Wells made a point all could agree upon. "I would like to emphasize that uprising or fighting in general," he said, "in no way elevates my stature as a survivor or diminishes the Nazi atrocities perpetrated on the victims whom they killed because they did not fight." Wells voiced his objection to what he called the "sheep theory" of Jewish victimhood, usually enunciated by those who had no idea of the conditions under which Nazi prisoners were forced to live and act.

The conference also dealt with a question much on the minds of the survivors at the conference: When and how well informed were the Allies about the ghettos and camps during the war, and why did they not come to the direct aid of European Jewry sooner than they did? In this final panel, the audience heard history-making individuals tell their own stories. Jan Karski, a member of the Polish underground who had smuggled himself in and out of both the Warsaw Ghetto and Belzec death camp, recounted the largely indifferent reactions of British and American journalists and officials when he confronted them with what he had seen. John Pehle, whose efforts helped create the War Refugee Board in 1944, an organization forthrightly committed to saving refugee lives and most famous for its sponsorship of Raoul Wallenberg's efforts in Hungary, explained how the Board came into being. Soviet General Vassily Petrenko, whose army liberated Auschwitz, described the shock, despite all the atrocities the Russians had suffered under the Nazis, at discovering the camp and its survivors.

These are just some highlights of the eyewitness testimonies and historic accounts that are contained in this volume. The complete texts reveal not only such individual moments, but an extraordinary mosaic of personalities and experiences that make the Holocaust more than a set of awful statistics and abstract victims. Rather one feels the force of individual human beings reliving their own histories and thereby recasting Holocaust history as the cumulative record of palpable human death, pain, and courage.

By the time the gathering reached its closing ceremonies, a bond had grown among the participants impossible to predict at the opening. No matter the gravity or intrinsic interest of its theme, a conference such as this can fall prey to ill-prepared or inarticulate participants, personality conflicts or political contentiousness, or distanced formality. Yet somehow the meetings came together; an intense but harmonious spirit encouraged frankness and sometimes personal revelation. In the hours between formal presentations and at meals, participants spoke to each other and came to know each other in ways none would have suspected possible but a day before. Whatever their differences, they shared a common purpose and, what is more, a common fate. For the liberators discovered what the survivors had always known: that they were among the last who could bear personal witness to a calamity whose lessons for humankind grew more indispensable with every passing year. Possessed of that awful but precious knowledge, liberators and survivors vowed to meet again.

CHAPTER I

OPENING

Chairman: Miles Lerman (USA): Businessman; Holocaust survivor; Chairman, International Relations Committee, United States Holocaust Memorial Council.

The Hon. Alexander M. Haig, Jr. (USA): Secretary of State.

Elie Wiesel (USA): Author; Andrew W. Mellon Professor in the Humanities, Boston University; Chairman, United States Holocaust Memorial Council.

Michael S. Gray (UK): Military Attache in Washington; Vice President, "Pegasus Brigade" Association; Curator, 6th Airborne Division Museum, Normandy.

Lt. Gen. Pavel Danilovich Gudz (USSR): Deputy Head, USSR Academy of Armored Forces.

The Hon. Jean Laurain (France): Minister of Veterans.

Institutional identifications are those at the time of the Conference.

MILES LERMAN

For the next two days, you, the liberators, and we, the survivors, will share some of the most vivid, the most personal, and the most anguished memories of the horrors that you discovered when you first entered the camps. Tonight, as I stand before you, my mind flashes back to the dreadful years of Nazi domination, for I am a survivor.

During World War II, I fought as a partisan in the forests of southern Poland. On the day of my liberation, I returned to my hometown on the top of a tank of the advancing Soviet and Polish armies. I should have been jubilant for Hitler's defeat was imminent, but I was not. How could I be? For of the 16,000 Jews who lived in my hometown before the Nazi onslaught, I found on my return home 11 surviving Jews, wandering around aimlessly, hoping to find some of their families alive. Unfortunately, most of them perished in the gas chambers of the death camp of Belzec. Among them were my mother, my sister and her husband, three of her young boys—ages six, eight, and 13—plus 29 other members of my immediate family.

I know that I am speaking not as an individual because my sad experience is not unique—not unique at all. Every survivor in this room could stand up and describe to you his own personal saga of misery, degradation, and mass murder. Yet, as I address you here tonight, I must share with you my deep sense of awe at having the honor of opening this historic reunion.

Little did I dream in the dark days when my people were being annihilated that some day I would stand in the assembly hall of the State Department of the United States of America, the symbol of freedom and hope, and fulfill the most fervent wish of those who perished—a wish to be remembered, a wish that we harken to their final plea that should any one of us survive, we were to bear witness and tell the story of their agony and their torture and their painful deaths.

How could I have dreamt that their final wish would be fulfilled at an assembly of 14 nations, nations who occasionally are at odds with one another, yet united here tonight in a historic commitment to memory and truth. I know that the next two days will be for all of us full, demanding, and rewarding—days that will allow us to recognize your achievements, to pay tribute to you for bringing freedom to all of us who were destined for death, but above all, to ensure that this shameful chapter in the history of mankind remains unaltered and undistorted forever and ever.

ALEXANDER HAIG

I am very, very honored to have been asked to participate in this evening's deliberations. I am very pleased to see so many of my former military colleagues, some of whom I have known in the past, and some of whom I am proud to be associated with in a common profession of arms.

Most important, it is with a very deep sense of humility that I address a very few remarks to this International Liberators Conference. The presence of great scholars and spiritual leaders adds a special dignity to this occasion, but we all share a unique honor. We are privileged to stand tonight in the same room with the survivors of the Holocaust and those who liberated them.

It is difficult to speak of the murder of the many millions whom we remember here tonight. Even Winston Churchill, who mobilized the English language and sent it into battle, lost his power of definition when he attempted to describe the Holocaust. He said simply that it was "a crime without a name." Yet it happened, and it happened in a century notable for the advances of science and technology, advances that should have ennobled life, not deprived so many of it.

A philosopher once wrote that a modern man lives on familiar terms with many contraries. We are modern men, and we live with a terrible contrary. We have achieved unprecedented progress for mankind, yet we carry the memory of an unprecedented crime against mankind. Even as we strive for the best, we know that man is capable of the worst. What are we to do with this memory? How can we bear it? This is the underlying problem that the Holocaust Council has set before this conference. This is the fundamental issue that we, the representatives of many nations gathered here, must confront.

I believe that we can bear the memory of the Holocaust only if we strive to prevent its recurrence. Let us, therefore, remember well the signposts on the road to genocide. First, individual rights were revoked. Then, individual dignity was denied. Finally, in the abyss of despair, came the murder itself. It began with the most defenseless, but it did not stop with them. And genocide succeeded because the defenders of individual rights allowed themselves to be divided because they sought refuge in illusion and in weakness. They failed to fight for their own principles. They betrayed not only those who lost their lives but themselves as well.

The victims and the survivors of the Holocaust have shown us, each in their own ways, that man need not succumb to this evil. Those who went to their deaths singing of their belief in God did not lose their souls. Those who fought against hopeless odds did not lose their dignity. Those who survived did not despair. I've seen for myself the stark testimony of the victims at Yad Vashem, the monument to the Holocaust in Jerusalem. I have also seen in Israel and elsewhere that the Jewish people have not lost their hope in God, in themselves, or in mankind.

The liberators, too, bear witness. You will tell us that the values we cherish become meaningful only if we are prepared to work for them, to defend them, and to fight for them. A generation unwilling to bear the burden of its own beliefs makes possible a Holocaust of its dreams. I know this as a former soldier, and we are all soldiers for our beliefs.

Let us, therefore, remember the Holocaust, not only to record the rapidly receding past, but also to prepare for the rapidly approaching future; not only to mourn the destruction of millions, but to strive for the rights of millions; not only to comfort ourselves with the memory that evil was once destroyed, but also to create a permanent structure of peace and of justice, both among ourselves and among the nations.

There is an old Jewish saying,"The memory of the righteous shall be for the blessing." As we remember the righteous today, let us resolve to act in such a way that we merit their blessing.

ELIE WIESEL

As Chairman of the United States Holocaust Memorial Council, it is my privilege to welcome you officially and thank you for having accepted our invitation to join us as we undertake a unique pilgrimage into history and its darkest convulsive nightmare.

Thirty-six and -seven years ago, we experienced together a moment of destiny without parallel, never to be measured, never to be repeated, a moment that stood on the other side of time, on the other side of existence. When we first met at the threshold of a universe struck by malediction, we spoke different languages. We were strangers to one another. We might as well have descended from different planets, and yet a link was created between us. A bond was established. We became not only comrades, not only brothers. We became each other's witnesses.

I remember—I shall always remember—the day I was liberated, and to think that one of you has been my liberator, of course, only adds to the emotion which, naturally, is mine today.

April 11, 1945. Buchenwald. The terrifying silence terminated by abrupt yelling. The first American soldiers, their faces ashen. Their eyes. I shall never forget their eyes. Your eyes. You looked and looked. You could not move your gaze away from us. It was as though you sought to alter reality with your eyes. They reflected astonishment, bewilderment, endless pain and anger. Yes, anger above all. Rarely have I seen such anger, such rage contained, mute, yet ready to burst with frustration, humiliation, utter helplessness.

Then, I remember, you broke down, you wept. You wept and wept uncontrollably, unashamedly. You were our children then, for we—the 12-year-old, the 16-year-old boys in Buchenwald and Theresienstadt and Mauthausen—knew so much more than you about life and death, man and his endeavors, God and His silence. You wept. We could not. We had no more tears left. We had nothing left. In a way we were dead, and we knew it.

What did we feel? Only sadness, and also gratitude. Ultimately, it was gratitude that brought us back to normalcy and to society. Do you remember, friends? You, the strong soldiers with weapons, with glory on your shoulders, and triumph in your eyes. In Ravensbrück, Lublin, Dachau, Stutthof, Nordhausen, Majdanek, Belsen, and Auschwitz, you were surrounded by sick and wounded and hungry wretches, barely alive, pathetic in their futile attempts to touch you, to smile at you, to reassure you, to console you, and most of all to carry you in triumph on their frail shoulders. You were heroes, our idols. Tell me, friends, have you ever felt such affection? Have you ever felt such admiration? Have you ever elicited such love?

One thing we did not do. We did not try to explain. Explanations were neither needed nor possible. Liberators and survivors looked at one another, and what each of us experienced then we shall try to recapture together now at this reunion, which to me represents a miracle in itself, and my good friends do we need miracles these days.

At this point, allow me to say a few words parenthetically about the Council whose Chairman I am privileged to be. Created by the President of the United States and enacted into law by the unanimous vote of both the House of Representatives and the Senate of the United States, our Council is essentially nonpolitical. It has not been used and shall not be used by any administration for any other purpose than to make our citizens and people everywhere aware of the unspeakable crimes perpetrated systematically and officially against the Jewish people—my people—and humanity. Our activities are manifold in nature and in scope.

The International Relations Committee, which coordinated this conference so ably and brilliantly and efficiently, is but one of the committees functioning within the Council. Another committee is in charge of gathering pertinent archives. Another is preparing educational programs for elementary and secondary schools and universities. There is a committee to prepare the annual Remembrance Day ceremonies; another to plan the museum; and yet another is engaged in raising funds to finance all these activities. What we all have in common is an obsession not to betray the dead—the dead we left behind—and who left us behind. They were killed once. They must not be killed again through forgetfulness.

This conference has its own history—Moscow 1979. Members of a presidential delegation met with certain high-ranking Red Army officers, and one of them in particular meant much to us—General Petrenko, who liberated Auschwitz. It was an extraordinary encounter. We exchanged stories. He told us of the preparations to break through the German lines, and I told him of the last day in camp, the last roll call, the last night, the last consultations among inmates, friends, fathers, and sons. What should one do? Hide? Stay in the hospital? Enter the hospital? Join the evacuation? The Red Army was so near, so near. We heard the artillery barrage; we saw the flames; we prayed.

I told General Petrenko, "We prayed for you and your men, and no believer ever prayed to his or her God with more fervor. We were waiting for you as the religious Jews were waiting for the Messiah."

While General Petrenko and I were telling each other tales of courage and despair—for, as far as I am concerned, they did come late, too late for so many of us—I suddenly had an idea of bringing together liberators from all the Allied forces—to listen to you, to see you, to be with you once more, to thank you, and—why not admit it?—to solicit your help once more.

My friends, we witnessed recently, in the last couple of years in many countries that you represent, a vicious phenomenon, which is so evil that it bears notice. There are groups all over the world that simply deny that it had ever taken place. They say we have not suffered and our parents didn't die and the murderers didn't murder. But where are the victims then?

I thought that since our testimony is being disputed, perhaps your voice will be heard. After all, you were the first men to discover the abyss just as we were its last inhabitants. What we symbolized to one another then was so special that it remained part of our very being to this very day. Here you are, friends, from so many nations, reunited with those who owe you their lives, just as you owe them the flame that scorched your memories.

On that memorable day, the day of our liberation, whether it took place in 1944 or 1945, in Poland or in Germany or in Czechoslovakia, you incarnated for us humanity's noblest yearning to be free and, even more, to bring freedom to those who are not free. For us, you represented hope, truth.

Six million Jews have been annihilated, and millions of brave men and women massacred by the Nazis and their collaborators. But we are duty-bound to remember always, that to confront the fascist criminal conquests, a unique alliance of nations—gigantic armies transcending geopolitical and ideological borders—was formed on five continents, and they went to war on behalf of mankind. The fact that millions of soldiers wearing different uniforms united to fight together, be victorious together, and alas, sometimes die together seemed to justify man's faith in his own humanity, in spite of the enemy and its inhumanity.

We thought of the killers and we were ready to give up on man, but then we remembered those who resisted the killers on open battlefields, from Stalingrad to France, to Normandy, everywhere. We remembered those who resisted them in the underground movements in France, Norway, Holland, Denmark, and the USSR and we reconciled ourselves with the human condition. We were—can you believe it?—naïve enough to think that we who had witnessed for a while the domination of evil would prevent it from surfacing again.

On the very ruins of civilization, we aspired to erect new sanctuaries for our children, that life would be sanctified and not denigrated, compassion practiced and not ridiculed. It would have been so easy then to allow ourselves to slide into melancholy and resignation, but we chose differently. We chose to become spokesmen for man's quest for generosity and his need and capacity to turn his or her suffering into something productive, something creative; and of this we are so proud.

We are proud that so many of these Jewish young boys and girls, who could have become nihilists, arrogant, demanding everything—and rightfully so—chose to go to the land of our ancestors, to Israel, and to build there a new society with ancient memories, a human society where everything is sacred. We had hoped then that out of so much torment and grief and mourning, a new message would be handed down to future generations, a warning against the inherent perils of discrimination, fanaticism, poverty, deprivations, ignorance, oppression, humiliation, injustice, and war—the ultimate injustice, the ultimate humiliation. We were naïve and perhaps we still are.

We, friends, we are naïve. Together we express human suffering which has no name and no end. Let us invoke it to avoid other suffering. Together we have the right and the duty to make an appeal to which no one can remain deaf, an appeal against death, against the degradation of man, against violence, and against forgetfulness.

We have seen what no one will see. We have seen the human condition trampled underfoot. We have seen what fanaticism can do—cruelty, imprisonment, slaughter on the scale of the state and of the planet. We have seen the metamorphosis of history, my friends, and it is incumbent upon us to bear witness to it.

When a people is sent to its death, all others are threatened. It is all humanity which is threatened. The plans of Hitler to annihilate the Jews could decimate the Slavs, and this already carried within it the germ of the end of all mankind. They killed the Jews, and it was mankind that was killed; and you, liberators, who stopped this process.

Be proud of it until the end of your days, and be thanked. Accept our thanks. If we unite our memories as we did before, everything is possible. The forgetfulness and indifference to complicity will be eliminated.

I address myself to you as brothers, friends. What unites us is powerful, durable. We make a community which is like no other, and it is getting smaller every day. Tell me, who will be the last messenger among us? The judgment which we make on past and future events we cannot fail to bring to bear. Our dignity depends upon it.

We are against prisons. We are against dictatorships. We are against fear, nuclear confrontation, and any other kind. We are living, vibrant proof that it is possible for men to unite to affirm the right to live and to live in peace. I am perhaps naïve, but I think with all my heart that if we speak loudly enough, death will retreat.

We looked deep into the abyss, and the abyss looked back at us. No one comes close to the kingdom of night and goes away unchanged. We told a tale, or at least we tried. We resisted all temptation to isolate ourselves and be silent. Instead, we chose to affirm our desperate faith in testimony. We forced ourselves to speak, however inadequately, however poorly. We may have used the wrong words, but then there are no words to describe the ineffable. We spoke in spite of language, in spite of the limits that exist between what we say and outsiders hear. We spoke and we spoke, and yet there were explosions in Paris, bombs in Antwerp, murderous attacks in Vienna.

Is it conceivable that Nazism could dare come back into the open so soon while we are still alive, while we are still here to denounce its poisonous nature as illustrated in Treblinka, which is its outcome? Again, we must admit our naïveté. We thought we had vanquished what Brecht called "the beast." But no; it is still showing its claws. Therefore, at best, what a gathering such as this could do is to shame the beast into hiding.

I am telling you, my friends, that if we succeed here—and I hope and pray that we shall—in rising above politics, above the usual recriminations between great and small powers, above simplistic propaganda, and simply tell the world what most liberators and liberated have seen, then something may happen and the world may choose to pay more attention to what hangs as a threat to its very future. I hope and pray that the liberators and the liberated succeed in putting aside what divides us because what divides us is, ultimately, utterly superficial.

If we dedicate ourselves, not only to the memory of those who have suffered, but to the future of those who are suffering today, we shall be serving notice on mankind that we shall never allow this earth to be made into a prison again, into a camp again, into a ghetto again. We shall never allow war to be considered as a solution to any problem, for war *is* the problem. If we succeed, then our encounter will be recorded as yet another of our common victories.

I speak to you as a citizen of the United States and as a son of the Jewish people, as a survivor. I know that our memories will traumatize history. I know that our knowledge is so awesome that it is impossible to receive it, but I also know that we must communicate it. We must give a meaning to our survival.

Friends, liberators, and brother survivors, if we do not raise our voice against hate, who will? If we do not raise our voice against forgetfulness, who will? If we do not raise our voice against war, who will? We speak with the authority of men and women who have seen war. We know what it is. We have seen all over Europe the burned villages, the devastated cities, the deserted homes, and a million murdered children of my people. We still see the demented mothers whose children are being massacred before their eyes. We still follow the endless nocturnal processions to the flames rising up to the seventh heaven, if not higher. If we shall not testify, who will? That is why we are here—to testify together, not to one another, but with one another and for one another.

Our tale is a tale of solitude and fear and anonymous death, but also of bravery, compassion, generosity, and extraordinary solidarity. Together, you the liberators and we the survivors represent a commitment to memory whose intensity will remain; and in its name, I pledge to you, and you will pledge to yourselves, that we shall continue to voice our concerns and our hopes, not for our own sake, but for the sake of mankind, for its very survival may depend on its ability and willingness to listen—to listen and to remember.

MICHAEL GRAY

Having heard this evening so many words, I feel it is good to be alive and to be here with you.

At the time all this was happening, I was a small boy at school, which I think puts in perspective the time that has passed. I remember the horror that I felt, even as a small boy, when I read in the newspapers and was told about what had happened and what was happening in Europe.

I therefore feel extremely humble but privileged to be with you and to represent Great Britain and indeed the British Army and those of my predecessors who fought across Europe to help eradicate the horror and liberate some of those of you who survived.

I would like briefly to introduce one member of the British delegation to you because I feel it is he who really should be leading this delegation.

Professor [G.I.A.D.] Draper and his wife have come over from Great Britain. Apart from being an international lawyer and a barrister at law, he was in the Irish Guards during the early part of the Second World War and was then seconded to the Judge Advocate General's office in 1945. He was a military prosecutor at the War Crimes Tribunal, and it was during this time that he personally arrested the commandant of Auschwitz, although that camp was liberated by the Russian Army. He will be speaking to you on Wednesday morning.

I'm sure that the French delegation here and others of you will know Mr. Robert Shepard, who is the President of the International Committee of Mauthausen. During World War II, he was a member of the SOE [Special Operations Executive].[1] He was caught by the Gestapo and was himself interned in that same camp, Mauthausen, and then ended the war in Dachau.

He and I worked together on a number of projects of this sort in France, and he has become a close friend. I mention this because it is quite by chance that I happen to be in my present appointment in Washington; and quite by chance also that I am here.

In 1978, he asked me if I would help him and another colleague, a man named Maurice Cordonnier, locate the officers of the

Grenadier guards who liberated the camp at Neuengamme in northern Germany. Many months later, in June, and after much research, we were able to locate and take a party of 10 of those officers over to Caen in Normandy for memorial weekend, as some of you may remember, organized by the International Committee.

It was indeed for me a memorable few days. I spoke again with Robert this morning, and I share his view entirely that events such as our gathering here this week are important in order to bring to the attention of a younger generation the horrors of those dreadful years —those, even like myself, who were at school, as I've already mentioned, during that part of the war. It is the responsibility of peoples of all nations never to permit the same to happen again.

I say all nations, too, because the prisoners who suffered the Holocaust were not only—as I read it—of the Jewish faith, but of many other creeds—members of resistance movements, political prisoners, intelligence agents, Gypsies, and many others from all nations across Europe and elsewhere.

Inevitably, I also believe there are disagreements about the preciseness of history in relating to the liberation of those of you who survived and the horror of coming away from those many death camps. Suffice it to say that I believe that their liberation came about through what, at that time, was a vital cooperation between Allies. It is a tragic narrative of almost unbelievable dimension which I know will unfold during the sessions which we are about to partake in during these coming days.

We from Britain are pleased to be with you to share and to remember, albeit very painfully, the experience of those of you who were subjected to such terrible fear, to the humiliation, the degradation, remorse.

I believe it was truly man's inhumanity to man.

*PAVEL DANILOVICH GUDZ**

Allow me on behalf of the Soviet Union to thank you for your participation in this first historical conference and to bring to the members of this conference greetings from the anti-Hitlerite coalition of all countries which contributed to the cause of the great victory over fascist Germany during World War II.

Hitler's fascism, the most horrible incarnation of the forces of darkness, caused innumerable sufferings and disaster to peoples. Tens of millions of people perished in action during World War II and in Hitler's jails and concentration camps.

The war left its terrible traces, its gaping, bleeding wounds over vast territories of our land and in the hearts of millions of mothers, widows, and orphans. We honor the memory of victims who perished in fascist jails and concentration camps.

This conference is being held at a time when, in my homeland, my people are celebrating the fortieth anniversary of the historic battle of Moscow. In October of 1941, the Red Army stopped fascist offensives and then inflicted a major defeat upon the German army for the first time in World War II, thereby dispelling the myth of its invincibility.

The main forces of Hitler's Wehrmacht were broken during the battles of Moscow, Leningrad, Stalingrad, Kursk, in Byelorussia, and in the Ukraine. The Soviet armed forces not only defended freedom and independence of our own Motherland, but brought liberation to other peoples and saved humanity from the threat of fascist enslavement.

Mr. Chairman, allow me to express

*General Gudz made his remarks in Russian. Printed here is the text of the English version supplied by General Gudz.

our most sincere thanks for the kind words which you spoke about Soviet soldiers and heroes who liberated these camps.

The decisive contribution of the Soviet people to the defeat of fascism was properly acknowledged by peoples in the countries of the anti-Hitlerite coalition, by many heads of states and governments in the West.

An important contribution to the victory over the common enemy was made by peoples and armies of nations which were members of the anti-Hitlerite coalition, namely the United States of America, Great Britain, France, and other countries.

The Soviet people remember and highly appreciate the courage and the valor of the soldiers of the Allied armed forces, the anti-fascist resistance fighters, and the troops in the liberation forces, partisans who heroically struggled against fascist invaders in occupied countries.

This demonstrated the possibility of an effective political and military cooperation of states with different social systems that is precisely what the Soviet Union was striving for to prevent World War II.

In 1945, mankind celebrated the great victory over German fascism and Japanese militarism. The peoples' trial in Nuremberg passed its weighty sentence condemning Nazi military criminals who unleashed the Second World War and who were guilty of mass deaths of millions of people.

In the after-war years, the Soviet Union remains steadfastly faithful to the ideals of the great antifascist struggle of peoples for their national freedom, democracy and a stable peace, for the implementation of the appeal, contained on the first lines of the UN Charter—to spare generations to come from the scourge of war.

It is appropriate to emphasize here that in the very first document issued by the government of the Soviet Russia—The Decree of Peace written by V.I. Lenin and adopted in October 1917—the young, at that time, Soviet state branded war of aggression as the gravest crime against humanity. The Soviet Union has been and is consistently following the fundamental guidelines of Lenin's peaceful foreign policy. The safeguarding of peace has been and remains the supreme aim of the foreign policy of the USSR. This is the aim of the Peace Program for the 1980s, adopted by the 26th Congress of the Communist Party of the Soviet Union. It embraces measures for reducing both nuclear missile weapons and conventional arms. It contains proposals for settling existing and preventing new conflicts and crisis situations. It is permeated with a desire to strengthen peace and develop peaceful cooperation between the countries of all continents.

In our nuclear age, dialogue and negotiations are needed equally by all. There is now no sensible method of solving disputed problems except negotiations. History taught a stern lesson. The peoples paid too dear a price for their failure to prevent war, to avert in time the threat which hung over the world. We must not allow any repetition of the tragedy. Everything must and can be done to prevent another world war. Peace belongs to all mankind and in our time it is also the primary condition of our existence. Only through joint efforts can and must peace be maintained and reliably safeguarded.

So may a stable peace and happy life of future generations become an eternal living memorial to victims of fascism, to victims of recklessness and adventurism in world policies.

*JEAN LAURAIN**

Please allow me to first thank the government and the Congress of the United

*Mr. Laurain made his remarks in French. This is the simultaneous translation.

States for having created this Council and to congratulate the members of this Holocaust Council for having had the idea of organizing this first international conference of liberators of Nazi camps.

Our common civilization about 40 years ago met a challenge, and if it did not succumb, it was due to all of you here. All of the countries that you represent we thank for having safeguarded the values of our civilization. This challenge to our common civilization was on behalf of the theory of the "master race"; it was a desire to destroy, to destroy all of those who were different because of their religion, their language, their ideas, their opinions. This eruption of a time of scorn and hatred first struck the German citizens, Communist, Socialist, and especially the Jews who had well served the state to which they felt they belonged. This spread throughout the continent was followed by the concentration camps, first built for Germans by Germans, which then received huge contingents of people from all over Europe, including resistance members from all over. They came before the same hangman.

The demoniacal aspects of the Holocaust of the Jews, however, took on dimensions that no one has the right to forget. It is healthy that this meeting should have been organized because it gives us all, despite the time which has gone by, a chance to remember, a chance to remind others who did not know the hideous face of Nazism to know this period of shame and misery. It is good for us to get together, those of us who liberated the camps and representatives of the survivors that were liberated at that time.

I think that their surprise was the same: the surprise of those who were fighting had no idea of what they were going to find behind the gates of those camps, and the surprise of the prisoners, who, no matter what their courage was, having been taken into this infernal machine, how could they ever have expected to be delivered. This deliverance came, and it was brought by these Allied armies that came together in a common struggle to free these people.

It is true that we will never pay enough tribute to those who delivered Europe, but we must always associate, in our memories, all of those who stood up with empty hands from the North Cape to Greece against this, all of those who opposed totalitarian ideology and spoke the healthy language of liberty and fraternity, which, of course, took on European dimensions. They fought on the soil of France, but the French also fought with all of those who were uprooted by war and for whom freedom had become the only homeland.

I think that we must adhere to the ideal of justice and its vigor, its strength, its ability to go against the forces of opposition and to finally triumph. It is important to recall this because we could yield to bitterness before the incapacity of our countries and our peoples to have prevented this Holocaust, this unprecedented massacre, which came in the implacable logic of a system and of its structures. We could yield to bitterness and cry with remorse, but we have this immense hope, which was given to us by all of those who, without uniforms, without a mandate, fought and fought so well. To our dead and our soldiers—we have a duty toward them. We have a duty to remember what they went through, what they did, why they made the commitment they did, why they suffered, why they sacrificed, and especially why they dared to hope.

This hope, we must cultivate altogether as a very rare and precious plant, a fragile flower. We must reaffirm, not only in our speeches but also in our acts, our faith in mankind and in his destiny, our faith in our ability to overcome difficulties as well as to overcome temptations and also to see to it that a new abyss does not reopen tomorrow. We must avoid totalitarianism, we have to say No to totalitarianism, No to racism, No to anti-Semitism, and we have to say Yes to fraternity. In doing so, we will be faithful to all of those dead without graves, to all of those whose deaths should not have been in vain.

Beyond survival our duty is also to awaken vigilance. This conference, seems to me to be a conference of vigilance indeed. We must do everything in our power so that such a phenomenon does not reoccur, and thus we must undertake an enormous educational enterprise, particularly vis-à-vis the young people. We have to undertake consciousness awakening; we have to become aware of the ideological origin of the concentration camps, of fascism, of Nazism; and we have to look to the dangers of a resurgence of this modern barbarity where all scientific and technological means are placed at the service of destruction of humanity. Because, as the German playwright Bertholt Brecht said, "the belly is still fertile and the beast can still come forth."

We have to learn a new way of life; we have to find a way to live without hate and with justice, where the respect for the human person, without aggression, without violence, will reign; then this new spirit, where reason prevails over instinct, and a world to which all men of good will must aspire, will become possible. The posthumous will of all the people in the concentration camps calls us to this vocation of the liberation of man.

Notes

Special Operations Executive. An agency established by the British in 1940 to organize and carry out sabotage in Nazi-occupied Europe. Many SOE operations were conducted in collaboration with native resistance movements, as well as with the U.S. Office of Strategic Services (OSS).

CHAPTER II

THE EYEWITNESSES

Moderator: Sigmund Strochlitz (USA): Businessman; Holocaust survivor; President, American Friends of Haifa University, where he endowed a chair in Holocaust Studies; member, U.S. Holocaust Memorial Council.

Dr. Leon Bass (USA): High-school principal; lecturer on the Holocaust; participated in liberation of Buchenwald as American soldier.

Capt. (Ret.) George Blackburn (Canada): Participated in liberation of Westerbork as an officer in the Royal Canadian Artillery.

Dr. Michal Chilczuk (Poland): Scientist; participated in liberation of Oranienburg.

Guy Fassina (France): director of Veterans Affairs; in charge of repatriation of deportees of France after World War II.

Maj. Gen. (Res.) Alexei Kirillovich Gorlinsky (USSR): Participated in liberation of Theresienstadt and in meeting of U.S. and Soviet forces at Torgau on the Elbe in 1945.

Col. (Res.) Dan Hiram (Israel): Member of Jewish Brigade in World War II; active in transfer of Jewish DPs to Palestine after the war.

Dr. Douglas G. Kelling (USA): Participated in liberation of Dachau as medical officer in U.S. Army.

Lt. Gen. (Ret.) William W. Quinn (USA): As commander of U.S. 7th Army Intelligence, investigated Dachau after liberation.

Alan Rose (Canada): National Executive Vice President, Canadian Jewish Congress; participated in liberation of Bergen-Belsen.

Rabbi Herschel Schacter (USA): As U.S. army chaplain, participated in liberation of Buchenwald and aided in resettlement of DPs.

Efraim Weichselfisch (Israel): Chairman, Disabled Jewish Veterans; veteran of Soviet Army.

Institutional identifications are those at the time of the Conference.

SIGMUND STROCHLITZ

Many years have passed since the Allied armies entered the camps. The Russian armies entered the camps in the East, being first to expose to the world the horrors committed by the Nazis and their collaborators. The English army entered the camps in the North and confirmed to the western world the brutal realities of death factories in the heart of Europe, next to big towns and small villages, while the inhabitants went about their daily work, unconcerned, undisturbed, and yet knowing very well that mass murder was taking place in their backyard. In the South, American armies entering the camps and suspecting that time may erase the memory of Nazi behavior, brought a high-ranking congressional delegation to record for posterity the atrocities committed by Nazi Germany.[1]

Survivors will never forget the valiant effort made by the Allied armies to save even those who were beyond help and to help restore a semblance of normal life to those who were at that moment not even able to respond to human decency or to react to human compassion. The same struggle, the defeat of Nazi Germany, enabled the Soviet army to liberate the camps in the East, as the western armies liberated the camps in the North and the South. We waited a long time for you to come, while life was ebbing out of us, and today we are meeting again in the secure surroundings of the State Department, but faced with a new threat.

I am sure that those who will be testifying today, recalling what they have experienced and what they found entering the camps, are as appalled, disgusted, and angry as survivors are with the proliferation of hate literature denying the existence of gas chambers and the murder of six million Jews—90 percent of European Jewry—and millions of others. The denial will be foremost in our minds today, but let's also remember that the danger that the Holocaust can be forgotten or become a matter of indifference—just a senseless, mindless crime—can only be ignored at the cost of great suffering and costly tragedies in the years to come.

But perhaps those eyewitness accounts should not be looked at only from those points of view. Those who fought in the last war and those who have been victims of hate, prejudice, and indifference owe it to present and future generations to sound the warning that we live in times when military forces of unimaginable destructiveness, religious fanaticism that caused so much misery in the past, and blind hatred that transcends boundaries are building up around the world that can in one summer day or winter day drive mankind to madness again. Let's hope, therefore, that today's eyewitness testimonies to acts of evil will stand as a permanent witness to an event that must be remembered and transmitted to younger generations, not only by us, the victims, but also by you, the victors. You and we are partners to a legacy forced on us by fate: to uphold the truth, to prevent the dead from being murdered again, and to save the conscience, the decency, and the humanity of mankind.

LEON BASS

I am very pleased to have this opportunity to share with you an experience that I had at the young age of 19. It was not an experience that I would have wanted, but it was thrust upon me. At 18 I enlisted in the United States army, and I began to find out at that time that in my great country I was set apart as something different because I happened to be black. Therefore, I was put into what we called then a segregated unit of the army, and I was told to deliver. I was told to go out and do battle, to change the world, to make it a better place for all of us to live. Most of my training took place in the South. At that time they were very overt in the way they treated those of color. I was constantly reminded, "Leon, you are something different." I had to rise above that. I had to be aware that in spite of the impingements on me that were denigrating and debilitating to me as a human personality, I had to be something better in order to make this world what it should be.

So I and my comrades went forth and one day we found ourselves in the Battle of the Bulge.[2] We found ourselves moving up under great stress, pushing the Germans back into Europe, until finally one day we landed at a place called Weimar, Germany. It was at that time that I began to take the blinders off. It was at that time I began to see that I could no longer have tunnel vision about human suffering. I could no longer be centered on what I wanted. The "Vitamin I" which I carried for so long had to somehow be eradicated. I was just ready to find out why that had to change.

No one had told me about the death camps. I went through many orientations, but no one shared with me what had been going on in Europe for so many years. On this day in April in 1945, with some of my comrades, I walked through the gates of a place called Buchenwald. I was totally unprepared for what I saw. Someone of 19 couldn't have been prepared, for he hasn't lived long enough. I was still trying to develop my value system. I was still trying to sort things out, and then all of a sudden, slap—right in the face—was the horror perpetrated by man against man.

I saw all the things that many of you have lived through who are survivors. I saw what most of you here who were eyewitnesses saw. I'm not here this morning to wallow in the horror story, because it's so painful for me, and I know it's painful for many of you. But, nevertheless, the story must be told. We must talk about the crematoria. We must talk about the dead. We must talk about the denigration of human personalities, how they tried to make people less than human. The purposes are beyond me. It boggles the mind for me to try to figure out why. Why would someone take millions of people and in a planned, organized, systematic way try to destroy them, exterminate them? I have yet to come to grips with that in my own mind. But I know that I must share this so that the history books really tell the story as it is, so that nobody sugarcoats the history as they did with slavery. Our secondary sources would make you think that all slaves loved the plantation, when this was not so. Even though the revisionists are out there today writing books and telling students that it never happened, we cannot ignore our responsibilities to tell the story. Yes, we must be graphic. We must use the media. We must come together like this to focus attention across the world.

But in the final analysis, my friends, if we want to avoid another Holocaust, if we want to make sure that this doesn't happen again, we have a personal responsibility to do something about it. I know it's nice to say that you're going to give a large sum of money to the NAACP[3] or you're going to give a large sum of money to B'nai B'rith.[4] But that's the easy way out. Yes, you can avoid a Holocaust because you must belong to organizations. You must contribute. But the tough part of the program is when you walk out of here and you go back to where you live and where you work. When you're on the job and your boss tells an anti-Semitic joke, do you laugh because you want to move ahead? When you're sitting around the bridge table and somebody talks about the dirty niggers or the spics moving in down the street, do you sit there quietly and never say anything? If so, you are contributing to another Holocaust.

It was James Baldwin who said, "God gave man the rainbow sign/No more water, the fire next time." You are throwing fuel on that fire when you keep your mouth shut. When you come to a large gathering like this, it is important that we talk about the things that we experienced. If, however, you go back to your job, back to your bridge table, back to your neighborhood, and you say nothing to people, you are sowing the seeds for another Holocaust. Trying to love the unloveable is the challenge, my friends. When we ignore the disinherited, the dispossessed, and the poor among us, we are contributing to another Holocaust.

So I come here today saying, out of my experiences, I can ill afford to pass by on the other side. I cannot ignore the young people who come into my school holding on by their fingertips, saying, "Give me a chance." Many of those who don't have enough money, who live jammed in poverty, will bite the hand that feeds them because they're so angry. Somehow they're still saying, "Help me," even though they call me an SOB. Even though they use all kinds of profanity to express themselves, they're still crying for help. And where am I? Where are you? Are we caught up in getting and spending? Are we so busy trying to move ahead, whether it's in the military, whether it's in the halls of Congress, or whether it's in our own community that we're trying to cater to people? Do we cater to them and ignore the morality that's striking us in the face? If we ignore those things, if we remain silent, if we pass by on the other side, we are sowing the seeds for another Holocaust.

I come here this morning, in the short time that's been allotted to me, just to say there's no easy way out. You must answer the question as I do every day. Is the price too high? You can't look at the person next to you, or behind you, you must answer that for yourself. Is the price too high? If you practice your Judeo-Christian ethics and dare to be a Daniel and go into the lions' den, you become vulnerable. I challenge you, all of you, to try to live up to those things that we see in the Ten Commandments, or in the Koran, or whatever philosophy you believe in. If you do, you're vulnerable, and you're going to take pain and blame for things you didn't create.

If we're going to survive, if we're going to make this world a better place, when we leave here we'll take the message back with us. We'll move out into the forefront where the battle happens to be waging, and that's with the disinherited and the dispossessed. I would like to remember again the words of James Baldwin who said, "Either we love one another/Or the sea will engulf us/And the light will go out."

GEORGE BLACKBURN

To label me a liberator of a concentration camp is just simply not true. No one person, no single unit, no division, not even the Canadian army, was capable of liberating a concentration camp. It took the full forces of the Allies crushing Germany from both directions to retake land and liberate people from those death camps and from those other horrors. I am very subdued, and I approach this all with a great sense of inferiority.

After listening to the first marvelous speech that was made on this subject, there is almost nothing left to say in terms of the purposes and the objectives of this great Conference. Please permit me to say, Mr. Chairman, on behalf of the Canadian delegation, that there is not a man on it—and I know from talking to them the last 24 hours—who does not feel a sense of inferiority being in the presence of people who have survived those horror camps.

I did not see a death camp. Westerbork was a collection center for the Jewish people of the Netherlands—supposedly identified as people of the Jewish faith—to be sent on to the gas chambers and the ovens. I was a forward observation officer in the artillery, and our job was to do a dash of six to 10 miles in behind the enemy lines to cut a road that was servicing a battle going on in the town of Assen and, in the dash, these kangaroos[5] came crashing by this camp. It was obviously a concentration camp of some kind. It had towers, the normal accoutrements of a concentration camp.

By the time my vehicle arrived, which had been falling farther and farther behind because of the lack of strength of the old engine, the people had run out of their huts—it was quite an extensive set of huts—and they'd clotted at the front gates. They had managed to get the barbed wire gates open, and they were coming out on the road and they stopped us. Of all the memories I have, and there are an awful lot of them from Normandy through to the top of Holland, nothing compares to the people yelling and screaming their gratitude for the liberation of their town, their farm. I can't call it crying; I can't call it screaming. It was more like the whimpering of an ill animal or a frightened animal, mixed with expressions of joy. My deepest memory will always be of these dozens and dozens of skinny arms attempting to touch us. They wanted to feel us and to feel the vehicle.

Even as we gave out the little bit of food that we could from our bren gun carrier to them, they seemed to be more preoccupied with feeling to make sure we were real. We had to go on forward. I mean, we had to catch up with those half-a-dozen kangaroos with the infantry in them, but we couldn't get these prisoners to move. I pulled out my pistol, and you can just imagine what went through the minds of these poor people. They were thinking, "My God, after all this, are you going to shoot us?" But this did quiet them down to the extent that we were able to get across in our pigeon Dutch—my driver could speak a little German—and English the fact that we were still attacking and had to keep going to chase the Germans. Then they opened up, and they reluctantly let us go. Really, that is all I saw. I didn't see the horrors of Belsen, except as we all have through pictures and eyewitness accounts.

But I suppose I must not occupy any more time, except to say that I, and everyone on the Canadian delegation, are a hundred percent behind the motivation and the purposes and the objectives of this conference. We must keep alive and vivid the memory and the horror that took place when people of a nation, a very enlightened nation, forgot to watch very carefully the movements of their morality and let a situation get out of hand, and even supported it, until it was too late. There's a real purpose, ladies and gentlemen, in what you're doing, and I can say on behalf of the Canadian delegation we're a hundred percent behind it.

MICHAL CHILCZUK

It is not too easy to speak without emotion in front of those who went through a cataclysm in history, civilized history. This cataclysm is based on a barbarian theory which was first implemented in my country—Poland. During the war, six million Polish citizens—almost half of whom were Jewish—were killed. I have come from the country where Nazis established over 2,000 different kinds of camps: military, slave, prison, extermination. Each day 2,800–3,000 lives were taken.

I have come from the country where the resistance movement started. Half-a-million citizens, together with Jews, participated in this movement which began in October 1939.

I am a representative of the Polish People's Army. In our battles, we liberated a dozen different kinds of camps. But in the limited time allowed me, it is impossible to describe all these camps; therefore, let me concentrate on one which the Polish Army directly liberated—Oranienburg, which some people call Sachenhausen.[6] Before the 20th of April, we had reached a suburb of Oranienburg. Together with my soldiers, I entered the concentration camp of Sachsenhausen on the 22nd of April.

It is not easy for me, Mr. Chairman, to reconstruct what I saw. Yesterday we listened as the Chairman of the Holocaust Memorial Council explained how he felt when he first saw the liberators. He remembers very well, but, Mr. Chairman, I want to explain what I saw from the other side.

I don't think any artist or any writer

exists who can reconstruct this picture. It is not only difficult for me in English, but in my mother language it is also impossible. You, sir, saw soldiers with nice uniforms, in good physical health. But what I saw were people I call humans, but it was difficult to tell they were humans.

I can never forget their eyes. There was a difference. Maybe they cried with joy because there was freedom for them. I will never forget one victim who I thought wanted to shake my hand because a little bit of him moved. And I took his hand. . .just now I can see this man with his hand in my hand.

After a few minutes, my soldiers also wanted to help as your colleagues did—with food. It was human instinct that they would want to share their food with the victims. They didn't realize that it could be a tragedy for these people to eat. But soon our physician explained to the soldiers that it could mean death to these people if a doctor didn't supervise the sharing of food. But they wanted to help—that was the first human reaction.

After that we helped these people with our medical care. We took them from their beds—some of you know what these beds were like. Who can describe these beds?

I went with one group who showed me the concentration camp, their township for murdering. I saw the crematorium. In this concentration camp we found only 5,000 people. There were 50,000 before our liberation. I heard from one victim that this crematorium, this industry for murder, was working two days before the liberation.

We then went West when on the second of May, I met up with American soldiers. But not all of us who participated in the liberation of Sachsenhausen and Oranienburg reached this point. A dozen soldiers, including Jews with Polish uniforms, died in the battle of Sachsenhausen. We fought together arm in arm in the liberation of our sisters and brothers from this concentration camp which was largely Jewish, Polish, Russian, Czech, Yugoslav, Italian, Belgian, Dutch, Greek, Spanish, and Latvian.

Therefore, if we want the world to survive, we should stop this hatred in people.

GUY FASSINA

When I received the honor to speak before you I though I would tell you just what a young man saw in 1945. I was an officer in charge of repatriation in the British Zone, attached to the British Army on the Rhine, the I Corps district. I was looking at the world with the eyes of youth, with the impression that I was coming to the assistance of people. Later, when I saw people wandering around in the streets where the Jews used to live in Paris, looking around, waiting for the people who had disappeared, disappeared forever, I realized that for some the deportation of the soul would never end.

But yesterday what the Chairman of the U.S. Holocaust Council, Professor Wiesel, said upset me a great deal. You [Wiesel] called upon the liberators to bear witness, and you said, "Say what you saw; you will be believed because your witness will not be doubted." They only saw a moment of your suffering, a privileged moment and a revealing one, but a very limited one. Should those who saw die before their eyes the members of their own families, those who followed with their glances their children who were held by the hand and led into the gas chambers, have to justify their witness and find a way to have this witness corroborated?

Here and there [there are] published texts which are astonishing. One is called *The Lie of Auschwitz*. People doubt the existence of the gas chambers, and if these people are challenged, their right to speak is defended. You can just say I don't share your opinion, but I will defend to the death your right to say it.

Youth listens attentively and is sometimes tempted by paradox and may at any time be misled. This is where, outside of the essential compilation of the witnesses, we must continue to work to introduce a new method of proof compatible with the language of today. Indeed, would the means of Nazi propaganda—the base calumny and slander, "The Protocols of [the Elders of] Zion,"[7] the caricatures—weigh heavier in the minds of some than the conviction that millions of Jews, Gypsies, and resistance and underground forces did go through the gas chambers?

We see in the years that have passed that sociological principles may have changed the truth, and things seem to disappear or fade. The concentration camps become historic facts and become just a part of people's memories. They become a secondary fact in the history of the whole Second World War. In the history books they are hardly mentioned, and sometimes there are sociological and literary aspects which are given more weight. The history books talk about myths, and this may make people reject the truth. That is why the literature on the resistance, as well as on racism or anti-Semitism, is so important to concentrate on.

Words change meaning because racism is used in different ways and is used to propagate lies. So what shall we do to leave to future generations the experience of these incredible facts? I think there are two different things we could do. The first thing is a kind of working program which has really been generally undertaken. The second is one which I would express as a wish to bear witness by looking at the original documents. In some cases there are as many as three million documents which have survived. These should be distributed in facsimile. Everybody should be able to see them. A German professor wants all of these documents to be disseminated because once they are known they can be fought. What can you say about these concepts, like the master race, the inferior race, people who deserve annihilation?

Language has served to place man in chains, and language can sound the alert. Let us listen to that language. And in conclusion, let me come to my wish. May every generation find men of the lyricism, the incantation, the magic which can serve to inspire by language, by music, by poetry, by plays, by painting, who can bring concern to their contemporaries in order to make people ask themselves and to doubt so that they can become better. May we learn the lesson of an unheard human drama and safeguard our liberty while not renouncing any of the moral standards which are the basis of the dignity of man.

*ALEXEI KIRILLOVICH GORLINSKY**

Mankind will always remember the bright days in the month of May of 1945 when the whole world heard the news about the victorious end of the war in Europe. The war ended where it had begun, and the long-awaited victory was ours. A great and happy holiday of all mankind had arrived. As events of the Second World War are fading away, the more significant and important appears the grandeur of our common victory.

One is terrified at the thought of what could have happened to the nations of our world and to all mankind if fascism had won. All the best that had been created throughout the centuries would have turned to ashes; many peoples would have been enslaved; freedom, honor, dignity, and independence of mankind would have been trampled and destroyed. I, as a participant in the Second World War and one who took part in the liberation of the inmates of fascist concentration camps, was a witness to the horrors and sufferings which fascism and war brought to the people.

*Mr. Gorlinsky made his remarks in Russian. This is the simultaneous translation.

On May the second of 1945, we liberated the fascist concentration camp of Terezin in Czechoslovakia and the 8,521 remaining survivors of this camp. The inmates were used there to construct an underground military plant. Hard labor, slave labor, hunger, disease, and humiliation caused great losses. From October 1941 to May 1945, 153,000 men, women, and children had passed through that camp from many countries of Europe. Fifty-eight thousand, three hundred and forty inmates, including 15,000 children, were killed in Terezin, and the majority was taken away and killed in other concentration camps. In all fascist concentration camps, especially great hardship was established for inmates from the Soviet Union, from different nationalities and different nations.

The Soviet War Veterans Committee, as a member of the International Federation of the Resistance Fighters and of eight international committees of former inmates of fascist concentration camps, takes an active part in the struggle against the revival of neo-fascism because fascism means terror, human-hating ideology, and war. In the struggle against fascism and war, the Soviet War Veterans Committee strives to expand and deepen friendly ties with veterans' organizations in the anti-Hitler coalition countries and with all those who contributed, together with the Soviet armed forces, to the achieving of our common victory.

I recollect this bright page in history, April 21, 1945, when our vanguard detachment met with a reconnaissance unit of the First American Army near Torgau at the Elbe River.[8] The meeting at the Elbe symbolizes the military Soviet-American cooperation in the war. We spoke the same language then, and that was the language of friendship. Soon after, the commander of the First American Army, General Hodges,[9] presented me with the highest military American decoration, that is the Legion of Merit, which had been awarded to me by the President of the United States. To me this decoration was the recognition of the immense contribution of the Soviet people and its armed forces to the cause of our common victory, of which Dwight Eisenhower said that the great deeds of the Red Army during the war in Europe have aroused the admiration of the whole world.

To me it was a sign of friendship in the war between the Soviet and American people and of the future peaceful cooperation between our states and between our people.

Soviet war veterans are still faithful to the "Elbe spirit" and to all the hopes which the victorious May of 1945 has given rise to. Many people in the USA, too, understand the historic importance of Soviet-American peaceful cooperation. "The more I think about our Elbe meeting," said General James Gavin, the former commander of the 82nd Airborne Division, "the better I understand its historic significance and its message. The older I grow the better I understand how important it is for our two countries to maintain good relations. I think it necessary to spare no effort to strengthen friendship and cooperation between our countries." This was said when General Gavin met a Soviet War Veterans Committee delegation in 1977 in Boston.

We fought to make it possible for our children, grandchildren, and all generations to come to live, love, study, work, and create without having to know what war is.

Recollecting the time which is part of history now, but which is so well remembered by us, I want to tell all our former comrades-in-arms in the past war, we who survived must do our best to prevent a new world catastrophe, especially a nuclear one. The Peace Program for the 80s adopted by the 26th Congress of the Communist Party of the Soviet Union, the Appeal of the Supreme Soviet of the USSR to Parliaments and Peoples of the World, the new peaceful initiatives submitted by the Soviet Union to the 36th Session of the United Nations General Assembly serve to achieve this noble goal.

DAN HIRAM

It is with a mixed feeling of humility and pride that I address this conference—the humility in meeting the delegates who represent the victims, that small residue of the Hitlerite hell on earth. The human tragedy of the extermination camps was such that the richest human language is much too poor to give any verbal expression to it.

For the members of the Israeli delegation, in addition to the human tragedy there was also a purely personal tragedy for every one of us: Parents, brothers, sisters, aunts, uncles, cousins, and families in their totality who disappeared forever from the face of this earth in this Holocaust, in this mass murder of six million Jews that was the personification of evil that no sane mind can ever understand, that Satanic and bloody tyranny called the Third German Reich, that incarnation des Geistes der stets verneint [of the spirit that always denies].

On the other hand, there is a feeling of pride, pride that our delegation stands here among the delegations of the Allied armies that took part in the liberation, pride that our national flag here is represented among the flags of the Allied nations who participated in the great victory of 1945. To achieve this, we had to go a long and hard way and breach many an obstacle.

As of September 1939, over 30,000 Jewish volunteers for the British Army, out of that very, very small community that was Jewish Palestine at the time, volunteered to fight shoulder to shoulder with the Allies against the Huns, against the German hordes. But, in the summer of 1944, the then-Prime Minister of Great Britain, Mr. Winston Spencer Churchill, decided to allow us to fight under our own flag, under the Star of David, within the framework of the independent Jewish Infantry Brigade Group. It was under our own Jewish flag that we met the battered remains of our people in Europe and helped them in every way we could to reach a safe shore, to find a new home for them in Israel. The flag of the Jewish Brigade was also the first and important step in the establishment three years later, in 1948, of the Israeli Defense Forces, the armed forces of the free Jewish state.

Since then, we have had to fight four more wars to secure our lives and independence, but what gave us the strength in body and spirit to hold out against all odds and every threat was the memory of Auschwitz, Dachau, Bergen-Belsen, Buchenwald, Majdanek, and Treblinka. The mere names make you shudder, the memory and the reminder that this must never happen again, nay, will never happen again, in any future generation, so help us God and our own fierce determination.

DOUGLAS KELLING

I am here today to relate what I saw and experienced at the Dachau concentration camp, which was located a few miles outside the city limits of Munich, Germany.

At Dachau concentration camp, 30,000 prisoners were liberated by the 45th Infantry Division and 42nd Rainbow Infantry Division. I was a physician in the 45th Division, the division psychiatrist. The camp was liberated during the spring of 1945; I believe it was April 29, I do not remember the exact date.[10] I entered the camp the morning it was liberated. This large camp was shaped in a rectangle form with a large bare center, about two or three blocks square. Wooden barracks and other buildings formed the perimeter of the square, and other buildings were behind these buildings. The barracks were one, two, and three stories high. Outside the camp, on either side of the streets, were mainly beautiful stone buildings which housed the Nazi SS officers and officials.

Electrified fences, walls, many guards, and large, vicious dogs kept the prisoners confined within this horrible camp. The camp was filthy, full of diseases, and literally lousy with body and other types of lice and vermin. Prisoners were dirty; their clothes were dirty, old, and tattered. The prisoners were starving, a forced starvation; many were sick. Their faces were depressed in a fixed stare; their appearance was one of resigned hopelessness. Their gait was listless, slow, and I am sure many at times wished that they were dead instead of being confined in such a cruel, unbelievable place.

Many of these prisoners weighed 70 to 80 pounds. I was told an average of 270 cases a day were dying from typhus fever, and many were dying from tuberculosis which was rampant, from other diseases, and from the forced starvation. The prisoners were fed a sloppy type food and bread which was made from small portions of wheat flour and a major portion of ersatz flour, which was powdered sawdust.

Now I take you to the crematoria. The eight large, vicious dogs which helped guard this area had been killed by our soldiers and were lying outside the shower and crematoria area. This area consisted of a large shower room, perhaps an area of twenty feet by twenty feet, in a one-story stone building. The shower room had multiple overhead shower heads; in the shower ceiling, there were small projections that looked like sprinklers for fire prevention.[11] Next to the shower area there was a battery of furnaces; about 50 feet away from this furnace area, there was another battery of furnaces in a separate building.

Outside the furnace area were three piles of dirt, in an inclined plane about 10 feet long. This inclined-plane area of dirt was used to kill prisoners by shooting them in the back of the head. After they had been blindfolded—some were, some were not—their hands were tied behind them in the back. After being forced to kneel down and place their face against this dirt they were shot. The dirt was very blood stained.

When I went to the crematoria area, the shower floor was still wet. Naked, clean bodies were piled on either side of the door which opened from the shower room to the crematoria area. One pile of bodies numbering perhaps a hundred, and another a few less, were on either side of the door. The bodies were piled like cordwood, straight. They were straight because they had been so recently killed that rigor mortis had not had time enough to set in. These bodies weighed perhaps 50 or 60 pounds, all about the same weight.

Now to the furnaces where the bodies were cremated. The furnaces were still warm. The odor of burned flesh and badly decomposed bodies was still strong, if that was the odor I smelled and experienced.

Besides the stacked bodies in the crematoria area, I saw hundreds of bodies on the floor of many railroad boxcars which were just outside the area. About 3,000 bodies, it is estimated, were in these boxcars. They were the European type boxcars that normally transported German soldiers 40 to a boxcar. These boxcars contained the bodies of approximately 100 each. The bodies, it appeared, had been thrown in these boxcars just any way, without any systematic order. Legs were hanging out the doors, heads were hanging out doors, bodies were along the side of the boxcars. They were dirty, clothed in faded white-and-black prisoner garments. Since they had been dead for some time and were brought to Dachau for cremation or disposal from the concentration camps and other countries besides Germany, rigor mortis had set in. They presented grotesque and contorted bodies in every imaginable rigor mortis state. Several unconscious prisoners were found among these bodies, and I was told perhaps one or two of these prisoners were saved, for at least a short time, by intravenous solutions.

What I saw and experienced at Dachau—the atrocities, the cruelty—was something which if I had not seen with my own eyes, I would not believe had happened in civilized nations. Cruel is not a strong enough word to describe the treatment of prisoners in Dachau by the Nazis during World War II. I pray to my God that this cannot happen again.

WILLIAM QUINN

I think that Dr. Kelling has pretty well described Dachau. I was there, too, within hours after the liberation and saw exactly the same things that he saw. What I'll do is go back a little in history to southern France or even before that to North Africa. I happened to have been the G–2 or the intelligence officer for the United States Seventh Army during the planning for and during the invasion of southern France. While in Algiers, our planning headquarters, we received information from G–2 as to the various prison camps, and we also heard and had reports of certain atrocities, but nothing in the reports would ever equal what I saw.

In any event, we invaded southern France and came across the Rhine near Mannheim, and the Seventh Army, being on the inside track, started down to Bavaria; then Dachau came in our particular area of interest and also became one of our targets and objectives for liberation. As Dr. Kelling has told you, the 45th Division on April 29 liberated Dachau, and oddly enough one soldier—you've heard that it would take a division to take—but one soldier actually caused this outfit to surrender. One G.I. and a jeep walked in, and the guards in the towers threw up their hands. They knew it was all over. They had been planning an evacuation, and they had partially moved some of the prisoners to the south of Bavaria. But transportation was slow, of course, and the German organization was in disorder. Consequently, the transportation facilities were not adequate, and many were not evacuated, as we well know.

On entering, I made the same tour that Dr. Kelling just told you about. Oddly enough, the impact was so great on me that I didn't really understand what I was looking at. I couldn't believe what I had seen. I was so astonished that I decided that right there and then I would document this genocidal aspect and also the torture and medical aspects of what I'd seen. After I went back to my headquarters, I called in three groups of people that worked for me. One was the captain or the head of the OSS, that is, the Office of Strategic Services; my prisoner of war and interrogating team; and the head of my Counter-Intelligence Corps. And I said, "I want you right now to get a team of photographers and your best writers, and I want you to go to Dachau, and I want you to document what you have seen." And they did.

I commanded them to break the reporting down into three categories. I was interested in the people of the town. It fascinated me that a peaceful, lovely town of Dachau could stomach the odors that came out of that camp for all of those years. I was also interested in the organization of the camp, who ran it, where the instructions came from, and so forth. The third category, of course, was the internees, what was happening and what did happen with them. This report came out two weeks later, and it was so vivid in its documentation and characterization of the camp that I decided not to weave the parts into one document. Instead, I wrote a foreword and left the reports in the three initial categories. That book was called *SS* and on the front of the book was the word Dachau.

It had pictures in it, and I had printed 10,000 copies of it, and some people in this room may have one or two. I only have one now, and they're trying to get it away from me for the museum. But, in any event, this book was certainly in all of Europe among the troops. Dr. Crawford of Emory University[12] came up to see me, and he had a copy which I believe he has reproduced because it's public property.

In any event, my final remark has to do with a group of people who are decrying the fact of Dachau or the other camps. It's just that if anyone says that there was no San Francisco earthquake, or a Chicago fire, he is not reading his history and he is trying to change it.

ALAN ROSE

I would like to say that I was 20 years of age in the British Army, a sergeant in the 7th Armored Division. I think those of us in those last few days of war saw the epitome of heroism on the battlefields after the second front and the abyss of mankind when we came across Bergen-Belsen. I can hardly speak today without being gripped with the emotion that seized me 35 years ago.

We had triumphantly liberated Brussels and Antwerp, and the British Second Army and anyone who served in it will recall the tumultuous welcome and the touching remembrances of the Belgian people after the liberation. We had heard inferentially about what had happened in Europe, but if you're a sergeant sitting in a tank and worried about meeting a German Panzer division, one's knowledge of what had happened was but sketchy at best.

The war was coming to an end. The invasion of Germany was about to begin, and the Second Army moved east through Aachen across the Rhine onto the great northwest German plain headed towards Hamburg and Kiel. Eventually it cut off the German forces that were descending across western Germany towards Denmark. The town of Celle,[13] which is adjacent to Bergen-Belsen, was taken after little resistance. I don't think that any human being could then conceive—certainly not I as a relatively innocent 20-year-old—what we saw as our tanks, almost by inadvertence, passed the gates and the rambling mass of buildings which was Bergen-Belsen. I think it would require the words of an Elie Wiesel or the pen of a Churchill to really comprehend what happened that day. I had intended to be an architect, but I decided then to spend my time doing what I could to restore the remnants of Jewish life.

The horrors of Bergen-Belsen—the litter of people who had once been human beings—and the abysmal conditions have been described, and I don't really think there's too much point in redescribing them to those of my colleagues and others here who have seen them for themselves. It was for me an indescribable sight, but I think there are certain things that we should learn from these descriptions which I will not weary you with. But I have certain simple thoughts that I would like to share with you.

In my innocence at that time, I really believed that any presence of fascism or anti-Semitism or racism of any kind surely must be expunged. Unfortunately, that is not so. As has been referred to this morning and last night, there is now an active school of revisionism which says, in fact, that the Holocaust never happened, that the camps never existed.

If the Holocaust never happened and the camps didn't exist, then all of us here are fraudulent, are we not, because we are being honored as liberators of camps. I think there is a particular duty incumbent on us who were privileged to liberate camps—if that is the understatement, and I come from a country of understatement—to perhaps devote our lives to refuting an abomination and an obscenity of this kind. I think it's particularly incumbent upon us—those who fought the war, those who were really the front-line soldiers, those who were at the sharp end—to do that. It's a duty we owe ourselves as much as the victims.

The other thing that I remember vividly is that for the first time—having served for some years in the British Army—I, of all people, had to threaten my tank driver. He was prepared there with his submachine gun to wipe out all the guards that were inside, or indeed any German, including the Bürgermeister [mayor] of Celle who, I'm given to understand, thought that, although the trains rumbled through Celle, the Bergen-Belsen camp was no more than a camp for the rehabilitation of wayward criminals.

The third thing I would like to say, and I'm sure you will understand me because I speak not only as a liberator but as a Jew, is that it never occurred to me in 1945, after the Jewish people had undergone the Holocaust—and after all, it's only existential that I was saved—that I could very well have been one of those who were in Bergen-Belsen and did not survive had my parents 100 years ago not come from Russia. Indeed, instead of sitting in a rather proud way as we did as tank commanders, I could very well have been any one of the people who were liberated. I never believed that I would have to go off and fight again in 1948 to defend the right of the Jewish state to exist—which had been established not only by historical demand and mandate, but by international law—as a member of the volunteer group that fought from all the countries of the Diaspora alongside our Israeli comrades.

So, I am both very happy and honored to have been spared to be among you, to be, as General Haig said, among comrades-in-arms. Today we forget the divisions that there may be between countries, and we come together rather as old comrades, together with all the survivors and those who are interested in the Holocaust.

I am deeply honored that that has happened. But for all of us who passed through the Holocaust, whether as liberators or as liberated, it leaves an indelible mark on us, and I would hope an indelible mark on mankind.

RABBI HERSCHEL SCHACTER

Dear friends, so very very much has been spoken. All of us here, I know, have seen so much, have read so much, and yet I am convinced that we can't begin to fathom the enormity of the cataclysm, of the tragedy that struck our people and so many other peoples of the world.

During the Second World War, I served as a young Army chaplain, perhaps not as young as Leon Bass or Alan Rose, but not much older than they at that time. I worked my way across with front-line combat troops through Europe. I was attached to the VIII Corps Headquarters of the Third Army.

The most unforgettable day of my life is April 11, 1945. I learned from some of the officers in my unit that early that morning our forward tanks had entered the notorious concentration camp called Buchenwald, outside of Weimar. I had heard the name before. My mind's eye conjured up all sorts of images. I quickly ascertained the directions and drove at high speed to Weimar and then to the camp.

As I drove up to the main gate, I was struck by the large German inscription over the gate: Arbeit macht Frei—what a tragic travesty. I drove through the gate into the open Appellplatz [inspection or roll call area] and there I was in Buchenwald. This was about 4:00 in the afternoon, just hours after the first columns of American tanks drove through and liberated that dungeon on the face of this earth.

I did not know where to go first. Happily, a young American Army lieutenant recognized my Jewish chaplain's insignia, and he approached me almost reverently. He urged that I follow him to see first the crematoria. We've heard descriptions. As I said, we've read, and we've seen pictures. As long as I shall live, I will never, never forget that gruesome scene that is indelibly engraved upon my heart and my mind. There simply are no words in the human vocabulary. Yes, our Polish friend this morning told us how difficult it was for him to find the words in any language.

I slowly approached the site of the huge ovens from which the smoke was still curling upward. I could smell the stench of the charred remnants of human flesh. There were literally hundreds of dead bodies strewn about. Dr. Kelling, you were right, but many of these bodies were not stacked neatly like cordwood. They were just scattered, waiting to be shoveled into the furnaces, which were still hot.

I stood riveted to this scene for what seemed like an eternity, tormented within with searing agony, until I finally tore myself away, my eyes burning from the smoke and, even more so, from my inner rage. I walked back from the crematoria toward the endless rows of barracks still dazed by what I had just seen.

I asked the young lieutenant who was there at my side, and who seemed to know his way around, whether he knew if there were any Jews still alive in this camp. He led me to an area called the Kleine Lager—the little camp within the larger camp. I hurriedly walked into one of the dilapidated, filthy, foul-smelling barracks, and there again I was smitten by an indescribable scene. There on a series of shelves—and again, you've seen the pictures of the series of shelves—were just raw planks of hardwood. From floor to ceiling were hundreds upon hundreds of men and very few boys who were strewn over scraggly straw sacks looking down at me, looking down at me out of dazed eyes. Last night Elie Wiesel so graphically and movingly described how he perceived our eyes. I remember their eyes, looking down, looking out of big, big eyes—that's all I saw were eyes—haunted, crippled, paralyzed with fear. They were emaciated skin and bones, half-crazed, more dead than alive.

And there I stood and shouted in Yiddish, "Sholem Aleychem, Yiden, yir zent frey!" "You are free." The more brave among them slowly began to approach me, as was just described, to touch my Army uniform, to examine the Jewish chaplain's insignia, incredulously asking me again and again, "Is it true? Is it over?"

Indeed, as Elie Wiesel said, I felt that love, that gratitude, that admiration. I ran from barracks to barracks throughout the whole area, repeating again and again the declaration, the scene, the experience. As I moved about, bands of Jews were now following me, pouring out tales of woe, asking me over and over, "Does the world know what happened to us? What will now happen? Where will we go from here?"

I stood among them. As I saw these men—brothers, flesh of my flesh, and blood of my blood—I could not help but think of the old cliche, "There but for the grace of God go I." Alan [Rose] was so right. If my own father had not caught the boat on time, I would have been there.

Thus started a period of about two months during which I spent every day in Buchenwald. I must confess that I paid little attention to the needs of American servicemen who really, at that time, did not need many of my services. I devoted myself—what little energies, what little ingenuity, what bit of initiative a young man could muster—to my new-found flock.

While I could never develop any accurate statistics, my estimate was that there were approximately 20,000 inmates, from every country in Europe, in Buchenwald at the time of the liberation, of whom only about 5,000 were Jews.

We know that Buchenwald was primarily built and maintained for the incarceration of political prisoners and was, therefore, less, less savagely brutal and torturous than the extermination camps in Poland. There were no gas chambers in Buchenwald, only crematoria. And the inmates who were then becoming my friends related to me in harrowing detail how every morning dead bodies were collected in the barracks and in the work stations and were carried off on wheelbarrows to the crematoria. And this was the less brutal? How much more gruesome could the other death camps have been?

It obviously would require much more time than I can take to describe all that transpired during the months, the weeks immediately after liberation. Just to highlight a few, I'll mention some of the programs that we undertook and developed with the aid of some American servicemen whom I found to be extremely sympathetic and cooperative.

The American army medics moved in with remarkable hospital facilities that literally saved the lives of thousands, but even then thousands perished. I set up a committee of inmates who were capable of administering some of the programs. We gathered lists of names and descriptions of survivors which I sent through military channels to Paris and then throughout the free world.

There were no postal services, obviously. We mailed many thousands of letters in order to unite families torn apart—to let the world know that these were still alive.

Many of them were enterprising, and they began to take off on their own—some eastward to seek their original home sites in the hope that they might find a relative, a friend, or to be able to retrieve some property. How sorely disappointed they were. Most waited, not knowing where to turn, where to go. The anxiety and frustration grew anew. Their eyes and hearts were turned to the free world—to the then-Palestine, to America, to the West, but how? When?

We organized a series of religious services which were remarkably well attended. The little U.S. army prayer books which I distributed were grabbed up and treasured as though they were made of gold. Only last night, Elie told me that he remembers the mezuzah[14] that I gave him and many others.

From among the Zionist groups we helped toward the establishment of a very noble experiment called Kibbutz Buchenwald, which existed, interestingly enough, until the entire group arrived months later in Israel, and there it was pulled apart. The remnants of Kibbutz Buchenwald are still in Kibbutz Netzer Sereni.

SHAEF, the Supreme Headquarters of the Allied Expeditionary Forces, put me in charge of a special transport of more than 500 children who were invited to Switzerland by a special arrangement with UNRRA.[15] This experience alone could provide material for books and articles and many more hours than I'm going to take. It was only upon my return from Switzerland that I found that Buchenwald and all that sector of Thuringia had been taken over by the Russians.[16]

Buchenwald was now empty of Jews who had all somehow been transported to West Germany and to the displaced persons camps until they did find their way to Palestine, to America, and to other lands.

Now, we are here to remember, to repeat, to keep alive the story. Why were we spared?—The problem agitates my heart and my mind as I'm sure it does the hearts and minds of thinking, sensitive people the world over.

We were spared for one reason, as has been pointed out by others—to deny Hitler the one posthumous victory. If we were to forget, if we were to become estranged, if we were to deny, to minimize, to negate our own Jewish identity as Jews and others as free human beings committed to the ideals of freedom, then Hitler will have won the war.

The Psalmist of old declared: "Lo Amut Ki Echyeh." "I will not die, but I will live." Seemingly redundant, superfluous repetition, but certainly not. It is not enough that we happily, gratefully were spared, that we are alive, that we did not die. We must live, creatively, courageously, and defiantly to tell the story to the world about us.

EFRAIM WEICHSELFISCH

The following comments by Efraim Weichselfisch are the simultaneous translation from the Hebrew by Gideon Hausner, who prefaced his translation with these comments: "I have agreed to translate, ladies and gentlemen, because I believe it is very fitting that the sounds of the language which was on the lips of the millions of our brothers and sisters at their last march when they professed the ancient profession of faith—'Blessed be. Listen, oh Israel, our God the Lord, our God is one'—be heard in this audience."

I enlisted in the Soviet army in Vilna,[17] was sent to an officers school, fought at Stalingrad, then joined the 1st Division, named after the famous Polish freedom fighter on whose flag of their division was written, "For our and your freedom."[18]

I bring to you the greetings of the war veterans, Jewish war veterans, from all over the world, who had fought under different colors in all the liberating armies. We were over a million-and-a-half. Had we fought together under one color, we would have probably been a very, very great army with many, many divisions.

We fought against Hitler who decided to exterminate the whole Jewish nation. He didn't succeed, but he did exterminate a third of our people, more than six million. We fought against Hitler throughout the Russian front.

I appeal to the Polish and Soviet delegations here to allow us to bring to eternal peace in Israel those of the fighters who were brought to burial in Trekobova.[19]

I have in my hands a book in which over 2,000 names of Jewish fighters in the Red Army, among them those who got the highest distinction of "Heroes of the Soviet Union" are named. But I will concentrate on the story of my fighting in the Polish army and how I came to Majdanek. Not far from Lublin is the camp of Majdanek where the Germans exterminated tens of thousands of my people and other nations. I crossed the big gate which is the boundary between life and death, and I stood there among the barbed wire. I smelled that. I smelled murder. I passed next to the towers of the guards who made sure that none of their victims would escape. The electrified barbed wire around the camp made it doubly sure.

I saw those wooden structures of three tiers on which these people had to live for years—500 on each structure—without any minimum sanitary installations. On the walls, I saw names in Yiddish and Polish and other languages—the last parting message of people condemned to death.

Every few weeks, new victims were brought here. Until they were killed, the last ounce of energy was squeezed out of them. They had to work like slaves. Many broke down. Many went insane. I have now before my eyes the pictures of this and the other camps and all those who fell on the battlefield. Among them I remember a rabbi who fell in the battle for Lena.

I invite you on behalf of the government of Israel and the veterans' organizations to a congress of amity and friendship of all fighters to be held in Israel.

SIGMUND STROCHLITZ

We survivors are often asked, "Do you have to live in the past?" No, but the past lives in us. And perhaps not only in us. Those testimonies today, this morning, are ample proof that the past is also a dread among those who entered the camps and were confronted with horrors never recorded in the history of mankind.

Notes

At least three groups of Congressmen visited Buchenwald in April 1945. Representatives Claire Booth Luce (R-Connecticut), John Kunkel (R-Pennsylvania), and Leonard Hall (R-New York) visited the camp on April 21, 1945. A larger delegation of members of the House of Representatives arrived at Buchenwald on April 22, consisting of the following individuals: Gordon Canfield (R-New Jersey), Carter Manasco (D-Alabama), Henry M. Jackson (D-Washington), Earl Wilson (R-Indiana), Albert Rains (D-Alabama), Eugene Worley (D-Texas), Marion T. Bennett (R-Missouri), and Francis E. Walter (D-Pennsylvania). Another delegation arrived on April 24. This group included: Senators Alben W. Barkley (D-Kentucky), Kenneth S. Wherry (R-Nebraska), Walter F. George (D-Georgia), C. Wayland Brooks (R-Illinois), Elbert D. Thomas (D-Utah), Leverett P. Saltonstall (R-Massachusetts), Representatives R. Ewing Thomason (D-Texas), James P. Richards (D-South Carolina), Edward V. Izak (D-California), James W. Mott (R-Oregon), Dewey Short (R-Missouri), and John M. Vorys (R-Ohio).

Various congressional delegations toured German concentration camps in subsequent months as well.

[2] On December 16, 1944, the Germans launched a major counteroffensive in the Ardennes region of Belgium and Luxembourg. The drive was successful at first, creating a "bulge" in the Allied line. Within 10 days, however, the German advance was halted.

[3] National Association for the Advancement of Colored People, a civil rights organization.

[4] B'nai B'rith is a leading Jewish fraternal, welfare, and civil rights organization.

[5] Presumably a reference to a type of armored car-troop carrier.

[6] Oranienburg was actually a satellite of Sachsenhausen.

[7] A forged document published and circulated widely in Europe beginning in the late 19th century, the so-called Protocols of the Elders of Zion has been used by anti-Semites to "prove" the existence of a world-wide Jewish conspiracy aimed at world domination. Hitler, for example, cited it in his own book, *Mein Kampf.*

[8] The link-up at Torgau actually took place on April 26, not April 21.

[9] Courtney Hicks Hodges commanded the U.S. 1st Army after the D-Day invasion of June 6, 1944. Although less well known than his colleague George S. Patton, Hodges usually has won high praise from military historians.

[10] The date given is correct.

[11] The Nazis often disguised the gas chambers in the death camps as shower rooms. The gas chamber at Dachau was not completed until 1945 and was never operational.

[12] Sociologist Fred Crawford, who as an American soldier participated in the liberation of concentration camps in 1945, later founded the Witness to the Holocaust Project at Emory University. The project has interviewed hundreds of ex-servicemen who participated in or witnessed the liberation of concentration camps. See Professor Crawford's remarks about the project in the chapter on the military.

[13] Celle, a town in northwest Germany, 25 miles northeast of Hannover.

[14] Part of Jewish tradition, a mezuzah is a small piece of parchment inscribed with scriptural passages and encased in a small tube, usually placed on a doorpost, but also often worn on a necklace, to signify Jewishness and faith in God.

[15] United Nations Relief and Rehabilitation Administration, an agency founded in 1943 to supply DPs with food, clothing, and other essentials.

[16] Thuringia, a region in central Germany encompassing Weimar and Leipzig.

[17] Vilna is about 250 miles northeast of Warsaw.

[18] The First Polish Division was named after Tadewsz Kosciuszko (1746-1817), a Polish patriot and general in the American revolutionary army.

[19] Trekobova (phonetic spelling) is a town near the present Polish-Soviet Union border where large numbers of Jewish fighters are buried.

On September 5, 1979, a symbolic urn of ashes of the Jewish fighters who died in the battle near the town of Oriol in the Soviet Union were secretly sent to Israel to be ceremoniously reinterred. See Isaac Kowalski (comp. and ed.) *An Anthology on Armed Jewish Resistance 1939-1945* (Brooklyn, New York, 1984), I, 628-630.

CHAPTER III

THE WAR CORRESPONDENTS

Moderator: Fred W. Friendly (USA): Professor of Journalism, Columbia University; Army correspondent in Europe during World War II.

Boyd Lewis (USA): War correspondent in World War II.

Col. (Ret.) Curtis Mitchell (USA): Writer, editor, film producer; media coordinator with U.S. Army in World War II.

Svenn Seehusen (Denmark): Leader in the Danish resistance.

Institutional identifications are those at the time of the Conference.

FRED FRIENDLY

I pondered for months after this invitation about which of those events of April 1945 that I lived through that I could share with you. Although I have a journalist's appetite to hear myself speak, I'm not going to speak. I'm going to play you a tape spoken by a man who died 16 years ago and who made this report from Buchenwald in 1945. His name was Edward R. Murrow. I was his junior partner.

The day that we went into Mauthausen in Austria was almost to the day when he went into Buchenwald. He was six years older than I was. We each filed reports. Those among us who are young will want to remember that there were three kinds of information that came out of that war: official information, censored information—every war correspondent who filed his copy, whether it was Murrow on a rooftop at the BBC or whether it was one of my colleagues on a bombing mission, had to send it through a censor—and then there was free information, which for mass communications could not exist; it was a declared war.

I want Edward R. Murrow's tape, which I play every year to students at the Columbia Graduate School of Journalism, to speak for itself. I call it the best piece of television journalism ever done, and obviously there are no pictures.

You may wish to close your eyes as you listen to part of it, for your mind's eye will transport you to Buchenwald swifter and with more accuracy than any television camera, electronic or film, could ever do. It runs about 19 minutes. It won't bore you.

I would warn you that because we had no satellites or cable in those days—it was short wave—the first three or four minutes may be a little difficult for you to hear; you will hear the carrier signal and the interference. Take my word for it—put up with it. Your effort will be rewarded.

One personal note. When I went into Mauthausen as an enlisted-man correspondent, of all the sights and sounds that stunned me, the weakness of the brave men and women who survived was the most memorable. I wrote about the thousands dead and hundreds alive in barracks—six high, four men in a bed. When we walked through, they shouted in various languages, "Viva Americanski." Then, to my great embarrassment, they applauded. But their hands were so emaciated, so much without flesh, that it sounded to me, I wrote, like seals clapping.

Murrow, whom I didn't know at that time, although we later became fast friends and partners, described the same event, hundreds of miles away, almost to the minute, as "the prisoners were so weak that it sounded like emaciated babies clapping."

You are familiar with the sound, "This is Edward R. Murrow, this is London." That battle is over. Ed is gone, but he lives, and I think he might introduce this by saying, "This is Buchenwald, April 15th, 1945." Please listen, even if it's hard.

VOICE OF
EDWARD R. MURROW
APRIL 15, 1945

"Permit me to tell you what you would have seen and heard had you been with me on Thursday. It will not be pleasant listening. If you are at lunch or if you have no appetite to hear what Germans have done, now is a good time to switch off the radio, for I propose to tell you of Buchenwald.

"It is on a small hill about four miles outside Weimar, and it was one of the largest concentration camps in Germany. And it was built to last.

"As we approached it, we saw about nine hundred men in civilian clothes with rifles advancing in open order across the fields. There were a few shots. We stopped to inquire. We were told that some of the prisoners had a couple of SS men cornered in there. We drove on, reached the main gate. The prisoners crowded up behind the wire. We entered.

"And now, let me tell this in the first person, for I was the least important person there, as you shall hear. There surged around me an evil-smelling horde; men and boys reached out to touch me. They were in rags and the remnants of uniforms. Death had already marked many of them, but they were smiling with their eyes.

"I looked out over that mass of men to the green fields beyond where well-fed Germans were plowing. A German, Fritz Kersheimer, came up and said, 'May I show you around the camp? I've been here 10 years.' An Englishman stood to attention saying, 'May I introduce myself? Delighted to see you. And can you tell me when some of our blokes will be along?' I told him, 'Soon,' and asked to see one of the barracks. It happened to be occupied by Czechoslovakians.

"When I entered, men crowded around, tried to lift me to their shoulders. They were too weak. Many of them could not get out of bed. I was told that this building had once stabled 80 horses; there were 1,200 men in it, five to a bunk. The stink was beyond all description.

"When I reached the center of the barracks, a man came up and said, 'You remember me; I'm Peter Zenkl, one-time mayor of Prague.' I remembered him but did not recognize him. He asked about Benes and Jan Masaryk.[1]

"I asked how many men had died in that building during the last month. They called the doctor. We inspected his records. There were only names in the little black book, nothing more. Nothing of who these men were, what they had done or hoped. Behind the names of those who had died there was a cross. I counted them. They totaled 242–242 out of 1,200 in one month.

"As I walked down to the end of the barracks, there was applause from the men too weak to get out of bed. It sounded like the hand-clapping of babies, they were so weak.

"The doctor's name was Paul Heller. He had been there since '38. As we walked out into the courtyard, a man fell dead. Two others—they must have been over 60—were crawling towards the latrine. I saw it, but will not describe it.

"In another part of the camp they showed me the children, hundreds of them. Some were only six. One rolled up his sleeve, showed me his number. It was tattooed on his arm—D6030 it was. The others showed me their numbers. They will carry them till they die.

"An elderly man standing beside me said, 'The children—enemies of the state.' I could see their ribs through their thin shirts. The old man said, 'I am Professor Charles Richer of the Sorbonne.' The children clung to my hands and stared.

"We crossed to the courtyard. Men kept coming up to speak to me and to touch me—professors from Poland, doctors from Vienna, men from all Europe, men from the countries that made America.

"We went to the hospital; it was full. The doctor told me that 200 had died the day before. I asked the cause of death; he shrugged and said, 'Tuberculosis, starvation, fatigue, and there are many who have no desire to live. It is very difficult.' Dr. Heller pulled back the blankets from a man's feet to show me how swollen they were. The man was dead. Most of the patients could not move.

"As we left the hospital, I drew out a leather billfold, hoping that I had some money which would help those who lived to get home. Professor Richer from the Sorbonne said, 'I should be careful of my wallet, if I were you. You know there are criminals in this camp, too.'

"A small man tottered up saying, 'May I feel the leather, please? You see, I used to make good things of leather in Vienna.' Another man said, 'My name is Walter Roeder. For many years I lived in Joliet—came back to Germany for a visit, and Hitler grabbed me.'

"I asked to see the kitchen; it was clean. The German in charge had been a Communist, had been at Buchenwald for nine years, had a picture of his daughter in Hamburg—hadn't seen her for almost 12 years, and if I got to Hamburg would I look her up? He showed me the daily ration—one piece of brown bread about as thick as your thumb; on top of it a piece of margarine as big as three sticks of chewing gum. That and a little stew was what they received every 24 hours.

"He had a chart on the wall, very complicated it was. There were little red tabs scattered through it. He said that was to indicate each 10 men who died. He had to account for the rations. And he added, 'We are very efficient here.'

"We went again into the courtyard, and as we walked, we talked. The two doctors, the Frenchman and the Czech, agreed that about 6,000 had died during March. Kerscheimer, the German, added that back in the winter of '39, when the Poles began to arrive without winter clothing, they died at the rate of approximately 900 a day. Five different men asserted that Buchenwald was the best concentration camp in Germany. They had had some experience with the others.

"Dr. Heller, the Czech, asked if I would care to see the crematorium. He said it wouldn't be very interesting because the Germans had run out of coke some days ago and had taken to dumping the bodies into a great hole nearby.

"Professor Richer said perhaps I would care to see the small courtyard. I said yes. He turned and told the children to stay behind.

"As we walked across the square, I noticed that the professor had a hole in his left shoe and a toe sticking out of the right one. He followed my eyes and said, 'I regret that I am so little presentable, but what can one do?'

"At that point, another Frenchman came up to announce that three of his fellow countrymen outside had killed three SS men and taken one prisoner. We proceeded to the small courtyard. The wall was about eight feet high; it adjoined what had been a stable or garage.

"We entered. It was floored with concrete. There were two rows of bodies stacked up like cordwood; they were thin and very white. Some of the bodies were terribly bruised, though there seemed to be little flesh to bruise. Some had been shot through the head, but they bled but little. All except two were naked. I tried to count them as best I could, and arrived at the conclusion that all that was mortal of more than 500 men and boys lay there in two neat piles.

"There was a German trailer which must have contained another 50, but it wasn't possible to count them. The clothing was piled in a heap against the wall. It appeared that most of the men and boys had died of starvation; they had not been executed. But the manner of death seemed unimportant—murder had been done at Buchenwald. God alone knows how many men and boys have died there during the last 12 years. Thursday I was told that there were more than 20,000 in the camp; there had been as many as 60,000. Where are they now?

"As I left that camp, a Frenchman who used to work for Havas in Paris came up to me and said, 'You will write something about this perhaps?' And he added, 'To write about this you must have been here at least two years. And after that, you don't want to write any more.'

"I pray you to believe what I have said about Buchenwald. I have reported what I saw and heard, but only part of it; for most of it I have no words. Dead men are plentiful in war, but the living dead, more than 20,000 of them in one camp—and the country . . . was pleasing to the eye, and the Germans were well fed and well dressed. American trucks were rolling toward the rear filled with prisoners. Soon they would be eating American rations—as much for a meal as the men at Buchenwald received in four days.

"If I have offended you by this rather mild account of Buchenwald, I am not in the least sorry. I was there on Thursday, and many men in many tongues blessed the name of Roosevelt. For long years his name had meant the full measure of their hope. These men, who had kept close company with death for many years, did not know that Mr. Roosevelt would within hours join their comrades who had laid their lives on the scales of freedom.

"Back in 1941, Mr. Churchill said to

me, with tears in his eyes, 'One day the world and history will recognize and acknowledge what it owes to your President.' I saw and heard the first installment of that at Buchenwald on Thursday. It came from men from all over Europe. Their faces, with more flesh on them, might have been found anywhere at home. To them, the name Roosevelt was a symbol, a code word for a lot of guys named Joe who were somewhere out in the blue with the armor heading East.

"At Buchenwald they spoke of the President just before he died. If there be a better epitaph, history does not record it."

BOYD LEWIS

The silence that followed Murrow's broadcast is the most eloquent applause I have ever heard in my life. I only wish I could add a little more silence to that which you gave as a tribute to one of the greatest reports I have ever heard.

I was a war correspondent in Europe at the time Ed Murrow gave that broadcast. This is the first time that I have heard it, and I tell you, I share the deep emotion that is within all of you.

Being asked to follow Murrow on this podium is like being asked to give a demonstration of painting after Rembrandt has just finished. I use that allusion because in my retirement life I am now a professional portrait painter. I wish I could paint many of the faces which came before me as I heard that broadcast.

What I wish to speak to in a very few moments is the question of credibility. It seems to me outrageous that one should have to speak, as was done in this meeting yesterday, of the fact that people sometimes doubt that there were those camps in Germany and Poland and the other countries.

I had a vivid description of this lack of credibility at the end of the war when the first reports from the men that I had assigned to the forward positions began to send back those awful words which the newspapers printed under sensational headlines. I was shocked a few days later to learn in messages from my home office that there was great doubt in many quarters in the United States that the correspondents had given a true picture. Many people, including many people in Washington, felt the correspondents had overdone it, that they had been carried away, that they had been overemotional.

So I was delighted to learn within a few more days that a delegation of VIPs was being flown over from the United States to "put the picture in perspective." They landed in Paris—a rather cocky lot. They were some of the best men in the communications industry. I don't recall all their names now, but one was my friend Lowell Thomas; one was my friend and neighbor Bill Chenery, the editor of the late, lamented *Collier's* magazine. There was the editor of *Newsweek* magazine. There were editors and publishers of large newspapers and newspaper chains.

They were a little patronizing as they went through the Scribe Hotel where the correspondents made their headquarters. They headed for those camps, which had been fairly well cleaned up by the time they got there. But, I tell you, when they came back at the end of the week and we greeted them at the door of the Scribe, we looked upon men who had gazed into the jaws of hell, and they believed. They believed. Believe you me, they believed.

So, if there is a theme for a war correspondent in speaking to you here in this marvelous gathering, it is, "Believe. Believe, and let us all do something about it."

CURTIS MITCHELL

This is a most solemn occasion and a most difficult one for all of us. We have heard all the things that cannot be put into words. We have heard that words are not adequate in any language to describe the things that happened on the eastern and western fronts.

I take exception to that to some extent because there are words that will describe it to somewhat better effect, but nobody can use them here. Nobody can use them except in his mind at night when he lies in his bed and he tries to say what really happened and how bad it was, and then somehow or other words of such filth and eloquence and pain come through the mind that you realize you can never utter them, even to the wife you have lived with for 50 years.

So I think all of us, certainly some of us, carry a burden of sorts. I wish I could liberate myself from that burden right here in your ears, but I cannot do that because of my cultural background, my inhibitions, and also, perhaps, because it wouldn't really accomplish what I would hope would be accomplished, because of the shocking effect.

However, I can tell you, as we have heard again last night and today, what I saw. But first, before I tell you that, I want to talk about something that I think will surprise our first speaker, who probably doesn't know that Ed Murrow was not originally headed toward the camp where he made that great report that you just heard.

I was in the Scribe Hotel also, representing the American War Department, and had been sent there on a War Department mission to see that the press was able to cover, with every possible liberty, the elimination of the Nazi system from the world. This meant censorship, opening up of censorship. This meant assisting in any way that I could.

During this period there came a time when we had crossed the Rhine—Montgomery in the North had crossed the Rhine; Patton in the South had crossed the Rhine. While there was no race literally between the two divisions because they were all under one command, there was, nevertheless, a rivalry between the people who wanted to be there first.

We had heard about these camps. There had been a few covert stories. A great reporter named Jimmy Cannon who published in the New York Hearst press at that time had hinted at these things.[2] One day I was in my room in the Scribe Hotel and Ed Murrow, whom I had known earlier, came to my room. He said, "I just heard that Belsen is probably going to be the first camp liberated." And I said, "Well, that's what I heard last night. Some people have just come down from General Montgomery's headquarters, and he's moving. There's a good chance that Belsen will be liberated." He said, "Well, I understand that you are trying to go in that direction." "Yes." "Can I go with you?"

So we agreed that we would take off for Belsen two days later. One day later, Patton broke loose. The American South front moved forward. Ed came back and said, "I'm sorry, but these are American troops. I am an American reporter for the American public, and I cannot go north to talk about the British occupying a camp. So I'll have to join the American correspondents."

And that he did. But for that change of plans, he would not have made that great reportage. It certainly is a masterpiece and a crossroads in the history of broadcasting—television or radio—of what really happened in the war.

To follow up on that a little bit, you have just heard that a group of newspaper editors were immediately flown over. One general up at the front had seen this for himself. I have forgotten his name. He called General Eisenhower and persuaded him to go immediately to see for himself. Then General Eisenhower sent word back to General Marshall in the Pentagon and said, "Get the newspaper editors over here as fast as possible." These editors were the first. Simultaneously almost, there was a group of, I think it was 10 or 12 congressmen—key congressmen, key committeemen—who were assembled.[3]

You wonder how stories get out. They get out because some eager beaver somewhere sees a great disservice to humanity and says, "Let's do something about it." And that is what was done. It started with an eager beaver somewhere down the line, and he said, "We've got to tell this story."

It went up the line, as it must in all army and military organizations, and the first thing we knew not only was this story being told in these interviews with these people who had seen the camps, who had walked into the extermination department, but we were also being told, "Get other people over here."

My station was here in the Pentagon. In our news division, we had an operation which consisted of reporters covering [for] the press, covering [for] the newsreels, and covering [for] the still pictures. Television at that time had not been invented—it had been invented but not made practical.

In turn, the Army provided large planes to take over groups of 20, 30 of these editors. I was able to also include the representatives of all the Hollywood production studios and distribution services so that if ever a picture was made someday, of which somebody would come along and say, "This never happened," the men around the studios would know what had happened and would be able to provide an antidote for that.

What is happening now is that most of my companions of that day, most of the generals, most of the studio heads, have passed on. They are dead or retired. We are bringing up another generation which doesn't know what really happened. That is the reason I want to add my testimony to what I have heard this morning and last night about the things I saw.

In kind, my testimony is pretty similar—not too different from what you have heard already. You have heard of bodies being heaped like cordwood. It is amazing that so many stories repeated the line, "They were heaped like cordwood." Why this is an American way of expressing the horror of bodies laid on bodies, I don't know, but there it was.

As I walked down the main street of Belsen after I entered it—I have forgotten the date, but it was early in April—here were bodies before every single barracks; women on one side, men on the other side, with the bodies heaped like cordwood.

Then came a truck—the process of removing those bodies. Do you understand that here was a world gone wild, a world gone hopeless, a world gone without any plans for what was happening? Usually there would be two Americans, or two, in this case, Canadian or British soldiers escorting the guards who had been the ones who guarded the camp. They would march their detail of these ex-guards to where the bodies were. One would get at the feet, the other at the head. Then they would reach down, they would grab the ankles, they would grab the sleeves or arms of the men. They would carry that body to the back of the truck, and they would swing it back and forth three times and then hurl it up into the truck where it was allowed to thump with a grievous sound.

That happened until all those bodies were removed, and the next bodies were removed. Finally, when my car got down to the end of that street, here was a huge open ditch which had in it, they told me, between 1,000 and 2,000 bodies which had been picked up from the streets in the last two days.

Beyond, I looked over and here were heaps of earth raised about three feet above the level. On each one was a white sign. On this sign, "Grave Number One—5,000 people," "Grave Number Two—5,000 people," and on through Grave Number Three and Grave Number Four.

It so happened that I had with me a camera crew from the U.S. Army Signal

Corps, and I took some of these pictures myself. Then it occurred to me, when they had thrown all of these bodies into this grave, that someday something like this [denying the existence of the camps and the Holocaust] might happen. And when it did happen, could anybody stand up and talk about it and have people believe them?

So, I told my cameraman, "Look, I'm going to stand over there by the edge of the grave, and I want you to take my picture." That picture is available in the Army Signal Corps files, and anybody who doesn't believe it happened only has to look at the picture. I'm not exactly the same face that I was 35 years ago, but there is some resemblance they tell me.

I am not saying, by any means, that this was what some people have called an extermination camp. We heard this morning that there were no gas chambers, I believe, on the western front, on the American front. I don't know anything about that. I only know that I saw those unburied dead and all of those graves. When I walked out of that place with my cameraman and an associate and into the first barracks, I saw in the distance something which must have been written by a medieval torture writer, because one-half of the building was completely demolished, the other half looked as if somebody had dumped a freightload of serpents on the floor.

Again, the words are most inadequate. As I stood there, they mistook me and the man with me, because he carried a pail, as the bringer of food. These people weighed only about 70 or 80 pounds and were so weak that they could neither crawl nor walk. When they saw food or what they thought was food, they took their mess kits, put them in their mouths, and started slithering forward on the floor until they had reached our feet. They wanted to touch us, and they couldn't.

One of the great tragedies, of course, in anybody's life is having a thing like that happen and then realizing that you cannot do anything about it. At every one of these camps, you may not know, there was a place where there was also a big training school where there were loyal German troops. If there was ever any trouble or a breakout, they could immediately get out the tanks. The tank school was right next to Belsen. They had put these people—those they thought could survive—in the empty tank school, and they had been so degraded, so depersonalized that they could no longer function as human beings. They couldn't hold food in their stomachs; they didn't know what to do. They broke up the furniture, the beds, and made fires in the middle of the room to keep warm by. This was the first chance they had had to do that.

They had never been outdoors for months or maybe years to go to a toilet; they used the corners of the rooms, although there were bathrooms down the hall.

All this leads me to a point that I think is awfully important and hasn't really been touched on here, and that is the walking wounded who survived. We have heard about the six million dead—gone but not forgotten, but beyond the pain of living. But as I circulated through the camp, I saw so many people who had paid the price of their imprisonment with their reason, their process of thinking.

Some of them were crawling around among the potato peelings one day when I passed by, fighting each other, taking their fingers and running them around the insides of the cans that the Canadian Army had opened and thrown out. They were fighting over these tin cans.

These people were let out of the place with no facilities for taking care of them. They wandered down the roads.

Afterwards, they were to establish things called displaced persons camps, and I visited a number of those. These were not organized except by the Allies. The DPs had to be taken care of. As one rode through the roads of northern Germany at that time, you saw nothing but DPs. At one corner I saw a three-story-high pile of bicycles. For reasons unknown, some general had given an order that the DPs could not have bicycles. They didn't want them to get too far away or they might lose control of them. They wanted them in containments where they could feed them, where they could heal them if necessary.

So they wandered around. They became their own law for a while. Some of those DPs and the children of those DPs are wandering around today. I don't know where they are, but they've got wounds. They've got wounds that will never heal.

If I may add just one more personal note to this. You may wonder what a professional newspaper man—who has seen bodies in the New York Police Department, dismembered, and who is so-called callous to these things—thinks about all of this?

There seems to be a psychological reaction called "numbing"—n-u-m-b-i-n-g. I see a head nodding because I am sure there are psychologists and psychiatrists among you. This numbing apparently preserved me from the worst. I think I'm lucky to have escaped this mystery, because I am not too acutely controlled by what I saw and what happened.

Today we have a Chairman here who married a woman who had been in these camps. I met her today for the first time, and I looked at her arm. There were the blue, the lavendar marks of the prisoners, the ones I had seen on thousands of people. Believe it or not, then it hit me. I began to realize that there are people all over the world who have these numbers tattooed on their arms, and that somehow this can't happen again. We're the only ones who can stop it.

So I hope you will join with the spirit, with the intent of this meeting and this organization which has organized it, so that this sort of thing can never come to humanity again.

SVENN SEEHUSEN

I have had no time to prepare my speech. I have not used my pen or my pencil so I ask you to listen to the sounds of my heart.

I went to the Danish resistance movement in 1941 as a young journalist. Denmark was occupied in April 1940. We accepted the German occupation after only a few hours' fight.

Very early, the young people started action against the occupying power. We started with underground resistance movement papers. In 1945, there were over 800 papers with 2.5 million copies in Denmark. The population at that time was only four million.

The Danish underground papers were very important in our fight for freedom. We had to give the Danish people the truth. We had to give information about what was happening in the world and what was happening in Denmark so they could fight for freedom.

The underground papers were important; they made the basis for the Danish newspaper service in Sweden. Through the Danish underground papers we could tell the free world what was happening in Denmark; we could talk about the Danish resistance movement.

I will try to tell you how I remember the last week of September and the first week of October 1943. At that time there were about 7,000 Danish-Jewish countrymen. We didn't know which of our school comrades and neighbors were Jews, but by the end of September, we knew who the Jews were.

I saw when I came here a map outside with millions of Jews who died in Europe during the Holocaust. But I never saw the numbers in Denmark. I would like to try to tell you why no Jews died in October 1943 in Denmark.

I remember the day we had a meeting of our regional underground group, and there was some rumor that something might happen to the Jewish people. About September 28 we got a message through a German officer from some political party people—two of them were later prime ministers in Denmark. The officer had gotten the message in his secret paper, and he went to these Danish politicians and said something would happen in connection with Yom Kippur [Day of Atonement] on the first of October, 1943.

The political people went to the resistance people and to the Jewish organization: "Something will be happening. Please be careful; please go from your homes."

What was fantastic was that our Jewish neighbors and countrymen didn't think it could be right. Many of them stayed in their homes. The resistance was sure that something would happen in the morning, so on the evening of October 1, they got a message through the papers and through the resistance organization out to all Denmark. The message was delivered primarily in Copenhagen, however, since most of the Danish Jews lived in Copenhagen. I don't know what happened, but all at once the whole Copenhagen population knew something was going to happen to their neighbors.

In the night, the neighbors would knock on the door of their Jewish neighbors and say, "Please stay with us tonight." Many of the Jews used the trains in the morning, and the Danes sitting beside them would say, "Please follow me home. You can be with me and we will help you."

I would like to be very honest and say that at that time, October 3, we in the Danish resistance movement didn't know how we were going to send out 7,000 people in two or three days. But we got them home. The truth about the Danish actions in 1943 was that they were helpful to the whole Danish population. Thousands and thousands of Danes were helped.

We in the newspaper worked very hard that night to send out information about what was happening. But there was not only the Danish people; there was the Church. The priests in the Church protested against what was happening to their Jewish countrymen.

We in the resistance movement went to the coast. We had a transport organization at that time. It was very difficult and very primitive, but after two or three days of going up the coast from Copenhagen, we got in touch with fishermen and boatmen and asked them to help us. I can tell you no one, no fisherman said no. They accepted this very dangerous task of crossing the sea to Sweden. We in the underground press and in the resistance movement were the organizers of the operation. But we could not hide our Jewish fellow countrymen for more than one or two weeks.

We were able to save our Jewish countrymen because we had a free Sweden; therefore, I am very sorry that there is no delegation from Sweden to this convention today. For me, Sweden was one of the most important countries during the war. It was a free country, a free country with hospitality to accept 7,000 Jews. We got them to freedom in Sweden in just one week.

My participation in this meeting today has been a very great experience. I have heard about how the Jewish people and the concentration camp people were forced to wear dirty clothes with lice, but I can say that we could see our countrymen come back to Denmark after the war, healthy and smiling. After listening to the testimony today, I have a little peace in my heart that I was among the thousands and thousands of people who together did their part for our countrymen.

We speak about the past for the future. Therefore, I am very happy to be here to attend this conference. I can promise on behalf of my Danish friends that we will support the efforts to tell the world about the Holocaust. But at the same time, I feel that perhaps what happened in Denmark in October 1943 can be an example for the future.

FRED FRIENDLY

The report from Denmark, what my colleagues have said, the legacy that Murrow left on that piece of tape, and what Elie Wiesel said last night, say it all.

I would presume on you only to share with you for a moment how I happened to be there. If you looked up my Army record, you would find that Fred Friendly was assigned to the China-Burma-India theater. I was a correspondent for the *C.B.I. Roundup,* which was the *Stars and Stripes* of Asia.

General Sultan who succeeded General Stillwell[4] early in April, said, "We are not going to win the war in Asia. We are not going to get to Japan via the Burma Road. The 400,000 Americans in India, Burma, China have to know what's going on there [in Europe]." I was suddenly called in to headquarters and given a letter to General Eisenhower. Two days later I was in Paris, and five or six days later I was at the front and at Mauthausen.

I was 24 years old. No one had ever begun to warn me that there could be anything like Belsen or Buchenwald or Mauthausen or Dachau. There I was, plucked out of China, plucked literally off the Burma Road, and dropped into Mauthausen, as Murrow went to Buchenwald.

I wrote a letter which I considered sharing with you, but better judgment told me to use the tape. It was to my wife, whom I didn't know yet, and to my six unborn children whom I could not even predict. Although I am not a very religious person, I wrote that letter to my mother, to those other people—my children and my wife—and asked that at every Passover it be read. And it is, every year, by a different member of the family—the oldest is now 35.

When I hear people ask, "Did it happen?" I don't understand. When I hear Murrow—and I've heard that maybe 70 times—the moment that clings to my heart, and I expect to many of yours, is the man from Vienna who asks to feel his wallet because he was a leather worker and he hadn't felt leather in six years.

I believe that little book I carry around, which is the only reference book I use very much—the Constitution of the United States and the First Amendment (which is sometimes honored more in the breach)—guarantees that events like Buchenwald—to give it one name, a generic name—will be remembered by history, by people who write about it.

But there is nothing like that first draft of history. Murrow didn't write that report a month later, 10 months later, 10 years later, or in his memoirs 35 years later. He was a very young man, and he wrote what he felt in his gut and his heart, which is what others of us tried to do.

He spoke in that tape of an epitaph for Franklin Roosevelt. I have never seen as many people listen to that Murrow broadcast as I did today. It's Murrow's epitaph, in a way. I would think that he would think that broadcast more important than what he did during the Blitz and the Battle of London and the McCarthy broadcast. I think he would like to be remembered for that, just as he suggested that we might want to remember Franklin Roosevelt.

In his speech last night, Elie Wiesel spoke about Buchenwald. Remember I said Murrow saw Buchenwald on the 15th of April. Wiesel talked about being a prisoner, a small boy, and seeing it on the 11th. They are opposite sides of the same coin, but that same kind of destiny said to all of us, "This happened." Wiesel wrote, "What we all have in common is an obsession not to betray the dead we left behind or who left us behind. They were killed once; they must not be killed again through forgetfulness. We cannot stand idly by, because what happened once could happen again—somewhere, someplace."

I've never said this before, because I've never felt it before, but Murrow's voice crying out to you, to my children, to my students, to my students' children, from his grave is saying, "We cannot let this be forgotten, because the consequences of forgetting is that we could allow it to happen someplace again."

Notes

[1] Eduard Benes (1884-1948), leader of the Czechoslovak government-in-exile after the German occupation of Czechoslovakia in 1939, first in Paris and later in London. Organized refugees from Czechoslovakia to fight on the side of the Allies. President of Czechoslovakia 1935-38; 1945-48.

Jan Masaryk (1886-1948), Czechoslovak statesman, served as Foreign Minister of Czechoslovak government-in-exile in 1940 and later as Deputy Prime Minister of Czechoslovakia. Deposed as a result of the Communist coup, he died in 1948 after a mysterious fall out of a window in Prague.

[2] Having distinguished himself originally as a sports writer with the *New York Daily News* and the *New York World-Telegram,* Jimmy Cannon became prominent as a commentator on other affairs as well, notably for the armed forces newspaper *Stars and Stripes* during the war.

[3] See note 1 in chapter on The Eyewitnesses.

[4] Lt. Gen. Daniel I. Sultan replaced Lt. Gen. Joseph W. ("Vinegar Joe") Stilwell as commander of American forces in China, Burma, and India in 1944.

CHAPTER IV

THE MEDICAL PERSONNEL

Moderator: Dr. Hadassah Rosensaft (USA): Survivor of Auschwitz and Bergen-Belsen; lecturer and author on the Holocaust; member, U.S. Holocaust Memorial Council.

Major General (Ret.) John Johnston (UK): British Army doctor who was senior medical officer at Bergen-Belsen.

Dr. Leo Eitinger (Norway): Professor of Psychiatry, University of Oslo; survivor of Auschwitz.

Marie K. Ellifritz, R.N. (USA): Treated liberated inmates of Mauthausen as nurse with U.S. Army.

Dr. Douglas G. Kelling (USA): Participated in liberation of Dachau as medical officer in U.S. Army.

Dr. George Tievsky (USA): Participated in liberation of Dachau as medical officer with U.S. Army.

Institutional identifications are those at the time of the Conference.

HADASSAH ROSENSAFT

The purpose of this session is to meet and to listen to some of the doctors and the nurses who served in the American Army during the Second World War and who came to the concentration camps soon after the liberation. We also have one doctor who is a survivor of Auschwitz.

They worked in the camps day and night, taking part in the intensive rescue operation which resulted in the saving of the lives of tens of thousands of survivors. We, the doctors and nurses, saw daily the misery, the tragedy, the suffering from all the diseases and epidemics; we saw deaths and recovery. We shall hear from members of the panel what they saw, how they felt, what they remember, and how the experience of those days has affected their lives and careers.

Before introducing them to you, allow me to introduce myself. I am Dr. Hadassah Rosensaft, a survivor of Auschwitz and Bergen-Belsen, and liberated in Belsen on April 15, 1945, by the British army. I was fortunate to have been able to work with the British doctors and nurses in Bergen-Belsen immediately after the liberation, and therefore it is an especially great privilege for me today to chair this meeting.

We all regret that none of the British doctors is with us today. I would like to call to your attention excerpts from a statement made by one of them. It is included in the brochure which you all have received. It is a statement by Major General John Johnston, a British army doctor who came to Bergen-Belsen two days after liberation. He was appointed by the chief medical doctor of the Second Army as senior medical officer at Belsen two days after liberation. He was appointed by the chief medical doctor of the Second Army as senior medical officer at Bergen-Belsen. General Johnson has asked me to express his regrets that he cannot be with us today.

JOHN JOHNSTON

Below is the statement written for the Conference by John Johnston, Major General (Ret.).

In the early hours of the 17th of April I was awakened by a liaison officer from Headquarters Second Army. He informed me that we were to proceed to Bergen-Belsen where there was a concentration camp which had been liberated by the 11th Armoured Division on the 15th. On arrival we were to initiate action to deal with the very large numbers of sick we would find there. He knew that typhus fever was present and that starvation was universal, but he could give me little information beyond this.

I decided to set off for Belsen almost immediately and instructed the unit to follow on behind and rendezvous with me at a point selected off the map close to where I had been told the camp lay. Although I had heard of German concentration camps I had very little idea what I was likely to find when I arrived there, but it was difficult to imagine how my 200-bed unit could hope to achieve much with the sort of numbers I envisaged we might encounter. Little did I realize that I was about to be faced with the greatest test of my career, with a situation that would remain engraved on my memory for the rest of my days and that would instill in me a lasting abhorrence not only of those who had perpetuated this crime, but also of those who had condoned it.

The camp was liberated, as we have already seen, on the 15th of April by the 11th Armoured Division. Brigadier Glyn Hughes, the deputy director of medical services of Second Army at the time, visited the camp shortly after its liberation. Just after his arrival and while he was interviewing Kramer,[1] he heard sounds of firing. Taking Kramer with him he went to investigate this and found SS guards shooting at internees by a potato patch. He ordered Kramer to have the firing stopped. Many dead and wounded were lying about with no attempt being made to do anything for the wounded. Judging from the number of dead with gunshot wounds that we came across later, this type of unprovoked shooting at random was a not uncommon occurence.

The dead lay literally everywhere—where they had simply fallen down and died, where they had been dragged and piled, and amongst the living inside the huts. Piles of dead. Some of these piles were three or four feet high and covered large areas of ground. They were most frequently in the women's Lager. When I was sent home in June to give a talk on Belsen at the Royal Society of Medicine I went to see a news film on Belsen which was then showing in London. One of the shots showed a pile of dead. A woman sitting just in front of me turned to her neighbor and said, "They must have been put like that for the picture." I had difficulty in restraining myself. What had happened was this. Until about March the dead apparently had been cremated, but during this month the mortality rate rose so sharply that the crematorium could no longer cope. The dead were then gathered into piles and burned in the open, but this was discontinued when military personnel in the adjacent barracks objected to the smell. Large pits were then bulldozed out and the dead were dragged to them for burial. But as the death rate and the physical incapacity of the internees increased, and this was most marked in the women's Lager, the dead were simply dragged as far away from the huts as possible and dumped. As exhaustion increased, the distance the corpses were dragged diminished and the piles around the huts grew. By the time we arrived, even this had got beyond the power of many hut occupants, and hundreds of dead lay in the huts amongst the living.

At first sight the task allotted to my small unit with its handful of doctors, sisters, and orderlies seemed totally impossible. At least 70 percent of the internees required hospitalization and one of the first things I did was to ask Headquarters Second Army for 1,200-bed hospitals although I realized that, with the war still in progress, there was no possible chance of getting them.

It was apparent to us that our capacity to deal with individual patients would be extremely limited and that our principal effort would have to be directed to preventing, as far as possible, further loss of life from starvation and disease. To achieve this aim there were several priority tasks. These were as follows: (a) to institute suitable feeding for all internees, and (b) to prevent the further spread of typhus and other infectious or contagious diseases by every available means.

The last of the sick in the "Horror Camp" were evacuated on the 18th of May. They were transferred to the building which had been the Officers Mess—now known as the Round House—which we had equipped to receive them. They were accompanied by the students and internee nurses who had been running the temporary hospital in the "Horror Camp" and who now became responsible for the Round House. Between the 21st of April when we started and the 18th of May we had admitted a total of 13,834 patients; of this number 1,844 died after admission.

On our recommendation the "Horror Camp" was then completely destroyed by fire. This was the only possible end to a place that had seen so much human misery, degradation, and terror and which was still heavily contaminated with disease-carrying germs. The burning was done by flame throwers, which accounted not only for the huts but for the rags and filth littering the ground. We had a ceremony for the burning of the last hut and I had the satisfaction of directing the flame thrower and pressing the button.

I have returned to Belsen on two occasions since. During the last visit with my wife in 1969, I was interested to see several bus loads of German schoolchildren being shown around. I should have been even more interested if I could have heard what was being said to them and been able to watch their reactions. Although it does not quite measure up to the garden of tranquility that I had hoped it might become, the place is clean and well cared for, a reasonable resting place for the thousands who lie buried there.

I have heard it suggested that now, after all these years and in the very changed international situation prevailing today, Belsen and all that it stood for should be forgotten and the area closed to the public.

I am utterly opposed to this proposal. In my opinion, Belsen and the other concentration camps must never be forgotten, not only because of the millions of Jews who suffered and were exterminated in them, but as a reminder of the incredible bestiality and cruelty which happened once "in this enlightened age" and which must never be permitted to happen again.

LEO EITINGER

I would like to say some words about one category of prisoner with whom I, for obvious reasons, am especially concerned. Their psychological reactions have been of extraordinary importance to their own possible survival and to that of their fellow prisoners. I am referring, as you understand, to the prisoners who were medical doctors.

Even they had to cope with the situation, very often by what we call in psychiatry "denial." Without using this defense mechanism, it would have been impossible for them to do their work and offer their medical help, insufficient as it was.

In spite of everything that has been said against becoming accomplices of the SS, the prisoners who were medical doctors alleviated countless sufferings and helped thousands and thousands of fellow prisoners to endure their fate.

The fact that there remained a few hundred thousand survivors at the end of the war, the fact that not absolutely all prisoners succumbed to the ill treatment, is partly due to the prison doctors' efforts.

We did nothing to boast of. It was the simplest of duties, and those doctors who were fortunate enough to be able to help were more than grateful for this opportunity to do so.

But from a psychological point of view, it was only their denial of the realities that made it possible for them to act and to work as if their human and medical activity was a normal one and of real help to their fellow prisoners.

This small example will perhaps illustrate what I have said. A colleague and I worked as prison doctors in the "infirmary" of a relatively small side camp of Auschwitz, where most of the prisoners did forced labor in a plant producing anti-aircraft guns.

One day a boy with terrible pains was brought to us from the factory. It turned out that he had a ruptured ulcer of the stomach. Under the most primitive of conditions, on the kitchen table, with shoehorns as surgical hooks, we managed to close the rupture. Improbable as it was, our patient survived.

But, as with other patients that we had to operate on under similar conditions, whom we could treat, he had to go back to his work and to his sufferings in the camp. Unfortunately, I am unable to say whether the operation was a real success, that is, whether the patient survived not only the operation, but also the war.

Fortunately, we have examples of prisoner-patients whom we treated against all possible odds and who survived not only their disease, but also the camp, and whom I have met subsequently in different situations after the war. These meetings with former patients whose treatment was possible or meaningful only when carried out under the complete influence of a denial reaction, while disregarding the realities and facts of life, belong to the most important and positive experiences in my medical life.

The fact that one can be of help in the most hopeless of situations and that this help can have long-lasting, positive consequences for others cannot be overestimated.

Another example: During the relocation of the prisoners of Auschwitz to an unknown destination, the staff of the camp hospital marched as a closed group, together with the other prisoners, on one of the seemingly endless and hopeless death marches. Late one evening, exhausted, we reached a sort of barn in which we could stay overnight.

A prisoner came to the camp hospital group because he had severe pains in his legs and back and asked for help. Hopeless as the situation was for everybody, for us just as for everybody else, he received some consolation and a pill against the pains. Without a complete denial of the actual facts of utter hopelessness and of the knowledge that everybody unfit to march along with the others was bound to be shot, even this very modest help would have been impossible.

Again, I do not know whether this fellow prisoner survived the march or not. But I know that the medical profession would have betrayed itself if this poor fellow had not received this small, perhaps pain-relieving tablet.

You know that emotional blunting has been described as a practically universal defense mechanism among concentration camp inmates. One deep and unchanging grief is the concern about one's nearest who has either been arrested at the same time as oneself or whom one worries about with the unknown murderous behavior of the guards. The killing of one's comrades, the floggings, and executions—in brief, all of the unvariable and incredible realities of daily life—had, to a certain degree, to be dealt with as if they did not exist. One tried to avoid the awareness of the difficulty of the situation by a type of psychic withdrawal from the realities.

It is true that basic psychology tells us that such primitive mechanisms are not very efficient and that even their moderate effectiveness is achieved only at great cost. We know that in normal life a problem cannot be solved when there is no awareness of it; but in extreme situations there was no realistic possibility of solving the problems, and denial of these situations was the only positive way of functioning.

Therefore, may I be allowed to say a few words on general coping in the camps? The group of people who were able to mobilize the most adequate coping mechanisms were those who for one reason or another could retain their personality and their system of values more or less intact, even under conditions of nearly complete social anomie.

Those who were most fortunate in this respect were, as mentioned, the persons who, thanks to their profession, could both show and practice interest in others and who could retain their values inside the camp at the same level as outside the camp. As you know, these few fortunate ones were some doctors and nurses. They were more preoccupied with the problems of their fellow prisoners than with their own and came through their trials in a better mental condition than the average inmate of the camp. Only a tiny minority, however, had this good fortune; the greater part had to find other ways of surviving.

I think it is necessary to stress that not every kind of denial had a positive function. The most tragic one was a prisoner's inability to assess how far he could go in using this as a medical excuse in order to avoid excessive hard work. While denial of the general death sentence could give positive results, denial of the camp's function was tantamount to being killed immediately.

After the first process of selection which took place immediately after the Jewish prisoners had left their cattle cars in Auschwitz, after their arrival in the camp, the prisoners were asked if they had some serious diseases. Those who really were chronically ill or hoped that they could get an easier life by stating that they were seriously ill were selected immediately and sent to the gas chambers. In other words, the prisoner who thought that he could gain some advantage by stressing, for example, his chronic sciatic pains or by aggravating fainting periods was in a very serious life-threatening situation.

Prisoners who denied their being in a life-threatening situation, who escaped into daydreams, who did not accept the grim realities of camp life and its immediate ghastly demands, and who did not try to find an operative adaptive mechanism were also selected very quickly.

In Auschwitz a prisoner who was not able to grasp the total tendency from the outset or who would try to escape reality by denial and fantasy would hardly survive the first working day.

It would be pointless to enumerate all of the situations that would have a fatal result for a prisoner who was not sufficiently reality-oriented. From the time the alarm sounded in the morning and the prisoners had to jump out of bed and correctly make the bed, stand at roll calls, march, and so on and so on, until the last distribution of the evening portion of the lukewarm watery fluid which was sometimes called "soup" and sometimes "tea" or "coffee," the whole day was controlled, and every moment full of danger. A fatal blow on the head was the most probable result of not assessing the bitter and grim realities of the moment or trying to escape them by any sort of denial.

Denying death could be life-saving under certain circumstances, while denying the small, seemingly unimportant facts of daily life and struggle would result in a certain and premature death. A more detailed analysis of the circumstances is involved, however, to enable us to explain the contradictions showing basic human values and positive human interrelationships that were of salient importance even under these most extreme situations.

MARIE ELLIFRITZ

I have been asked to tell you how it was from the medical liberators' point of view. Let me try to remember. After all, it has been 36 years since I was subjected to that experience. It will take some effort for me to play that mental videotape I have stored in my mind and impressed upon my soul and that has become the emotion I know today, the one that makes me more caring for others, more compassionate, more loving, and also makes me deplore those things that threaten the world's freedom—not democracy as Americans know it, for that is the fabric of our heritage. We may disagree with your politics, but we want everyone to have the freedom of choice as we know it. Perhaps that is not necessarily what you may want, but it is something we want you to have, a gift we may have to die for in order to give to you.

Emotion is one of the strongest complex reactions of man that can manifest itself as love, hate, fear, and anger. It is a feeling that one can be easily moved by. It causes tears, frustration, depression, or elation. As nurses, we attempt to deal with the full gamut of emotions, both in our own lives and in the lives of the people we try to serve. The emotional trauma caused by our medical participation in the liberation of the European concentration camps was beyond belief.

As Americans, and as women, we had never before been subjected to such inhumanity to man, and my initial feeling was of a tremendous job to do. To take in 1,500 patients into a 400-bed hospital had to be madness. That fact became our madness, and it proved to be a tremendous, overwhelming job.

Clinically, it was a matter of sorting the dead from the living, deciding who would live for at least three days or more, and to make all those we found comfortable. We began the process of treatment by attempting to keep the patient dry and supplying an air mattress to give him a place to lie down, a blanket to help him keep warm, pajamas to give him some dignity, a small amount of food to nourish him, and plasma to preserve the remaining life and begin him on the road back to living.

Precautions we threw to the wind; in combat there is little one can do to avoid danger—it is everpresent. In liberating a concentration camp, you dig in and start where you are. The danger of disease and the emotional trauma you may suffer is not a primary concern, for that will come later. Disease and emotion can be treated; the saving of human lives from mistreatment and starvation was the paramount concern.

Some of us did get sick from the dysentery that the patients had, from the TB exposure, from the emotional trauma, but most of all, it was the sickness of the heart, of being a witness to the results of man's inhumanity to man.

We wondered if we could save any of them, and if we did, what would we save them for? Would there ever be the chance that life would be "normal" for any of them? We had to try, and we had to succeed.

Everyone had work to do. The patients themselves helped as much as they could. We deloused them, we moved them out of the camp into our tent city, and we let fresh air, the sunshine, the space, and, most of all, their freedom do its work. Survival was always the name of the game.

I well remember my reaction to the arrival of my first ambulance of patients. I had never before seen a naked man, and I was assigned to the men's wards. I did not control my reaction to the scene very well. The patients weren't really reactive to me. Their exhaustion, their apathy, and their many years of imprisonment made them incapable of reaction. I was embarrassed at emotions the patients had not enjoyed for a long time. However, my recovery time was very short.

It was a new experience for most of the nurses to begin to understand the emotional needs of our patients. For some patients, trust came early. After all, we were Americans; we had a heritage. We had an agreement with our Allies that we would win this conflict, and it was only a question of time. When would the winning become a reality? Who among the patients would survive long enough for the winning to help them make it meaningful?

It seemed to take one to three days for us to convince some of them that they were truly free at last, and when that reality came, they simply closed their eyes and died in peace and freedom. Some of the patients seemed to know immediately that they were free once again, and so they were able to rejoice and begin to make plans for their future. Life force for these patients had begun when the camp gates were opened by their liberators.

Man's inhumanity to man—how far can it go? You, the victims of the concentration camps, have been there. You know only too well. I can speak only of our perceptions of the patients' reactions to liberation.

Liberation. When will it come, and who will do it? Where will you go, and how long will it take? And then it happens. The bomb sounds are closer. The enemy begins to rattle, movement in and movement out. Something is about to happen, but what? Recent rumors in the camp were that liberation was coming soon, but could you dare believe it? You had believed the rumors before, and they turned into your lost hope. Maybe this time it might be true.

And suddenly it happens. The gates are open, and your liberators are facing you. "Is it really true? Are you really Americans? Dare we believe it?"

"It really is true." But how long will it take for the reality to be meaningful to each of you? Some of you are too close to death to be able to accept the enormity of your final freedom.

I cannot believe it either. The sights before me are truly unbelievable. We are hearing rumors, also. The nurses are hearing them from our medical personnel. Are the bodies really stacked four across and four high?

It was so terrible that our commanding officer called us together. He gave us a choice—you can go in and help, or you can stay out and support your colleagues. The choice was ours, for he could not bring himself to subject American nurses to the horrors he had seen and knew would face us.

How much could he expect us to take? We had already earned two battle stars for combat. We had already nursed the liberated U.S. army air force prisoners of war at Moosburg, Germany.[2]

Americans as individuals are not too good at listening; we must be able to see for ourselves. We are travelers, we are survivors, and we are doers. And so 40 American nurses from the 130th Evacuation Hospital rolled up sleeves and went to work.

If patient experimentation was done at Mauthausen, I was not made aware of it. I remember coming home to the United States in August of 1945. I was 22 years old. I wanted to tell everything I knew and tell everyone I knew about the horror I had seen. They listened politely, looked quizzically at me, and changed the subject. Behind my back they told my family that I must be losing my mind to come home with such stories. Repression came quickly, not to my family, for they believed me, but to everyone else. I smiled and said my combat experiences were unbelievable, and for them that was enough.

What we as nurses suffered from is now known as "burn-out syndrome," and "burn-out" is the result of unresolvable conflict and stress. It is exhaustion as the result of making excessive demands on energy, strength, or resources. It is the giving of too much, too soon, over too short a period of time. It has been experienced, also, by those nurses who served in the Korean and Vietnam conflicts. We have a name for it now, but we need to seek help for those who suffer from it.

History will attest to the 11 million victims of Hitler's atrocities. Six million were Jews, and five million were victims of political oppression, of not being one of Hitler's group, of just not being what Hitler would allow. Dictatorship was his game, and if you opposed his view, you, too, became a victim.

In 1977, I returned to Mauthausen. The walls of the camp still stand today, and I'm glad I went back. My visit was a quiet one. The birds sang a cheery greeting in bright rays of sun along the blowing green-grass carpet there. Monuments abound in remembrance.

I found peace for myself upon my return. Thirty-two years of carrying a burden of mixed emotions had to be put to rest, so I left them there. I have no need to go back again.

When people speak of concentration camps, they speak of the horror of man's inhumanity to man, the works of the devil, of hatred, of fear, and of anger. I would like to leave with you a more pleasant thought, for some of us discovered love there. Love is the nicest of all the emotions, because by simply being, it causes elation, brotherhood, companionship, and beauty, since no bride is ever more beautiful than on her wedding day. But most of all, love leaves us with a tingling sensation of the heart that can last a lifetime.

As patients, as liberators, and as medical personnel there was a post-traumatic stress disorder that affected us all. Medically, I would like to know the answers from those of you who survived. I would like to know the average length of your lifespan. I would like to know the cause of your eventual death. I would like to know where most of you survivors now live and what major occupational jobs are now held by former inmates. Did subjection to camp life and punishments cause these people to become stronger or weaker mentally and emotionally? How much do the children of these camps remember, and why do they remember? How much bitterness, and towards whom, do you still hold in your hearts?

We know the figures of those who died. What are the figures of those who survived? For how long did they live after liberation? How much, how deeply, and how long this post-traumatic stress disorder affects you depends upon the other traumas that life has dished out to each of us.

Let us put life's stresses into perspective and move on. Let us move from hate, fear, anger and frustration into the emotion of love, for only there will you find peace for your troubled soul, and only in love can you forgive. Survivors we are, so let us be loving survivors.

It is my prayer for each of you that God in his great wisdom will grant you peace; love for each other; freedom from want, fear, and loneliness; and most of all the joy of sharing together the promises He gave.

*DOUGLAS KELLING**

As far as some of the medical problems [at Dachau are concerned]—and I will just speak of a few because there were multiple types of diseases—one of the prevalent diseases there was typhus. I think everybody in the camp had body lice, and typhus fever is carried by body lice. I was told that on an average each day 270 patients died from typhus fever. Many patients died from tuberculosis. It was rampant. Many patients died just from starvation, this forced starvation.

It looked as if these people were trying in every way to be more cruel, in any way that they possibly could, thinking of these devious, cruel methods to destroy innocent people.

When I entered the camp, the prisoners had taken over. Now the SS guards were the prisoners and were being turned over to our military personnel. Many of these liberated prisoners were wandering aimlessly about the camp, apparently not believing what was happening. Many were crying with joy, and all were appreciative. To show their appreciation, they gathered in this exercise area in the middle of the rectangle in national groups, and that was a pitiful sight to see these poor, sick, emaciated people in tattered dirty clothes showing their appreciation. It made you want to cry, and I did cry.

They had been treated cruelly, as you know, from the time they entered this camp. But the important thing, their pride, self-esteem, was still there. They were so happy to be liberated that their foremost thought now was to return home to their relatives and friends. But now, the true realism presented itself. Their homes had probably been destroyed; their relatives and friends had probably been killed or possibly were in other concentration camps. Although liberated and now free, ill with various diseases, and emaciated by this diet, many, and naturally so, became quite depressed. We all would. They could not be termed "mentally ill." They were acting just as any normal person would act in a similar environment. I considered them weak physically, but very strong mentally, to have endured the tortures they had undergone.

Having been subjected to such brutal treatment and now liberated at last, these prisoners could, in my opinion, adjust to their new freedom, experiencing depression, despondency, sorrow, weakness, physical impairment, and disease in a better manner than most of us could. They were naturally angered, and hated those who held them captive and treated them so cruelly. I am sure they were all hoping, thinking, and wanting to bring these guilty persons to justice. I'm

*Dr. Kelling repeated here much of his statement made during the session entitled "The Eyewitnesses." That material has been removed here for reasons of space.

sure they were thinking, how could such things have happened and what can we do to keep this from happening in the future?

As Division psychiatrist, quarters were set up for me in the camp where I could continue to treat our military personnel when needed and offer my services to the former prisoners of the camp. I was consulted only very infrequently by an occasional former prisoner about personal problems. It seems to me that the thought of getting out of this terrible camp probably suppressed some abnormal mental states and thoughts for the immediate time being, which might surface later on.

Some of my other duties were camp inspections to suggest means to improve the prevailing camp sanitation. The necessary medical treatment of the prisoners was cared for by the prisoner physicians and by medical units from the services, such as the field hospitals and evacuation hospitals, which were brought in to help with this problem.

Would that I could erase my memories of Dachau forever.

GEORGE TIEVSKY

By way of background, I was 28 years old at the time. I had just finished my internship at the local municipal hospital, which is like any municipal hospital in a large city—one sees the bottom strata of society, the lowest level, sometimes the animal level. I had seen malnutrition; I had seen drug addiction; I had seen, I thought, the worst that society could present. I was horribly surprised.

The 66th Field Hospital was a unit which is now known as a "Mobile Army Surgical Hospital," MASH, for short. It was used for critically injured soldiers who could not be transported. We were outside of small fire range but within artillery range, so we saw massive wounds. This was something that I thought would help me later, although I did not know what I was going to see later.

We crossed the Rhine very early, within the first day or two, and followed the forces right behind the infantry into Bavaria and ended near Munich. At the cessation of hostilities, we were bivouacked in a very pleasant green pasture. On May 2, we received orders to proceed to a town by the name of Allach. Allach turned out to be a subcamp of the Dachau complex, about 2.8 kilometers, or roughly two miles, from there.

We set up our station; within two hours we were receiving patients en masse. A field hospital is a small hospital—it is divided into three platoons. Each has 20 beds. Each has 11 nurses and, as I recall, about eight physicians, with an attached surgeon. So our medical personnel was not great. We were inundated with patients immediately.

During this period of time I wrote letters daily to the girl who was to be my wife, who is my wife of 36 years. I have a letter here. We were at Allach for six weeks. We were ordered out on June 10th to be shipped to the Pacific, to the Philippines, for the invasion of the home islands of Japan. The letter I have here is dated June 4, 1945. I summarized to some extent our experiences at Dachau. I begin:

"We were sent to Dachau, or perhaps I should say rushed, just several days after the Americans had taken it. What they found there was the same as in any other concentration camp—human beings living in indescribable filth and utter neglect. Dead bodies lay about unburied, and the stench was almost unbearable. The sick were in buildings called 'hospitals'—revieres they called them—fifty or sixty to a small room, in beds three tiers high, and with two, sometimes three, persons to one bed.

"There were no blankets, even during the coldest part of the winter. Sanitary facilities were practically nonexistent, and the floor was slimy with excreta. The odor was horrible.

"Food was practically nonexistent and medicines even scarcer. There were many doctor prisoners, but they weren't given anything with which to work.

"These were the conditions in the compound, that is, the main area of the camp.

"We moved into the area, Allach, used by the SS guards and other camp personnel, and this wasn't quite so bad. In this area were a few buildings in which prisoners had been housed, and these we used as our hospital—after much cleaning out.

"Our primary reason for having been sent there was because of an outbreak of typhus in the camp. I haven't stressed that because I didn't want you to worry. The term 'typhus'—that is, of the epidemic type—is one of the diseases that even medical men face with some qualms because of its extreme contagiousness and severity under these conditions. During the immediate postwar period of World War I, millions died of the disease in the Balkans and Russia. The Army is quite concerned about the disease and has typhus teams that work in all areas in which typhus is found.

"Our first function was to set up a ward, which was formerly a gymnasium or theater, for the typhus patients. The diagnosis was made in the compound, and they were then sent into us. The 3rd Platoon was in this ward, our platoon having nothing to do with it. When the patients were received there, they were bathed, their clothing discarded, and their entire body dusted with DDT—the new marvelous insecticide. They had previously been deloused in the compound, but no chances were taken.

"We were all surprised at the relative mildness of the disease and few deaths. True, the patients would have high fevers—103 to 104 degrees—and severe headaches, but almost always recovery would occur. The answer was quite simple—we were seeing patients after the disease had been active for nine months. Remember the mortality curve in an epidemic? It always tapers off after a little while because of a number of different reasons.

"The 2nd Platoon—ours—took general medical and surgical cases. The most immediate problem in these patients was that of starvation; the complications could generally wait until that was licked.

"I think I have already written descriptions of the living skeletons that were carried into our building. It was incredible to look at them and think that they might still be living. We fed them soups and gruel at first and added solid food little by little. Some could take nothing. And to these we gave plasma, sometimes orally, later. All of them had very severe diarrhea, with eight to twenty stools per day. It was primarily on a nutritional basis, for with paregoric and a little food almost all of them responded promptly.

"I had an opportunity to see the vitamin-deficiency diseases in their classical textbook pictures, something that is very rarely seen. We saw the hyperkeratasis, thickened skin, of A-deficiency, and the night blindness which accompanies this deficiency. One of my patients was totally blind in dim light. Most of the patients had bronchial conditions due to A-deficiency. Thiamine and B-1 deficiencies were manifested by peripheral nerve disturbances and weakness of the extremities. I even saw one case of wet beriberi, an extremely rare condition in this part of the world. The patient was edematous up to the clavicles and in addition had much fluid in his left chest. Nicotinic acid (B–2) deficiency was manifested by his characteristic dark brown skin pigmentation, diarrhea, and mental disorders.

"Sevatomic acid deficiency showed up as areas of bleeding beneath skin and gums. Most of the patients showed mixed pictures of the deficiency diseases so our primary problem was that of feeding them and administering large quantities of vitamins.

"Things proceeded smoothly for a while, and then the Army—which had sent us there—found out that the patients we were feeding were not GIs and refused us food and medicines. That's right! It sounds incredible, doesn't it? We were sent there to salvage a few souls, and we were expected to do it with our bare hands.

"The patients were reduced to two very skimpy meals a day, of a quality totally unfit for persons in their condition. The black bread they were given was alone enough to induce their diarrhea again. This went on for seven to 10 days, and my ward rounds during this time were not very pleasant. The patients just couldn't understand what had happened. All that they knew was that hunger was gnawing away at them again. 'For six years we waited for the Americans to come; are we to die of hunger now?' I can still hear ringing in my ears their 'Nicht essen?' (Nothing to eat?) and the hungry look on their faces. It made us all feel so bad and so angry and so helpless, and all because of incompetence and red tape some place. That's the Army.

"Finally, things improved, and by the time we left there was adequate food. Medicines we were still having difficulty getting.

"I took care of about 70 patients, 25 or 30 being women. I will write about them more than about the men, as I have written in former letters about the men.

"Ward G had 11 patients. The first bed on the right was that of a pretty young girl with far-advanced tuberculosis. I was just about to segregate the tuberculosis cases when we moved out. Next to her was a very nice, intelligent, middle-aged woman who had been brought over with her two daughters, one 16 and the other 14. We didn't want to separate them. When I left, the mother had been running a fever for some days, and I was afraid that she had typhus.

"In the corner on the right was a malnourished middle-aged woman, and beside her a very pretty 14-year-old child, quite healthy. Six years of her childhood had been spent in the ghetto and in concentration camps, and in spite of it she was still a darling child.

"Next to her was one of the most vivacious, spirited persons that I have met in a long time—a very pretty woman in spite of all she had been through, and one with a great deal of spirit. And that was the most remarkable part, that her spirit was unbroken.

"The girl next to her, also young, had an infection of the leg—probably tuberculous in origin. Also a very nice personality.

"And then there was the woman who had been wounded in the buttocks by shrapnel. I always used to tell her that she would get a medal for her wounds, and she would laugh at that.

"I walked into the infirmary at the main compound on another day and met there a very striking character and one whom I shall remember for a long, long time. His name is Dr. Joseph Heller, and he was the chief doctor in the Jewish section of the camp. He is an older man and practiced gynecology and surgery for 20 years before the Germans came. He was rounded up with all the other Jewish doctors.

"In this one compound there were originally 164 of them, of whom only 59 are now living—one year later.

"The Germans gave him no medicine. A chimney sweep smuggled these to him every week. He improvised surgical dressings. Gummed paper was used as adhesive tape. He had one hypodermic syringe.

"One night a man with an abdominal wound was brought in, and the commandant refused to allow him to operate at first. After much persuasion he agreed, but meanwhile the patient had been transferred to a place 10 miles away. So Dr. Heller walked the 10 miles at night, carrying his instruments, and operated. And he said the patient lived, with a great smile.

"I invited him to make rounds with me the next day and sent over an ambulance for him that morning. He was very happy, very happy, to have a chance to learn a little of the progress that medicine had made during the war years in the world outside the Germans' sphere of influence. And I felt humbled, very humbled, before a man who had done so very much with nothing at his disposal and with death at his elbows at all times.

"His first question was about penicillin, and I told him as much as I knew of its use. Then he asked me about the yellow fluid the patients had been receiving intravenously. For a moment I did not understand, then—plasma! Of course. We made the rounds and enjoyed it immensely. I took him to my room to wash up before dinner, and after he had washed I saw him looking intently and at some length into the mirror. 'This is the first time I have seen my face in a mirror in several years.' The white-breaded lunch brought comment, as did the preserved cherries he had for dessert.

"My last rounds were quite hurried, as we were to leave in a few minutes, and I didn't have much time to spend. A number of the patients were standing outside, and they stopped me to shake my hand and to express their appreciation. They all wished me a speedy return home; they knew that I was not going back to the United States. 'Time will pass, and it will all be over soon,' one of them said. 'Yes,' said her friend, 'that is what she told me when we rode the freight cars for days, and that is what she said all the months in the concentration camp.'

"'Jews will always live', added the first. 'Auf Wiedersehen! Auf Wiedersehen!'"

DISCUSSION

RAY KANER: I am Ray Kaner from the Center for Holocaust Studies. I am a survivor of Lodz ghetto, Auschwitz, and Bergen-Belsen. I don't have a question, but I have a story I would like to tell.

I was in Bergen-Belsen from late December 1944 to April 1945. In late March I was very, very sick. I had typhoid; I was unconscious, dreaming only about water. We didn't have water. We didn't have anything. I was in a barrack, and I couldn't get up, and I was beaten every day.

I said to my sister "Go to the reviere, go to Dr. Bimko[3] and please see if I could go into the hospital. At least I could lie down and nobody is going to beat me up."

She smuggled herself in from one camp to the other and pleaded. She said, "Doctor, my sister's dying after so many years of living. Please give her a chance. She's a little girl."

Dr. Bimko said, "No, there is no room. Do you see what's happening? Three in a bunk—three in a bed." But then she took pity and she said, "Bring your sister under one condition—you have to wash her when you bring her. We have water here."

My sister came back. I couldn't walk. Somehow she dragged me through from one camp to the other, to the reviere. We came in, and I felt, "Now, if I'm in a hospital, I won't get lice. I'll have some water to drink." It wasn't so, but she washed me, and naked she brought me into Dr. Bimko. They didn't think I would live through the night. As a matter of fact, they had some glucose, and they had to decide to whom to give this injection. They decided that I was not good material. I would not survive, and it was a waste on me. They put me on top, because this was the only place. Somehow, maybe because of this cold water that my sister washed me in, my temperature dropped. I did survive the night.

On the other side of this place was another survivor from my camp. Dr. Bimko saved her. Her name was Sima Kaplan Heishrick. She wanted to save me, too, so she pleaded with the doctor. She said, "This is my student from high school. Would you let her lay next to me so I could keep an eye on her?" It was permitted, and I was brought in, and I lay down in a bed that was a very narrow little cot with two more girls—both unconscious, both having diarrhea, and I with them.

I just want to tell you there was very little that a person could do. But if a person did so much good in saving others, we have to recognize this because it was such a bad time.

[To Dr. Rosensaft] I looked for you for many years—36 years.

UNIDENTIFIED SPEAKER: This will just take a couple of minutes. I asked the chairperson if I could interject my representation on this panel for just a couple of minutes because unlike all of the very distinguished professionals that you have heard from, I was a 19-year-old surgical technician. I had one semester of pre-med as a freshman and served in five different camps in Europe: Hemer[4], Oberhauf;[5] Branau;[6] Ebensee,[7] of which I have some pictures at the far end of the room; and Wels,[8] but most of the time at Ebensee.

You asked at the very beginning what our reactions might have been, and as you have seen from the distinguished panelists it is very difficult for any of us in the room to talk about these things without feeling, without emotion.

Nineteen years old is very young. Someone asked me the other day when I spoke to a group of children of survivors in the San Francisco area, "What was your first feeling the first day you drove into one of these camps?" And I said, "Nothing. Blank. I felt nothing." I couldn't let myself feel anything, and I didn't feel anything for 15 years after, emotionally. Then it hit me and I got busy in the Jewish community and have been very involved since.

I think I just want to add this to our medical panel. Because of our involvement in these camps, more on a personal basis than as a liberator—and I dislike that word intensely; it's embarrassing—I think that from this point on we had better get busy on the outside and see that this never happens again.

UNIDENTIFIED SPEAKER: I also wanted to say I am a survivor of Bergen-Belsen. I was a witness to getting rid of all the dead people, how they took rags and tied them to the ankles of the dead, tied them to their necks, and dragged them. I was assigned to it, too, but I couldn't do it. They told me I would get the next soup to eat, but I couldn't do it.

I saw a man who cut a dead body open and took something out, and he ate it. He was then kicked to death, and he was dragged to the grave, to the mass grave. This was where our camp was. That is where we were sleeping.

UNIDENTIFIED SPEAKER: I have a question, and I don't know whether the people who are here know the answers.

We know about the problems—as Walter Laqueur's book has it, "the terrible secret."[9] In other words, the secret that everybody knew that wasn't shared appropriately or acted on. My question is, were any of the medical personnel briefed in any way as to what to expect, and how to prepare for the camps? After all, our intelligence people did know about the camps; they had information. Were any of the medical people given briefings to know how they could go in and cope?

UNIDENTIFIED PANELIST: I can't answer for the entire panel, but I would say, no. We were not briefed. This was an entire surprise and entirely different to medical knowledge we had experienced in medical education and in practice. Essentially, no.

UNIDENTIFIED SPEAKER: The question follows the one that Dr. Eckhardt just asked. Did psychiatric problems develop in the men who came into the camps as a result of what they saw?

DR. HADASSAH ROSENSAFT: May I answer this? I am not a psychiatrist, and at that time I knew even less about psychiatry than I know now. But at the beginning of the liberation, we couldn't even deal with these problems because the disease and epidemics were so great. There were, for an example, in Bergen-Belsen, 17,000 sick people who were dying every day, and we had to take care of this problem first, to stop the epidemics and then to take care of other problems.

In concluding, I know that I'm expressing the feelings of all of the survivors of the camps when I say that the work of doctors and nurses who came to us from the Allied armies remains a ray of light in our memories of those dark years. They may have the satisfaction of knowing that those who remain alive, thanks to their tireless efforts, are everlastingly grateful to them.

As for the work of our own doctors and nurses, it remains forever a great example of self-sacrifice and human devotion. It is incomprehensible how they found the strength and energy to care for others when they themselves had not recovered.

Notes

[1] Josef Kramer (1906-1947), SS officer employed from 1934 in concentration camp administration; commandant of Auschwitz-Birkenau (May-November 1944) and Bergen-Belsen (December 1944-April 1945); condemned to death by a British military war crimes tribunal and executed in 1947. See *The Belsen Trial* (London, 1949), pp. 156ff.

[2] Moosburg is on the Isar river, about 30 miles northeast of Munich.

[3] The person identified here as Dr. Bimko is Dr. Hadassah Rosensaft, the chairperson of this panel.

[4] Hemer, a town about 15 miles southeast of Dortmund, was the location of a POW camp. When American troops liberated Hemer in April 1945 over 23,000 POWs were rescued, the vast majority of them Soviet. The prisoners were in such poor condition, however, that hundreds died after their liberation. See Charles B. MacDonald, *The Last Offensive* (Washington, 1973), p. 366.

[5] There was no camp with this name. The speaker may be referring to Oberdorf, Oberstdorf, or Obertaufkirchen, all of which were satellites of Dachau.

[6] There was no camp with this name. The speaker may be referring to Burgau, a satellite of Dachau.

[7] Ebensee was a satellite of Mauthausen.

[8] Wels was a satellite of Mauthausen.

[9] Walter Laqueur, *The Terrible Secret: Suppression of the Truth about Hitler's "Final Solution"* (Boston, 1980).

CHAPTER V

THE MILITARY

Moderator: Julian E. Kulas, Esq. (USA): Attorney and banker; Chairman, Helsinki Monitoring Committee of Chicago; Chairman, Interfaith Group of the Jewish Federation of Chicago; member, U.S. Holocaust Memorial Council.

Prof. Fred Crawford (USA): Director, Witness to the Holocaust Project, Emory University; participated in liberation of concentration camps as American soldier. (Deceased 1982.)

Lt. Col. (Reserve) Dan Dagan (Israel): Wounded in combat in Italy as member of Jewish Brigade in World War II; helped organize and carry out migration of Jews from DP camps to Palestine after the war.

Brig. Gen. (Ret.) Franciszek Skibinski (Poland): Fought with British Army in World War II; Chairman of Polish-Belgium Friendship Society.

Lt. Gen. Pavel Danilovich Gudz (USSR): Deputy Head, USSR Academy of Armored Forces.

Col. (Ret.) Lewis H. Weinstein (USA): Attorney; accompanied Gen. Eisenhower during the latter's visits to liberated concentration camps in 1945.

Brig. Gen. James L. Collins (USA): Chief of Military History, U.S. Army; participated in liberation of Nordhausen as officer in U.S. Army.

Institutional identifications are those at the time of the Conference.

JULIAN KULAS

This morning we heard a very interesting eyewitness account from various individuals who had been in numerous concentration camps and we heard their impressions of the horrible realities of the liberated camps.

However, little was said about any plans or preparations and courses of action by the various military commands who liberated the victims. Was there such a plan? Were our combat troops prepared to enter a camp, or did the fighting units simply stumble upon the camps, never anticipating the horrors locked behind the steel gate of these camps? What did they feel? What had they expected to find in the camp? Did their experience change their lives in any way? These are only a few questions that our panel will attempt to answer.

I know that it is very difficult for many to understand what really took place during these evil years in Europe. We read, we hear, and yet we have difficulty believing the scope of the Holocaust. Recently I visited Yad Vashem in Israel, and I confess to you that I came back a changed person. I hope that this conference and this panel will in some way help all of us to better understand, to remember, and to pass it on to our future generations.

FRED CRAWFORD

This is one of the most important and serious events in the 20th century, following as it does upon the meeting of the survivors in Israel last summer.[1] What I really want to emphasize is the role of the American soldier, and I should say the citizen soldier. We were not career military people. I joined the Army on my 18th birthday. My middle brother was in the Army when he was 20. My oldest brother had been in for some time, and by the time he was 23, he was a major.

We came from our status as students, as people working in garages, as people who worked on farms. We came from all over the nation, and we were molded into an army to fight Nazism. The sacrifices that had been made by our families and by the men who fought are being recognized at this conference, and for this I am extremely grateful.

We did know what was happening to the Jews in Germany. In 1942, in a magazine called *The Churchman,* published by a Christian group in this nation, William Kernan wrote to beware of the Hitler weapons: first hate and then murder.[2] He mentioned at that time that more than two million Jewish men had already been murdered by the Nazis. At the end of this little article, which was brought in by one of my students, and I'm quoting now, is, "Stop anti-Semitism and you stop Nazism dead in its tracks!" If there is a message that I bring it is simply that we fought the Nazis and we destroyed that particular political system, but we did not destroy anti-Semitism.

After the "Holocaust" series in 1978,[3] we decided to find the American liberators and let them tell their story. The first man that we located happens to be sitting here at the table with us, Dennis Wile from Florida. Dennis is a liberator of Buchenwald, and he was beginning a research effort that has brought us into contact with 500 American men and women who saw through their own eyes, their own lives, what the concentration camps were like. They have given us their testimonies. They have brought their photos, and some of the men behind me now have photographs of Buchenwald; one has the Dachau booklet that General Quinn talked about this morning. We have been given documents like the Dachau book which we have reproduced, trying to tell the truth to a generation that really does not know the story. The American soldiers tell this truth.

I did see Dachau, but I had seen the way that the Hungarians treated the Jews long before. When I was captured in 1944, they thought I was a Jew and they lynched me.

My life was saved when they broke my dogtag chain, and put the rope around my neck. There was a small, little cross on the chain, and they stopped lynching me and put me in a prison where I saw the loading of the boxcars, knowing now that they were on their way to Treblinka or to Auschwitz.

We have had tremendous success in finding these unimpeachable witnesses. Curtis Mitchell, who is at another session, was a colonel on General Marshall's staff, and it was he who arranged for the congressional commissions to go to see the concentration camps in April and May of 1945. We were told this, and I sent one of my students to a library and found the document, the report of the congressional commission that went. We checked the names and found one person who was still alive, former Congressman Edward V. Izac from San Diego, California, a graduate of Annapolis in 1914 and a World War I Medal of Honor winner, who tells the truth about what this American delegation actually saw as they went.

We have presidents, senators, congressmen, mayors, and millions of American soldiers who saw what it was like. No, we were not prepared at that level. We have interviewed everyone from privates to generals—the higher you go in rank the more they did know. The vast majority of us who fought the war were not prepared at all for what we saw when we came to the concentration camp, and I think that the 45th Infantry Division's newspaper of May 2 sums it up pretty clearly with a headline that simply reads, "Dachau Tells Us Why We Fight." They had seen Dachau and up until that time we were fighting a war against an enemy, and it was kill and be killed. But after seeing the concentration camp, the American soldier understood that this was different, that these kinds of murders were really beyond anything that the human society had experienced.

As we talked to these men, they responded so eloquently—even when it hurt—with their stories, with their testimonies. We are all doing it for the same reason and that is for the dead who died in those concentration camps and for the living, the survivors who keep that torch high and tell us that truth is necessary. It is for them that we must bear the witness that we do for the Holocaust.

DAN DAGAN

As you might know, the Jewish Brigade was a military formation within the British Army. I myself am Israeli-born, but I dare say that the majority of the volunteers from the Jewish community in then–Palestine under the British Mandate weren't Israeli-born but were Jews who came from all over. Everyone had his special story to tell, and of course there was no question that we had to take an active part in the fighting against the Nazis.

As I mentioned, we all voluntarily joined the British Army because Palestine was under British Mandate at that time, and there was no restriction by the British government then. It was a short time after the White Paper[4] was issued when Mr. Ben Gurion, who became the first prime minister of the State of Israel, rallied the Jewish community of Palestine to join the British army and fight the Nazis as if there were no White Paper, and to fight the British about the White Paper as if there were no war. I think those words show exactly how the condition was at that time.

Myself and my brother were part of those approximately 35,000 volunteers among the Jewish community of around 600,000 that volunteered to various units within the British army. We didn't have a very easy life in Palestine at that time or during the past decades, and the Jewish community was fighting for its existence all along. One of the major things we were aiming for was to be accepted as a fighting Jewish unit and be recognized as such. That was not the case at the beginning. At the beginning they were dispersed over the various units of the British army mainly to perform guard duty and all sorts of odd jobs, but they were not allowed to fight.

That didn't come about until September 1944, when Prime Minister Winston Churchill took the political decision that fighting Jewish units would be recognized and organized as such, and only then did the Jewish Brigade Group, which was organized as a fighting unit, come into being. The minute that this decision was taken everything was done rapidly, and in a very short intensive month of training the Jewish Brigade fighting unit was ready for the front and took part in the fighting in the northern region of Italy. When the fighting in Italy stopped and Germany surrendered there—it was a short while before they surrendered in Europe—that was the end of our actual fighting, and we were at the north part of Italy.

Of course, we heard and knew what was happening in Nazi-occupied Europe, mainly to our Jewish brethren, and one of the questions of this panel is: Was there any plan ahead to try to get in touch or contact to do something. But, as I mentioned, we were just a part of the British army, and we ourselves couldn't do much planning. As you know there were a few parachutists dropped behind the lines who were able to make contact with the partisans, but I don't think anybody succeeded in reaching a concentration camp or deep in the part of the occupied territories. I think I'll leave it to the other members of the panel to discuss whether the armies or the governments made any actual plans about what was going on in occupied countries.

Just in a few brief words I'll tell you what we did and how we did it. I think the main object for us was to reach those remnants of mainly Jews that were left after the abolition of the German army. We heard a lot from many speakers here about the physical facts, but I think the sense of feeling is something that is more important than the physical aspect of the contact between liberators and those who were in the camps. I think the major role for us was to reach out and make contact. I do not think one has to explain what it meant to be wearing a uniform with a Magen David [Star of David] on it and I think just for that reason the justification of the direction of the Jewish Brigade was right. It really brought, first of all, hope that there was a free Jewish world existing and there was hope in the future, but we didn't stop at that.

We were part of the British army, and actually we shouldn't have done all that we did, but today it is history so it was told and it can be told. All we did was illegal and forbidden by our British commanders, but all we did was organize. We organized the DPs of the camps with the main stress on the children, and we organized various mini-camps, hidden camps. But I must point out that without the aid and understanding of the various armies—I see an American general in front of me, and the French and all the others who actually knew and said they didn't but they did and they helped—all those things couldn't have happened. Without their help, we could not have gotten large groups of people across borders, illegally, in illegal convoys and then passed them through their countries to the southern parts of France and Italy where they boarded illegal ships and emigrated to Palestine. That transporting couldn't have been without a real organization that all of us took part in and the understanding and aid of our fellow soldiers in the various armies. This really wasn't a political issue, just a human issue, and they understood exactly what was happening and they helped us a lot. To summarize what we were and what we did, we were there at the right moment of this tragic time of history and we brought hope and a new life to the remnants of the Jews that survived the camps.

FRANCISZEK SKIBINSKI

There are two soldiers in our Polish delegation, Professor Chilczuk and myself. Professor Chilczuk told us about his experiences in 1945. I stress the fact that he was coming from the East as a platoon commander of the Polish People's Army, fighting with the Soviet troops. I came to Germany from just the opposite direction, through France, Belgium, and Holland as a commander of a brigade in the Polish 1st Armored Division. It may be difficult to understand why the Poles were coming this way to France—through Belgium and Holland—and how they found themselves in the West together with the British and American armies. That is part of the history of the participation of the Poles in the Second World War, and I feel it my duty to acquaint you in a few words with this history because I don't know whether everybody knows how it was.

We were the first who told Hitler, "No," after his bloodless victories over Austria and Czechoslovakia. We first started to shoot upon the German troops as they were advancing into Poland in 1939. We, of course, lost the campaign, but we were quite certain that we did not lose the war. Therefore it is a fact that from the first of September 1939 to the eighth of May 1945 in no anti-Nazi theater was there ever lacking participation by any of the Polish armed forces. At all times we maintained quite a powerful air force and navy and a powerful army during the battle of Norway in 1940, the battle of France in 1940, and in the Western Desert.[5] In the Italian theater, we had an army corps of two divisions and an independent armored brigade. In northwestern Europe, we maintained a very strong armored division whose brigade I had the honor to command. On the eastern front, we had two armies of 20 divisions and independent brigades of tanks, cavalry, sappers, and artillery.

All together, in the last months of the war against Hitler, we had about 100,000 soldiers and navy men on the western front and over 300,000 soldiers on the eastern front. In terms of land forces, of course, we can't compare our war effort with such mighty countries as the United States of America, Soviet Russia, or even Great Britain, but we exceeded those of such a big country as France.

Concerning my experiences with liberating the concentration and POW camps, it happened in the 10th month of the offensive in the west, after the big battle of Normandy. After the push towards Belgium and the Netherlands and after the liberation of northern France, we entered Germany near the Dutch border. We had been told that on the road through Europe we would come across the German slave labor camps, concentration camps, and prisoner-of-war camps, but exactly where we were never told. Every time we met such a camp, we were surprised. As a point of fact, my brigade did meet many such camps, but the most prominent camp was near the town of Papenberg.[6]

It was a single camp, a sort of chain of concentration camps, so-called hard labor camps, situated on the very bad marsh country where we liberated about 3,000 to 5,000 prisoners of all nationalities: French, Dutch, Belgian, Russian, and a lot of Jews from all countries. Of course, the sight of this camp was just such as has been described by the speakers in the previous meetings. I shall not describe it because they were too terrific sights to remember too many times.

We were all so shocked, and as we are very good people, we thought our first duty was to shoot on the spot all the SS men guarding these camps. It was our first good deed. Afterwards, of course, we reported the presence of this camp and asked the civilian government that was following the armies to take care of the prisoners.[7]

The most touching experience of our brigade was the liberation of a prisoner-of-war camp close to Papenberg because there we found about 2,000 Polish women soldiers who were kept in these camps as regular prisoners-of-war. We, the Polish soldiers, never expected to find the Polish prisoner-of-war camps and especially this camp with 2,000 Polish women. Among them, we found a lot of acquaintances and relatives. Of course, we helped these prisoners out to the extent we were able to since we were still fighting and attacking towards the Elbe River.

So, that is the story of the professor and myself and one of the instances of the history of the Poles fighting in the East and in the West, meeting in Germany and liberating German camps on the way.

*PAVEL DANILOVICH GUDZ**

Forty years ago the peoples of the world suffered a great tragedy. German fascism unleashed the Second World War which took tens of millions of human lives. The war inflicted enormous damages on productive forces in many countries, on the whole of world culture, and civilization as a whole.

In carrying out their criminal designs, the German fascists resorted to barbaric methods of annihilating people. The death factories were a monstrous creation of fascism. There were concentration camps built on the territories of many European countries and in Germany itself. Contemporary data indicate that there were tens of such industrial factories of mass annihilations. They contained more than 18 million people, of whom approximately 11 million were exterminated.

Mass atrocities were perpetrated by the Hitlerite invaders on Soviet land. On temporarily occupied Soviet territory, the fascists set up scores of temporary camps. When we came to the United States of America, we did a certain amount of calculation, and we calculated that there were 95 camps where the peaceful Soviet population and prisoners of war were executed en masse.

Hitler's bandits in these camps killed and tortured to death six million Soviet citizens and approximately four million Soviet prisoners of war. Such is the scope of the appalling atrocities perpetrated by German fascists.

Mankind, and first of all we Soviet people, cannot forget and forgive these crimes and atrocities perpetrated by the fascists. It was precisely the Soviet people that withstood the main thrust of the barbaric fascist invasions. The Great Patriotic War lasted almost four years. This was a gigantic battle which extended along the front line of up to 6,000 kilometers.

Soviet forces threw off the Hitlerite invaders and achieved a radical change in the war and liberated their own territory. In the course of these victorious offensives, we liberated inmates of fascist concentration camps, at first on our territory and then on the territories of Poland, Czechoslovakia, Germany, and other countries.

We consider it also to be our duty to stress here that in the Soviet Union we highly value the contribution of the Allied armies in the defeat of the fascist Germany—the armies of America, England, France, Canada, and other states. We will never forget the days of liberation—Soviet soldiers driving the enemy from our land and helping peoples of other countries to get rid of the fascist occupation, seeing pictures of terrible devastation, seeing the fascist machine of mass annihilation of people in action. The whole world became an eyewitness to these fascist mass atrocities and to these millions of victims of the camps.

We revere the memories of millions of

*General Gudz made his remarks in Russian. This is the simultaneous translation.

the victims of German fascism who died in concentration camps. We, the Soviet people, cannot forget that the great victory cost our country 20 million lives and the people of the world paid over 40 million. Paying tribute to the heroism of the fighters against Nazism and the victims of fascist concentration camps and those who gained victory, we are obliged to remember the lessons of the past war.

The memory of the sufferings and horrors of the war calls on us to do everything to prevent their repetition. Taking account of the destructive, deathly effects of nuclear weapons and the scale of their production and stockpiling, we must all pool our efforts to achieve mutual understanding between peoples in order to prevent nuclear catastrophe. It is vitally important for mankind that the energy of the atom not be used against life but for life, for the progress of science, for raising the living standards of people, that is, exclusively for peaceful purposes.

In the struggle for peace, for the prevention of a new, atomic war, we are solving—as was noted by the Chairman of the Presidium of the Supreme Soviet of the USSR, the General Secretary of the Central Committee, Leonid Brezhnev—"the problem of a truly global nature. For at present there is nothing more essential and more important for any nation than to preserve peace and ensure the paramount right of every human being—the right to life."

In the break between the preceding sessions, a correspondent of Associated Press came up to us. He asked us a few questions. Among them he asked what we were doing to guarantee the right of every man to life. We consider it to be our duty to report to you gentlemen that for the achievement of this great goal, the Soviet Union is making a number of new peace initiatives, among them: To continue negotiations with the United States without delay on limitation and reduction of strategic armaments, preserving all the positive elements that have so far been achieved in this area; to renounce the production of neutron weapons, if they do not appear in other countries; and to conclude an agreement banning them. The Soviet Union reaffirms once again that it wants normal relations with the USA. There is simply no other sensible way from the point of view of the interests of our two nations and of humanity as a whole. We consider that there simply is no other sensible path.

World civilization has achieved great progress in all spheres of human endeavor—in the development of productive forces, sciences, culture, and the bringing of peoples closer together. We must not allow our planet to turn into a gigantic graveyard for mankind and for civilization. We are very concerned with the present situation.

I repeat, we cannot allow our planet to turn into a gigantic graveyard. Peace is the precious asset of all people of all countries, of all nationalities on the earth. It is the precious asset of all people on the earth, an essential precondition of progressive development of countries and nations. It has been achieved at a high cost.

We war veterans know the cost of peace. And we must do everything for the future of mankind to be bright and peaceful, for people to never experience the horrors of war. To insure further prosperity of humanity, culture, and civilization, preservation of life on our planet through strengthening peace—this is our historic goal.

LEWIS WEINSTEIN

I was asked specifically to talk about the first camp liberated by the American Army. It was actually in Ohrdruf, right near Gotha,[8] and it was the first camp that we liberated on April 4, 1945. It wasn't until about April 1, maybe March 31, that I saw war maps in our situation room with the words "death camp" stated there. We had heard all kinds of rumors and stories, but they were so horrible they were incredible; we just couldn't believe them. I had a great guilt feeling when I actually found out about what happened in these camps. I had talked in terms of possibly a few thousand having been murdered, but thinking in terms of six million, 20 million murdered—I was obviously very much taken aback.

I remember when I saw this first announcement. The 4th American Armored Division was heading towards it. I remembered that I knew a medical officer in that division, a Major Levy. I called him and I told him that I was attaching myself to his division because we had to have information firsthand. I was then a lieutenant colonel. I was chief of the liaison section of the European Theater of Operations of the United States Army. I was then 40 years old, having enlisted in the Army at the age of 38.

I then approached General Walter Bedell Smith[9] who was chief of staff to General Eisenhower. I said, "It's terribly important that as soon as we learn what it's all about, you and the General head toward this camp (Ohrdruf) and see with your eyes, smell with your own nose, and hear with your own ears exactly what has transpired there, because it will be so horrible." By this time, I was getting more and more information every moment as to what was happening there. He said he doubted very much whether General Eisenhower could come. This was the beginning of the last month of the war; you know how fast the movement was at that time, and every moment was precious. Then, Eisenhower eventually saw me, and he said to me, "I know how important it is to you, but I just can't make it because of my activity." I said, "It's not that it's important to me, General. The issue is the world must know the atrocities; the world won't believe them if they come secondhand, but if General Eisenhower and others like him are there on the scene and can relate exactly what happened, that will make a great deal of difference."

In any event, he just could not make it on the fourth of April when Gotha was liberated. I am not going to repeat what I saw then. You have heard similar stories. You have heard them told very effectively, and it is very moving for me to have lived through what I lived through. But, from the field I called General Bedell Smith and General Eisenhower. When I called General Eisenhower, he told me again that he could not come but would try to arrange something for the 12th, and we did arrange it. Only when I got here yesterday did I see, a photograph on page 28 of the book that was issued especially for this meeting, a picture of General Eisenhower, General Patton, and General Bradley looking at what was left from eight days earlier—bodies lying in the middle of the camp right next to the gallows, right next to the whipping table. I did not know such a photograph existed.

But, the important thing is this: I saw General Patton so moved physically that he vomited. I asked General Eisenhower if he could not get word so that members of Parliament in Great Britain, members of the Chambre de Deputés in France, members of Congress in America, and high-ranking journalists taken at random, representing really the media of America and the media of these other countries, would be able to come there. He told me later, that very night—he had been staying at General Patton's headquarters of the Third Army—he had sent messages suggesting what I had previously said to him, but which did not need to be said to him because he felt the same way.

There is one quotation in this book, a letter that I had not seen before, a letter to General Marshall that General Eisenhower wrote: "The things I saw beggar description. The visual evidence and the verbal testimony of starvation, cruelty, and bestiality were so overpowering as to leave me a bit sick. In one room where there were piled up 20 or 30 naked men, killed by starvation, George Patton would not even enter. He said he would get sick if he did so. I made the visit deliberately, in order to be in a position to give firsthand evidence of these things if ever, in the future, there develops a tendency to charge these allegations merely to 'propaganda.'" Now that's the story of Ohrdruf.

In your opening remarks, Mr. Chairman, you referred to other events and how much soldiers knew and what we were doing about preparing for what we would be confronted with. A school of military government was established in Charlottesville, Virginia. We didn't get very much information from Europe, but we saw information that came from Japan. We had captured Japanese documents relating to how they treated civilians, and we were beginning to learn more and more or beginning to fear more and more that there was a much worse situation in Europe. We did write many articles and books and leaflets to give to enlisted men and to a G-5, which was first established at that time. We always had our four Gs: personnel, intelligence, operations and training, and supplies. But this was a G-5 to deal with military government and civil affairs. A big part of civil affairs dealt with what to do with displaced persons, what to do with people we found in the camps, and how to organize for that. There was material, but the trouble was in disseminating that material down through the ranks. It did not trickle down as quickly as we wanted to. When I first came to the 4th Armored Division, I talked practically that whole night with people about how they were going to prepare for this. They had not even heard of the manuals that we had prepared and the suggestions that we had made.

I must close with one other story, the liberation of another place—Paris. You referred to it, Mr. Chairman, in the opening. This was not the liberation of a death camp, but the liberation of a huge city which the Nazis had occupied for a long time. There was an immediate need to feed the people, to cheer the people, to get them out of their feeling of apathy into a feeling that they could help the war efforts as well. I tell you that these experiences cannot be concentrated into 10 minutes.

JAMES COLLINS

Really, I feel that I am here on somewhat false pretenses because I was not the first liberator of Nordhausen. I did not arrive there until several hours after the event. But let me back up just a little. At that time, I was a lieutenant colonel commanding a battalion of 155-millimeter howitzer field artillery. We had come from across France and Belgium through Remagen[10] into Germany, and after we got into the upper end of the Ruhr,[11] we started to uncover small labor camps, mainly agricultural. In other words, there would be four or five people who were working on a farm. Normally, these were prisoners of war, but, in effect, they had volunteered to work on the farms so they could get out of the POW camps. As a matter of fact, their life was not all that hard. They worked hard and their diet was not all that good, but it was still better than the diet they got in the POW camps.

Having seen these people, who really were not so badly off, I thought, well, these camps are not so bad. In fact, I remember one little camp of about six or eight people who were mainly New Zealand prisoners of war who were engaged in refining sugar from the local sugar beet fields.

I talked to the corporal who was in charge, and he was telling me what they were doing and so forth. I was directing him to move on back down this road where he would find a collecting point and get taken care of. Just as I was about to leave, he said, "Colonel, don't eat any of that sugar." I asked why, because we were a little short of sugar and other things during the war, and I was about to scarf up a 100-pound bag for the battalion. He said, "No sir, don't eat it. I always had my men 'schack' in it before we finished it."

So, coming up to Nordhausen, which was just south of the Harz Mountains, we were completely unprepared for what we found. I had a forward observer with the leading elements of infantry of the 104th Infantry Division at that time who, in conjunction with the 3rd Armored, uncovered the camp after a slight fight in Nordhausen.

My forward observer called me on the radio. This was getting towards the afternoon. And he said—my code name was Jealous 6—"Jealous 6, this is Jealous 23. You gotta get up here right away."

I asked, "What are you talking about, and besides, you're breaking radio silence and security."

He said, "Sir, I don't care. You just gotta get up here. You won't believe it."

Still not really understanding what was going on, I said, "Well, what's the matter?"

He said, "We found a death camp."[12]

I got in my jeep and went forward and got there about 6:00 or 7:00 in the evening. I will not bore you with the description because you've heard many descriptions today; but it was really mind-boggling.

This had such an effect on me that I made arrangements with some of the troops there—the 104th Division—to start taking care of these people—feeding them. There already was a medical detachment on hand.

The next morning, before we left in pursuit of the Germans, I had my whole battalion go through that camp to see what it was like. This made a tremendous impression on these young farm boys from North Dakota because it was a North Dakota National Guard Unit I was commanding.

Each year—or I should say every other year—the battalion has a reunion, and at that reunion are displayed the scrapbooks, the pictures, the albums, the photographs of our wartime service, of which a large part is made up of photographs of what we found at Nordhausen.

So, I can assure you that the fact of the Holocaust is being kept alive.

DISCUSSION

JULIAN KULAS: General Collins, did the fact that your troops saw the slaughterhouse and you went through it in any way change their feeling or your feeling towards the local civilian population?

JAMES COLLINS: Yes, it did. As a matter of fact, the 104th Division organized most of the males—or a goodly number of the males—left in Nordhausen to come out and dig trenches and carry the dead and bury the dead in these trenches.

My unit, when it went through there, saw these Germans, and they had to almost be physically restrained from attacking them; it certainly made them, shall I say, less friendly towards the populace. Of course, this was the 11th of April, and the war was over less than a month after that.

But it certainly altered their view of the Germans because my men felt the Germans could not live in practically the same town with all that was going on without knowing it; and if they knew about it in Nordhausen, other Germans in other parts of the country must have known about it. Therefore, they were pretty hard on them.

JULIAN KULAS: We've heard from General Skibinski, of course, that the camps came as a complete surprise, and you indicated that as well. I would like to ask General Gudz of the Soviet Union: Had you had any prior knowledge of the actual location of these camps and were you prepared to cope with the findings?

PAVEL DANILOVITCH GUDZ: About certain concentration camps, we had certain preliminary information. Our intelligence, our operatives, spies, and our military spies produced this sort of information, but in each large concentration camp—as we know now—there were certain branches. Such branches numbered 50 or 70 or 75 in certain camps, but we did not know about all of them. But as far as the mass annihilation of people, we also knew something.

JULIAN KULAS: And also were these matters communicated to the general population of the Soviet Union at that time?

PAVEL DANILOVICH GUDZ: We immediately, as we discovered such terrible phenomena to which we had not been accustomed, broadly discussed this in the press. Much was published. Many photographs were printed and published, and there were also oral instructions, particularly among the attacking troops and later among the population. We not only made photographs, but we also made many films. Today, we have brought several films. At approximately 8:00 p.m., we with great pleasure will present these films to your organization as a gift.

JULIAN KULAS: If any member of the panel would like to pose any questions, feel free to do so, please.

UNIDENTIFIED SPEAKER: I'd like to ask the American delegates, at what stage was it actually known that such death camps existed? To this very day, discussion goes on whether anything could have been done militarily about it.

LEWIS WEINSTEIN: I had access to Top Secret materials. In England, I was even given a security clearance for access to material on target areas and target dates, and yet I never saw anything until on or about April 1, 1945, indicating that there was such a thing as a death camp. If I had access even to newspapers of the world, I might have known it because, later on, I learned of newspaper stories, but whenever the question—and I can only talk of myself personally—was put to me, I said it was incredible.

I might tell you that one time, in the situation room, General Eisenhower and General Bedell Smith were there, I pointed out to General Eisenhower that there was a small railroad and that if it were bombed, maybe the death camp wouldn't receive its supply of people or other supplies.

He said our orders from above were that we were never to deviate one bit from victory, that we would destroy the Nazis with our Allies, and until then we could not deviate for any purpose whatsoever. He then put his finger up to his lips and nose and made a gesture, meaning not to talk about that any more.

That is when I became very suspicious as to how much was known and was not told. I was not very high-ranking—I was a lieutenant colonel—but I did have access to information. I often went to the G–2, the intelligence files, and we did not know it. You may know that a special commission has been appointed, of which Justice Arthur Goldberg is the chairman, for the purpose of determining what the American Jewish community might have done and didn't do within the capacity of knowledge.[13]

UNIDENTIFIED SPEAKER: Mr. Weinstein, were you personally able to relate to the survivors?

LEWIS WEINSTEIN: Well, when you see a man talking to you, his mouth swollen and with sores and pus, and he says, in broken Yiddish and German, that yesterday his brother had been shot, and then a medical officer, a captain, comes over and says he has to feed this man some glucose intravenously, and the man dies just as the medic is about to insert the needle, you can't help relating to an incident like that.

With many of the people, there wasn't much time, but you could get into conversations with some of them. Their liberation came to them as a shock. They did not expect it to happen, that is, those to whom I spoke—I did not speak to everybody obviously. It was a combination of both terror and joy that is indescribable.

JULIAN KULAS: Professor Crawford, I know you have done an extensive oral history, taking statements from our military personnel and also some of the survivors. What was the feeling of the survivors towards their liberators in general?

FRED CRAWFORD: Those who had the physical ability to even move would try to crawl out of whatever so-called barracks they were in just to see these liberators coming in. There were no tears. The tears had been cried out years before. It was the shock of suddenly realizing that they might live another day, because one of the things that was so very hard for many of us to understand was that the Nazi murders did not stop even as the war was being won. Even after Hitler committed suicide, for those next eight days the inmates in concentration camps were still being murdered every day.

One of the things that our liberators had told us—in a sense, a feeling of real accomplishment—was their getting to the camp when they did. It kept some more from being murdered the next day—just maybe an hour or five hours. If they had been delayed another short period of time, there would have been other murders in those same camps.

Our men understood how important that was. Certainly, someone knew. There is also in this booklet that has been prepared for this conference on page 22 an aerial photograph of Auschwitz. We have them of Dachau. We have them of Buchenwald. So, aerial reconnaissance certainly had adequate information about the location of these concentration camps and about what was going on in them. The break came only a month ago when, finally, the writers who are now revealing what the British intelligence system had done with the German code—ULTRA—are admitting that from about 1942 on they were receiving over the German radio the actual counts of people being moved into concentration camps every day.[14]

This has never been revealed before. So, there are two facets to this question: The one, what we knew as soldiers, what the men on the battle line knew; and then secondly, what was known up at a very high level.

JAMES COLLINS: May I add that the very day before Ohrdruf was liberated, 3,000 Jews were killed and were so-called buried in a shallow trench; and that's where most of the stench came from when we arrived there.

JULIAN KULAS: I would like to ask General Gudz, if I may, other than the Jewish populace in Treblinka and Auschwitz, what other national groups did you find in those camps?

PAVEL DANILOVICH GUDZ: This question, we believe, still has to be clarified since there are various data. According to these data which we have, there were almost all nationalities there who were taken there by the Hitlerites.

Notes

1 A major gathering of Holocaust survivors took place in Jerusalem, June 14-18, 1981.

2 William Kernan, "Beware of the Hitler Weapons First Hate, then Murder." *The Churchman* (October, 1942).

3 A reference to the fictional mini-series "Holocaust" first broadcast by the NBC television network on April 16-19, 1978.

[4] The British White Paper of 1939 declared Britain's intention to create an independent Palestinian state, in whose government Jews and Arabs would be represented proportionately according to their populations. The White Paper placed severe restrictions on Jewish immigration to Palestine as well as on the legal purchase of land in Palestine by Jews.

[5] The reference is to the campaigns in North Africa.

[6] Papenberg, on the Ems River, is in extreme northwest Germany, near the Dutch border.

[7] The reference is to one of the Civil Affairs teams that followed combat troops into Germany in order to establish occupation government.

[8] Gotha, in central Germany, lies 35 miles west of Weimar.

[9] Once described by Eisenhower as the "general manager of the war," Walter Bedell Smith held a number of key positions in the American military hierarchy. In 1945 he was Chief of Staff of SHAEF.

[10] Remagen, on the west bank of the Rhine a few miles south of Bonn, was the location of a strategically important railroad bridge captured by American troops on March 7, 1945.

[11] Located in western Germany, the Ruhr was (and remains) Germany's most important industrial region.

[12] Historians usually refer to Nordhausen and similar installations as concentration camps rather than death camps in order to distinguish them from extermination centers such as Auschwitz and Treblinka.

[13] For the conclusions reached by this commission see Seymour Maxwell Finger, ed., *American Jewry and the Holocaust*. A Report by the Research Director, his Staff, and Independent Research Scholars Retained by the Director for the American Jewish Commission on the Holocaust (New York, 1984).

[14] The issue of Allied intelligence gathering on the Nazi extermination of Jews has been discussed most recently in Raul Hilberg, *The Destruction of the European Jews*, 3 vols., 2nd ed. (New York, 1985), III, 1109 ff.

CHAPTER VI

THE HISTORIANS

Moderator: Prof. Raul Hilberg (USA): McCullough Professor of Political Science, University of Vermont; author of *The Destruction of the European Jews*.

Dr. Jorgen Haestrup (Denmark): Historian of World War II; author of *Passage to Palestine: Young Jews in Denmark, 1932–1945; Secret Alliances;* and *European Resistance Movements, 1939–1945: A Complete History*.

Brereton Greenhous (Canada): Military historian; author of *Out of the Shadows: Canada in the Second World War.*

Gen. Henri Raguet Brancion de Liman (France): Military historian; survivor of Flossenbürg.

Dr. Yitzhak Arad (Israel): World War II partisan; Israeli general; scholar; Chairman of the Directorate, Yad Vashem.

Dr. Yehuda Bauer (Israel): Professor of History, Hebrew University of Jerusalem; author of numerous books and articles on the Holocaust.

Institutional identifications are those at the time of the Conference.

RAUL HILBERG

In a certain sense, this panel is a little different from the others. It is more philosophical and more contemplative, more reflective. The victims in the camps and the liberators who stumbled upon them have a different view, a different impression, and a different remembrance from that which generations henceforth will have—the pictorialization of the camp network. They saw it; they smelled it; they felt it; they suffered from it. Their view was microscopic, immediate. They saw the detail as no one else will see it.

The historian, on the other hand, who is just venturing into the totality of this vast epoch, has a macrocosmic view. He sees a context that could not very well be understood by those who lived through that time. He is able, for one thing, to see the great variety of camps: the 2,000 in Poland alone that we heard of a short while ago; the prisons; the labor camps; the Stalags,[1] the camps through which prisoners of war passed and in which several millions died of starvation under the care of the German Army; the regular concentration camps of which Dachau is the prototype; and the special death camps, such as Treblinka.

The historian has to understand what produced this profusion of camps for many different people and many different purposes. He also has to understand something about method, the method of the perpetrator hidden from the view of those who experienced the events immediately. He has to come to grips with a modern society that, through its instrumentalities and technology, was capable of creating such a system. One may be overwhelmed by the extraordinary events of that period.

But little has overwhelmed me personally more than the sense that so much of what was done is so ordinary: that there were legal condemnation proceedings before the Auschwitz camp was constructed for the purpose of transferring real estate to the SS; that there was a regular allocation of war material for the erection of barracks and of other facilities in Auschwitz by the Ministry for Arms and War Production headed by the late Reich Minister, Albert Speer; a vast transport system by rail, which brought millions of people to their deaths in these camps; that the German railways charged the Gestapo four pfennige per track kilometer one-way for the deportees, half the rate if there was what they called group travel—400 or more—and round-trip fare for the guards; that this was done as a business as if the transported people were about to go on a vacation.

The historian has to take all of this in. Last but not least he has to understand not only the variety, not only the complexity, but also the psychological consistency of the entire process. It is very hard to grasp. It will not do for the reflective historian to call these events demonic or satanic; they are of this age. They were performed by men who, to outward appearances, looked like us and acted like us. Yes, they had a conscience, and they had to deal with their consciences every day of the week, so much so that in the final hours, they were not only able to, but insisted on, erasing the traces of their deeds.

What I am about to do is introduce to you some short presentations by a very distinguished panel that has come from this continent and from two other continents. This is not a topic that has engaged very many people over the last 30 years. But these men have spent a long time in study, and some of them have been personally involved in the events that they have studied. They are not merely document specialists; they're also individuals who have been through it in one way or another.

JORGEN HAESTRUP

I shall in a few minutes try to describe the fate of the Jews in Denmark during the occupation. As you probably know, the

Danish picture is somewhat brighter than the picture in most of the other European countries under German yoke. Let me give you a few figures. The Jewish community in Denmark comprised about 7,000 people, most of them totally assimilated into the Danish society. Many were born in Denmark, and many families had been assimilated over several generations. They were Danes, generally highly respected, and many had contributed greatly to Danish cultural, political, and economic life.

To these 7,000 people must be added a comparatively great number of young Jews and teenagers who, during the 1930s, had come to Denmark as members of the Jewish He-chalutz[2] or Youth Aliyah[3] organizations to learn farming, gardening, or fishing in Denmark. The total number in these groups was about 1,850. They were all dedicated Zionists or they became Zionists during their stay in Denmark. In that respect, they differed from the people in the assimilated Jewish community who, nonetheless, helped financially to sustain their stay and their location in their temporary Danish home.

After training in Denmark on Danish farms and in Danish schools for a year and sometimes more, they proceeded to Palestine as soon as they could obtain British certificates for immigration to the land of their only hope. But when the war broke out and the Germans occupied Denmark, about 550 found themselves stranded in Denmark without any possibility of reaching their destination. They were stateless fugitives, spread on farms all over the country. They had much fewer contacts in Danish society than 7,000 assimilated Jews, who mostly lived in or near Copenhagen.

When the crisis came in October 1943 in the form of German attempts to arrest all Jews in Denmark and deport them, their situation was even more desperate than that of the homeborn Jews in Denmark. Surprisingly, nothing happened to the Jews in Denmark in the years 1940 to 1943. The reason was that the Danish government, yielding under protest to the occupation, made it absolutely clear to the Germans that it would not tolerate any anti-Jewish action in Denmark. So the Jews could continue in a normal way of life as if nothing had happened. But when the Danish government, under pressure from the active resistance supported by the people, had to resign on August 29, 1943, this political shield disappeared. The Germans were then free to decide upon action against the Jews in Denmark as they did in all other countries.

The action was to take place in the night between the first and the second of October 1943. Broadly speaking, the action became a failure. Warnings to Danes and Jews had been given by a brave man in the German administration, a Mr. Duckwitz.[4] With a warning of 48 hours, the Danish people managed to take countermeasures. Out of about 8,000 Jews, only 284 were apprehended. The Jews went underground in the following two or three weeks. An escape organization to Sweden was improvised based on the resistance movement. It was imperative in those days that the Swedish government had declared Swedish willingness to receive any Jew coming from Denmark. The overwhelming majority of the Jews in Denmark, a little more than 7,000 people, were brought to safety to Sweden in a few hectic and dramatic weeks. Some were, of course, caught during the crossing.

What then was the final result? Alas, 464 were deported to Theresienstadt. Of these, about 40 died during transportation and from hunger and disease in the camp, whereas more than 400 of them survived to be brought back to Denmark in April 1945 by a Swedish-Danish rescue expedition.[5]

Is it possible to explain this comparatively bright outcome of a disaster? I think so. From the very first day of deportation, the Danish civil servants who carried on the Danish administration pestered the Germans in Copenhagen and in Berlin with protests and almost daily inquiries as to the names, whereabouts, and situation of the deported persons. In time, actually after only a few weeks, the Danish administration managed to get Red Cross parcels brought to the deported. In June 1944, they pressed through a German permit to inspect the camp. I think this constant pressure was all-important; at least the Germans knew that they were under constant observation from Copenhagen and they could not secretly retransport the Danish Jews to Auschwitz or other real extermination camps. The young, stateless Jews were, as a matter of fact, considered as Danish subjects and got the same help as any other Jew.

Were there any other casualties among the He-chalutz Jews in Denmark? The answer is yes. Three young Jews from the He-chalutz organization drowned on their way to Sweden. One was killed by a stray bullet during a riot in Copenhagen in September 1943,[6] and six young Jews from He-chalutz were caught when they rather desperately tried to smuggle themselves through Europe to Turkey and finally to Palestine. They were hidden under or in a train. These six were taken to Auschwitz, and only one of them survived after a death march to Buchenwald where he managed to contact Danish prisoners to get part of their Red Cross parcels.

To sum up briefly, out of about 8,000 Jews living in Denmark in 1940, about 50 died—these were mostly the weak or the very old. Ninety-nine percent survived in some way or other. It might illustrate what might have been done. But, of course, Denmark had special opportunities.

BRERETON GREENHOUS

There is at least one sense in which I stand here under false pretenses. Canada didn't have any extermination camps on its soil. Its part in the liberation of the camps was limited because the Canadians on the extreme left flank of the western Allies' advance were not in the geographical line which took them through many of the camp areas. You heard this morning from one member of this delegation who was a liberator of the one camp, as far as I know, that the Canadian Army did liberate. Individual Canadians may have played a part in liberating other camps under other auspices, but the Canadian case was virtually limited to the camp of Westerbork, which I understand was primarily a collection and transit camp. I say I understand, because I myself am not a historian of the Holocaust. As far as I can discover, Canada has no historian of the Holocaust. I'm a historian of the Second World War who stands here today because in one of my books there were a couple of paragraphs about the liberation of Westerbork.

However, there is another sense in which I feel that I do have something to contribute to this session, and it is a wider one which really applies to all historians. One of the reasons, I take it, that we are gathered here is to try and bring home to the world-at-large once again the realities of the Holocaust. As several speakers have mentioned earlier, there has in recent years been an increasing flood of literature, some of it pseudoscholastic, arguing that the Holocaust never existed, that the whole thing is a figment of propaganda machines.

To the extent that that information is accepted by some people, it seems to me historians have failed in their duty. I agree with the late British historian Sir Herbert Butterfield, who was also a very devout Christian, that in this modern age, when we no longer pay too much attention to our prophets, the historian has to become the moral guardian of his people. To the extent that propaganda suggesting that the Holocaust did not occur is permeating society, all historians have failed.

Our chairman, when he introduced this session, discussed briefly the difficulties that the historian has in taking in the vast extent of the documentary material, not to mention the terrible demonic nature of the incidents that he must look at if he is going to examine the Holocaust. He has to do more than that—he has to explain it to the people in general. In that respect, it seems to me from my limited reading in these fields that historians have failed. They have given the facts, but they have not explained how or why these things have come about in sufficient detail. They have not considered how, as the moral guardians of their people, if you are prepared to accept that definition of the historian, they are going to set about seeing that it does not happen again.

There are a whole range of possibilities here, which I am certainly not qualified to go into. However, one of the points I think which certainly needs much more consideration, as well as the hard bitter facts of the Holocaust, is the way in which the German people were able to live with it. We have heard at various sessions of the effect that it had on the liberators when they found Germans, ordinary German people, living cheek by jowl with extermination camps and apparently ignoring it. It seems to me that that must have something to do with the ability of the human mind to compartmentalize reason. Emotional people cannot compartmentalize. It is impressed upon their total personality.

But when we get to matters of reason, people can divide their life up into official and unofficial segments. They can divide up their business life from their home life, their government duties or their civil duties from their personal and private duties. That is surely one of the problems which societies today all over the world face. If that trend continues or develops, it will not be impossible to have another Holocaust.

Therefore, it seems to me that historians have a duty to investigate issues like this, to try and work out ways in which we can restore man to a whole personality, a whole integrated personality which would stop this sort of thing from happening, not just in Germany, but anywhere at all. As I said, this is only touching the fringe of an immense subject. But I do feel quite deeply that this is one of several respects in the modern world in which historians have, up to this point in history, failed.

I would like to leave this thought with you in the hope that perhaps somebody somewhere, a graduate student who is here present, perhaps several if we are lucky, will decide to devote himself to this sort of study in order that we can ensure that there will never again be another Holocaust.

*HENRI RAGUET BRANCION DE LIMAN**

I am simply going to tell you something that I lived through myself. I think my modest contribution can lead to a better understanding of what we are trying to do here because it seems to me an exemplary story and one which can lead to better information on what happened 35 years ago.

One evening in April of 1945, in the Leitmeritz camp in Czechoslovakia, a Yugoslav prisoner went into Block 5. He was looking for a Frenchman. Leitmeritz is the Germanized name of the Czechoslovak city, Litomerice, on the Elbe. It is not far from Terezin. In Leitmeritz there were never many French and there were still fewer at that point because most of the camp had already been emptied by the transports. Each of the camp chiefs tried to get rid of all of the prisoners to escape punishment so there were only three French prisoners in Block 5. Our Yugoslav friend was looking for a Frenchman who had a stomachache. This was not uncommon. But this Yugoslav was only a simple nurse, a military nurse. Out of his pajamas, out of a piece of paper, he brought a few grams of charcoal. He had stolen a bit for this Frenchman who had a stomachache. This prisoner

*General Brancion de Liman made his remarks in French. This is the simultaneous translation.

was myself. I am alive, and I was saved by this Yugoslav comrade, perhaps not by the charcoal but by the extraordinary witness that he bore. All the prisoners there knew that being there was less bad than being elsewhere. When someone came to Block 5 with some stolen charcoal from an almost empty drugstore or pharmacy, he was risking all sorts of punishment.

Yesterday I think it was said here that to survive in the camps a kind of a miracle had to happen. This miracle was, of course, a voluntary miracle, a miracle of will—you had to have will to want to live, but you had to be lucky. For me, these grams of charcoal were my good fortune. Indeed, you had to overcome this human degradation which the creators of the camp wanted and which was applied rigorously by the jailers. One had to overcome weakness, the lack of food, the lack of sleep, the work weariness, and especially this lack of faith which could come upon any of us at any time and could really do us in. Fortunately, there was friendship, friendship among the prisoners, the comrades in the underground, and others, friendships which came inside the camps, above and beyond any national solidarity, between people of all social classes. This Yugoslav taught me a lot, too.

At the present time, there are people who deny the existence of the camps. It is by proper teaching, by fact, that we can and that we must all combat this denial, this incredible denial. We must endeavor, of course, to remember, to recall this period, but we must, above all, teach, tell what happened to all, especially to the young people. For that, we have got to develop appropriate teaching methods. I think that as a follow-up to this conference we all must reflect and meditate about what we can bring to bear on the intelligence of our young people. All historians from this frightful period must compile the facts, and the people who are specialists in teaching young people must work hand-in-hand with historians to carry out this very essential task.

YITZHAK ARAD

At this conference, we have heard testimonies of the liberation of camps by the Allied forces that evoked emotions, and the shocking conditions in which the liberators found the surviving prisoners. These were camps mainly on German soil which the Allied armies reached in time to find survivors just before the Nazis collapsed and before the SS guards had had time to liquidate the remaining prisoners. But there were camps which the liberating armies reached too late to rescue the inmates. In some of the major death camps and places of murder, where millions of people, millions of Jews, were killed, the liberating armies found no survivors, and they could not easily discover the traces of the atrocities carried out there. This is the reason why we did not hear a witness report this morning on the liberation of Treblinka, Sobibor, Belzec, or Chelmno, because there was no such liberation.

Since the Summer of 1942, a special operation had been carried out by the SS with the aim of eradicating the traces of the mass killings and the burning of the bodies of the murdered in the death camps, and in the valleys of mass murder in Soviet-occupied territories. How did this operation begin? What had Himmler and Heydrich, the heads of the SS at the early stages of the war, to fear from the future in the Spring of 1942 when the German armies were advancing on all fronts? Did they all just suspect that the war might not end with a Nazi victory but in defeat and that the mass killings would be discovered and they would face personal, national, and historical responsibility for the crimes committed by Nazi Germany?

The answer to these questions is to be found in the defeat of the German army in the Winter of 1941–1942 when the Nazis were forced to retreat from vast territories in the Soviet Union. Himmler was afraid that the mass graves of the murdered Jews in the Soviet-liberated territories would be found. In a speech Himmler gave before high-ranking SS officers in Posen on October 4, 1943, he said, in relation to the extermination of the Jews, "This is a page of glory in our history which has never been written and which is never to be written." [7]

Therefore, in the Spring of 1942, after the Winter defeats, Himmler decided the corpses of the Jews shot in Nazi-occupied territories and buried there in mass graves should be removed without leaving any traces. The same should happen to those killed in the death camps, which had started functioning at that time. Heydrich, chief of the Reich Security Main Office (RSHA), was entrusted with this task.

The beginning of this operation was postponed for about two months because of Heydrich's death. But in June 1942, the head of Gestapo, Kaltenbrunner, appointed Paul Blobel to the task of the eradication of the traces of mass executions.[8] This operation was given the code name Kommando 1005. Blobel's duty was to find the appropriate technical methods for the destruction and disappearance of the bodies of the victims and to coordinate and supervise the whole operation.

After his appointment, Blobel started his experiments for the burning of the bodies. The place of these experiments was Chelmno, the first death camp which had been operating since the end of 1941. At that time tens of thousands of Jews from the large area were killed there and burned in pits. The first experiments with burning the bodies were made with incendiary bombs, but this caused big fires in the surrounding woods. Then they started to cremate the bodies with wood in open bonfires. The bones left after burning were destroyed by a special bone-crushing machine. The ashes of the bodies and small fragments of bones were buried in the pits from which the bodies had been taken.

After these successful experiments, the SS found a simple and efficient method of erasing their crimes. About 350,000 bodies of Jewish victims murdered in Chelmno were burned. In August, after the experiments in Chelmno, Blobel came to Auschwitz and handed over to Rudolf Hoess,[9] the commander of the camp, Himmler's order to burn the bodies, and told him about his experiments at Chelmno. Hoess visited Chelmno to learn the methods adopted there. At the end of September 1942, the burning of the bodies in open bonfires began in Auschwitz. The bodies were arranged in layers, sandwiched between layers of wood, and burned, about 2,000 bodies in one bonfire. Simultaneously with the burning of the bodies in open bonfires, in the summer of 1942 the SS began building crematoria, and the first crematorium was in operation by the end of March 1943. The last of the four crematoria was built in June 1943. The capacity of the four crematoria in Auschwitz reached up to 8,000 bodies within 24 hours. The number of people gassed exceeded this number. When the Hungarian Jews were brought for extermination in 1944, they also used, in addition to the crematoria, open bonfires. The bones that remained after the burning were destroyed by hammers and together with ashes taken on lorries and thrown into a river or a lake in the vicinity of Auschwitz.

About two million people, mostly Jews, but also Poles, Russians, Gypsies, and people of other nations, were burned in Auschwitz. The removal of the corpses from the pits and gas chambers and their cremation was carried out by a special group of Jewish prisoners, the Sonderkommando, who were murdered after a period of work and replaced by another group to be killed in turn later.

In the three death camps of Operation Reinhard,[10] Belzec, Sobibor, and Treblinka where the gassing began in the months of March and June of 1942, the corpses of the murdered were buried in pits until the beginning of the winter of 1942. Globocnik, who was in charge of these camps, opposed the eradication operation ideologically.[11] In August 1942, when he was asked why the corpses shouldn't have been burned instead of being buried, he replied that "if ever a generation should arise so slack and soft-boned that it cannot understand the importance of our work, then of course our entire National Socialism will have been in vain." He was of the opinion that "bronze plaques should be erected with inscriptions to show that it was we who had the courage to carry out this great and necessary task."[12]

Despite this stand of Globocnik's, the commanders of the death camps of Operation Reinhard received directives regarding burning of the bodies based on experiments carried out in Chelmno. The decision to carry out these directives was left to the camps' commanders. Indeed, the burning of the bodies had started in Belzec in the winter of 1942.

At the same time, the burning of bodies in Sobibor was begun. The reasons there were different. By the end of the Summer of 1942, due to the heat, the mass graves in which tens of thousands of bodies had been buried began to crack open. The smells and liquids which were escaping attracted large numbers of vermin; an unbearable stench prevailed all over the area. The camp's commanders, fearing that the drinking water would be poisoned, decided to burn the bodies. In Treblinka, the largest death camp of these three, they went on burying the bodies without burning them.

The German victories on the eastern front in the Summer of 1942, as they advanced up to Stalingrad and the Caucasus, aroused hopes among the Nazis of a German victory. The wiping out of all traces of the crimes was not given priority at that time. But the outcome of the battle of Stalingrad in the Winter of 1942–1943, which ended with a big Soviet victory, changed the whole situation. Vast areas of Nazi-occupied territories in the Soviet Union were liberated in the first months of 1943. The fear that mass graves would be discovered by the advancing Soviet Army forced the SS to start again with urgency the Operation 1005. At the end of February 1943, Himmler visited Treblinka and found out that in the camp hundreds of thousands of murdered Jews had been buried in huge pits and that no system of cremation had been introduced there. He gave orders to start the burning of the bodies there.

From this time on, starting in March and April of 1943, all the mass graves in Treblinka were opened, the corpses burned in bonfires, and the bones destroyed by the methods similar to those used in experiments in Chelmno. The ashes were mixed with earth and buried in the same pits. Having completed this operation of the erasing of the traces of crimes, the Nazis dismantled the three camps of Operation Reinhard: Belzec, in Spring 1943, and Sobibor and Treblinka in the last months of 1943. The whole area was fluffed up, trees were planted there, and fields were sown so that the camps would look like peaceful farms.

When the Soviet and Polish armies liberated these camps in the summer of 1944, no survivors and only a few corpses out of about 1.7 million Jews murdered in these camps were to be found. There were only signs of the pits in which there were ashes mixed with earth. The burning of the bodies of the victims was accomplished successfully by the Nazis.

But they didn't succeed in hiding or erasing their crimes. There remained witnesses, liberators, local people, and survivors who told the story. Even the Nazi criminals admitted the enormity of these crimes in their trials. The extermination of the millions of Jews, of millions of other people, the "page of glory," as Himmler called it, are written in the history. Let the Holocaust be a warning to mankind that it should never happen again.

RAUL HILBERG

Not only did the Germans eradicate camps, but they tried in every possible way to maintain the camp system until the very last moments of the war. We have heard already this morning about cremations going on even just two days before liberation. There were actions in the removal of camp inmates from the Stutthof camp very late in April prior to the arrival of the Red Army. There were incredible attempts in the last hours of the Nazi regime to maintain the concentration camp system and to kill off more inmates. One of the most bizarre stories in this chapter are the so-called death marches.

YEHUDA BAUER

By examining the death marches very briefly, I would like to point to a few of the historical problems that we face when we discuss the whole system of Nazi terror. At 10 o'clock a.m., January 12, 1945, the forces of Marshal Konev,[13] the First Ukrainian Front, broke out of the Baranov[14] bridgehead over the Vistula River to open the offensive that was to destroy the Nazi armies on the eastern front. Within seven days, they and their comrades from the armies commanded by Marshal Zhukov and Rokossovski[15] had liberated Warsaw, Lodz, Radom,[16] and Cracow.

On January 17, with the Russian guns booming in the distance, the last roll call was held at Auschwitz, and 66,020 prisoners were counted. The sick were left behind, 2,810 being liberated by the division commanded by General Petrenko, who is with us today. The rest were taken off. From then on, until one day after the end of the war, hundreds of thousands of inmates of concentration camps were marched without clothing in the winter months in Europe, with sandals of wood or barefoot in rags, without food, or they were put on wagons on railways without food or water for days, weeks, months.

That is the story of the death marches. Nazi figures tell us that in January 1945, there were 714,000 inmates of concentration camps. Like so many historians, I accepted that figure too. I think one ought to question it. In the last weeks of the regime, tens of thousands more prisoners were put into the camps. Sixty thousand Hungarian Jews alone were brought into Mauthausen, and tens of thousands of Soviet prisoners of war were put into the concentration camp system. By that time, the differentiation so carefully maintained until then among the different types of camps and their administration was breaking down, and the death marches began to encompass other types of camps apart from concentration camps. I don't know how many hundreds of thousands we are talking of—maybe 800,000, maybe 900,000, maybe more.

How many died in those marches? There is no record, but the only research that was ever published on the death marches was published in 1965 in Prague. During 13 out of the 52 marches recorded in that book—and the book says it only covered a small portion of them—69,000 people started off and of these over 40,000 died, 59 percent. If this is any indication at all, and I think it is, of what happened with the rest, we come to an amazing conclusion: Of those who were in the concentration camps (this does not include Soviet prisoners of war, of whom vast numbers died—the lowest figure is 2.5 million—or the five or so millions of Jews who were killed in extermination camps, shot in trenches, or died of hunger and disease in the ghettos), over half supposedly working for the German machine were killed. This means that within three months and a-half in the death marches and their follow-up in the last weeks and days of the camps' existence, more people died than in all the rest of the time that the concentration camps existed from the very beginning of the Nazi regime.

What was their intention? Why did the SS march these people away? Were they trying to hide the atrocities? But if they were, why did they leave 2,810 people in Auschwitz? Why did the commander of the camp in Stutthof give an order in January 1945 that everybody was to march except for the sick? Maybe a partial explanation is that they were trying to work them. Yes, some of those who were marched inside Germany were put to work, but many were not. They were too weak, and they were being marched for months and not put to work anymore. Do you realize that the Nazi machine at the very end had 2.5 million working prisoners of war and 8.6 million foreign workers in Germany, over 11 million in all? So what difference would the few hundred thousand starved prisoners of concentration camps have made? That is a partial explanation at best.

I think there are two explanations. One, there was the inertia of a system which saw in these people enemies of the Reich who must never fall into the hands of the Reich's enemies. They must never be liberated. The other thing is that it was another way of killing. The mass destruction process in gas chambers and total shootings had stopped for various reasons, but the way in which the death marches operated shows quite clearly what the intention was. If you operate a train from Ellrich,[17] in mid-Germany, up to Hamburg, down again to the railway line next to Bergen-Belsen, there is no other reason behind it but to kill—the fewer of those who were on the train who arrived at Belsen, the better. Do you realize what that meant in a Nazi Germany fighting on its last legs? Train space, wagons, troops—German troops were fighting on both fronts against the advancing Allies, and here was a train going for weeks with large numbers of wagons backwards and forwards through Germany with the only intention being to kill the people inside!

The problem arises when we speak of the SS system of ice-cold killing, of emotionless action devoid of all human moral sentiment. We always used to say, and still do, that in a certain way they were sadists. Of course they were sadists, but that wasn't the main line. But what do you say about the death marches when, in the Czech town of Lobosice,[18] they put in charge of a transport a local German head of a sugar factory, and he killed? What do you say when they take a housewife from Plauen[19] and put her in charge of a women's death march and she flogs the women to death? What do you say about the kind of evidence that shows that during the last stages of the war when everybody knew that it was going to end soon, suddenly—or is it suddenly?—something quite different appears than what we used to talk about? I would not answer these questions, even if I had hours to talk, because I am still looking for the answers.

The aim of research—do I have to spell it out?—is not only to examine past history, but to examine future history. What about the victims? What could they have done? Could they have run away? I will give you one example. It will stand for hundreds. I already mentioned the name of the town, Lobosice. There was a Czech gardener there at the railway station. His name was Josef Pilney. He described a couple of weeks after liberation what happened. There was a train with thousands of men and women in the station who were being starved to death and no water was being given. This was in a Czech town, and he said that in at least one wagon the women were all Czech. By a great persuasive action, he managed to get the commander of the railway station to permit him to use his garden hose to put water on the prisoners, on those women. Not one escaped, and this is in Bohemia, among their own people, 50 meters away from freedom. Why? Terror. Young, brutalized by 16-to-18-year-old SS boys. The problem is—where to run? And yet some did escape.

But there is another problem. What did

the Allies know, and what did the Allies do? I went through, I think, most of the SHAEF records, Intelligence, Chief of Staff, and so on. Not a word. I went through the whole of the western press. There is one article. The April 15 issue of the *New York Herald Tribune* quoted a Polish press release in Moscow relating to the death march of women from Stutthof which just had been liberated. About seven or eight lines on page 4—that's it. Nothing else. But there is any amount of material about the POWs. They knew exactly that 180,000 Allied prisoners of war were being marched from Stalag so and so into Germany. They were in the same echelon with the death marchers. They went on the same routes. They were treated slightly differently, not very much differently. The Allied Expeditionary Force in March 1945 sent teams of parachutists who were dropped behind enemy lines to save prisoners of war from the same marches that the concentration camp victims were on. Not a word about the concentration camp victims.

It's a problem, isn't it? I don't want to be too easy about this. This was the last few weeks of the war. They had to win it quickly; by arriving quicker they saved more people. There is no doubt about that whatsoever. Maybe that is an explanation. Maybe it isn't. There was one attempt and one attempt only to save the death marchers. In Geneva, Gerhart Riegner, the secretary of the World Jewish Congress, contacted Jaromir Kopecky, the Czech representative in Geneva, and together they set up a committee of representatives of all the European states that were under German control. They pressed the International Red Cross to move into Nazi-occupied territory to save people from the marches, and they knew about them and the camps. Mauthausen was saved from being blown up by a Swiss Red Cross worker. There were other instances of that kind. The International Red Cross was very hesitant about it. It came late.

I have to end. Sometimes I am told that we are overdoing this, writing too many books, and dealing with a subject in a way that will disgust people to the point where they don't want to read it anymore. Many people feel this is not really a historical discipline, that it is something that happened and it is time to forget about it. You may have gathered that I do not support that view. I think we are at the beginning of research. The survivors give us material, or part of it, and the archives give us the material, or part of it. It's got to be an effort by all.

Notes

1 Stalag was the German term for a prisoner-of-war camp. The word is a contraction of *Stammlager*, meaning "branch camp."

2 He-chalutz was a movement begun in 1917 to prepare young Jews to settle in Palestine in cooperative farming communities. The young people, called Chalutzim ("pioneers" in Hebrew) were trained on special farms throughout Europe.

3 Aliyah, literally "going up," is a Hebrew term denoting permanent relocation by Jews to Israel. According to Jewish tradition, Aliyah is tantamount to a return from exile to the Jewish homeland. Youth Aliyah was an organization for mass immigration of Jewish children and youth for settlement in Palestine. It started in 1934, after the Nazis came to power and it became necessary to provide refuge for Jewish children.

4 Georg F. Duckwitz (1904–1973), was a German businessman attached to the embassy in Copenhagen as a shipping expert, who maintained clandestine contacts with Swedish officials and Danish resistance leaders.

5 Through the influence of Swedish aristrocrat, Count Folke Bernadotte, the Swedish Red Cross and Swedish Army were allowed by Himmler to rescue Scandinavian deportees imprisoned in German concentration camps. Beginning in April 1945, a convoy of white busses transported Danish and Norwegian prisoners from a collection point at Neuengamme into Denmark.

6 Cophenhagen Riot of 1943: The year 1943 saw a widespread upsurge of resistance and sabotage activity against the Nazi occupation of Denmark. In August 1943 riots broke out in Copenhagen and other cities. In response, the Germans inaugurated a new, more repressive phase of occupation, declaring martial law and interning the Danish king.

[7] Nuremberg Documents, PS-1919.

[8] Paul Blobel had been commander of Einsatzkammando 4a, which, among numerous other atrocities, executed 34,000 Jews near Kiev in 1941. After the war he was condemned to death by an American military tribunal and was executed in 1951. Nuremberg Documents, NO-3947.

[9] SS officer Rudolf Hoess was made commandant of the Auschwitz camp complex in 1941. After the war he was tried in Poland and executed in 1947. His memoir, *Commandant of Auschwitz* (London, 1959), provides a chilling account of the killing operation at the most notorious of the Nazi camps.

[10] The operation was named in honor of Reinhard Heydrich.

[11] Odilo Globocnik supervised the camps in his capacity as SS and Police Leader in Lublin. He committed suicide in 1945 after his arrest.

[12] On this statement by Globocnik and the document in which it is reported, see the first edition of Hilberg, *Destruction of the European Jews* (Chicago, 1961), p. 628.

[13] Ivan S. Konev, sometimes spelled Koniev. He won several major battles during World War II, and participated in the capture of Berlin. Konev was made a Marshal of the Soviet Union in 1944.

[14] Baranov is about 75 miles northeast of Cracow, on the Vistula River.

[15] Soviet General Konstantin K. Rokossovsky was one of the great tactical innovators in World War II, especially in the area of armored warfare. Troops under his command halted the German advance before Moscow in 1941, annihilated 22 German divisions at Stalingrad in 1942–43, and captured Berlin in 1945. Rokossovsky was made a Marshal of the Soviet Union in 1944.

[16] Radom is about 60 miles south of Warsaw.

[17] Ellrich is about seven miles northwest of Nordhausen.

[18] Lobosice is about 35 miles northwest of Prague.

[19] Plauen is about 55 miles south-southwest of Leipzig.

CHAPTER VII

THE CHAPLAINS

Moderator: Rev. Franklin Littell, Ph.D. (USA): Professor of Religion, Temple University; honorary chairman of the board, National Institute on the Holocaust (now the Anne Frank Institute); member, U.S. Holocaust Memorial Council.

Rabbi Judah Nadich (USA): Rabbi of Park Avenue Synagogue, New York City; advisor to General Eisenhower on matters pertaining to Jewish DPs; author of *Eisenhower and the Jews.*

The Rev. George B. Wood (USA): Participated in liberation of Woebbelin as chaplain with U.S. army.

Rabbi Herschel Schacter (USA): As U.S. Army chaplain participated in liberation of Buchenwald and aided in resettlement of DPs.

Father Edward P. Doyle (USA): Participated in liberation of Nordhausen as U.S. army chaplain.

Rev. John P. Pawlikowski, O.S.M. (USA): Professor of Social Ethics, Catholic Theological Union; member, U.S. Holocaust Memorial Council.

Institutional identifications are those at the time of the Conference.

REV. FRANKLIN LITTELL

I have been struck by the various paths through which we have come to this place, through which some of us have come to concern for the Holocaust and the lessons of the Holocaust. First we had a generation in which a few poets and novelists and sensitive interpreters told the story, and now we are beginning to speak of certain lessons of the Holocaust that need to be learned by all peoples.

I think of the event as like that of the Exodus or of Sinai—originally something which happened to a particular people, but which, taken seriously, speaks to the conditions and the needs of all peoples and all nations. We have a unique event which is like Amos' plumbline which can be held against other cities and other societies, other times and places, but the uniqueness must remain.

My own experience was one in which I was first concerned to know what the churches were doing or not doing in the time of the rise of Adolf Hitler and the establishment of the Third Reich, and then, finally, the terrible events which we call the Holocaust. I ask myself why in Christendom it was possible for a heathen system and a heathen religion—an ersatz religion—to carry away tens of millions of the baptized.

In an experience which was almost like a conversion—if I may use a Wesleyan word, for I am a Methodist—it came to me that the great event for Christians as well as Jews in our time—the great event which, when you have once confronted it, changes your whole life and your whole perspective—is the Holocaust. Ever since then, for those of us who have made that path—and I find more and more Christians who are wrestling with the lessons of the Holocaust—nothing is ever the same again.

Some of you will remember—it was reported at the time, and then more recently it has been referred to again—that with the opening of Dachau, General Eisenhower sent a cable to General Marshall and said to send congressmen, journalists, educators, and churchmen because it was simply unbelievable. He was afraid that if these witnesses did not come, the facts would be denied.

We've come to a time when the facts are being denied, and the reason why people repress facts can be a discussion in itself. They repress facts because they cannot face them, but we say that Christians and Jews and persons of conscience, humanists—whether believers or not—have to come to terms with the Holocaust; for example what it has to say to our universities in the corruption of university training, as with those great German universities, and what it has to say to our religious institutions and the breakdown of control systems.

In our panel today, we have four men of the cloth—two rabbis, a Catholic priest, and an Episcopal clergyman who have something to tell us out of the days when they were younger but something which they still remember and I suspect has been a definitive event in the personal life as well as in the history of our time for them also.

RABBI JUDAH NADICH

I must first put my remarks in a particular setting to explain exactly where I was and how I came to see what I did.

I came to Europe during the summer of 1942 as the first American Jewish chaplain ordered to the European Theater of Operations. I served in northern Ireland with the first American troops sent to Europe. When they later left for the invasion of North Africa, I was transferred to England, and I covered the United Kingdom for the next year-and-a-half. I went into Normandy and later into Paris. In Paris I received an order to come to Frankfurt to serve as adviser on Jewish affairs to General Eisenhower, the commanding general of the European Theater of Operations.

That position, which was and is unique in American military history, came to be because American war correspondents had been visiting the displaced persons camps and were struck by the fact that not enough was being done to help the people in the camps who were Jewish. The American army advance plans called for the speedy evacuation of any survivors found in the concentration camps, but the plans did not reckon with the fact that there might be people who would not want to be returned to their original native countries. Those who were not Jewish—who were French or Belgian or Greek—were returned within 90 days from the concentration camps to their own countries.

But the Jews who were in the concentration camps did not want to return to their lands of origin, principally lands of eastern Europe, because they were aware of the fact that the populations in their native countries were virulently anti-Semitic and had in many instances cooperated with the invading Nazi armies in the decimation of the Jewish population. As a result, the Jews who were transferred from the concentration camps quickly to the DP camps were receiving very little consideration.

The war correspondents reported this situation, and as a result of their stories, President Truman appointed a commission headed by Earl G. Harrison, the Dean of the Law School of the University of Pennsylvania.[1] The commission came to Europe, studied the conditions in the DP camps, returned to Washington, and reported to the President.

General Eisenhower immediately received a summary of the findings of the Harrison Commission and was asked by President Truman, in the light of the very critical report, what to do? General Eisenhower replied that he would immediately appoint his senior Jewish chaplain to the post of adviser to him, to move around the various camps and return and make recommendations as to how to improve the conditions in the DP camps. And he suggested that if the President wished to send a high-level civilian adviser, he would be pleased to receive him.

This explains the background for the creation of this unique position in American military annals—a Jewish adviser to an American commanding general. Now, the first concentration camp that I visited in my new duties was Dachau. I want to make it clear that I did not visit Dachau upon its liberation, or shortly thereafter. Yet, when I did visit Dachau, it had not as yet been prettied up. The corpses had been removed and buried, and the sick had been taken to hospitals, and those who were comparatively well, even though suffering from the effects of malnutrition and from various other conditions in the concentration camps, had been moved to displaced persons camps.

When I came into Dachau, I saw soon after entering a large enclosure in which there were dog kennels. In my naïveté, I thought that the dog kennels must have been kept for the pets of the German officers of Dachau.

I was soon disillusioned when I was told that these kennels were for guard dogs who were deliberately kept famished, and a prisoner in the camp, for some infraction of the rules, in some cases not even for an infraction of the rules, was tossed into that enclosure. The dogs were let loose to leap upon the poor victim and the victim was torn apart. That was my introduction to what I was to see later in Dachau.

I moved on in the camp and came to the anteroom to the gas chamber, and the anteroom had some hooks for the hanging of clothing, with a large sign in German on the door leading into the gas chamber itself reading "shower bath." I went through that door into the gas chamber and tried to imagine what it must have been like to have been packed like sardines into that area and suddenly to have begun smelling the gas that was to take away one's life.[2]

One cannot really imagine it, because one cannot put oneself in that position. But then I looked at the inside of the door, and I saw thousands of scratches upon it, scratches that must have been made by the fingernails of so many men and women and children because the scratches covered the entire door, from high up all the way down to a low position.

I went from the gas chamber into the next area, which was the crematorium, and looked into the mouths of the furnaces into which the bodies were shoveled, one after the other, and burned in the fires.

My attention was suddenly caught by some sacks that looked like potato sacks standing at the side of the crematorium. I went over to the sacks to see what they were. On the front of them was stamped the German word for fertilizer, and I looked into the sacks and what I saw there I soon realized was human ash that had been taken from the furnaces in the crematoria, ready for shipment to German farms in order to make the soil more fertile to grow more crops for the Herrenolk [master race].

I plunged my arm into one of the sacks up to the elbow and pressed the "fertilizer," the human ash, with the fingers of my hand into my palm and ground it into my palm so that I might never forget what I had seen there.

And I have never forgotten, and I gladly accepted the invitation to be here today and to speak this testimony because I feel it to be a part of my responsibility to tell the story, to keep telling it, until the day I die.

REV. GEORGE WOOD

I brought out some pictures so that I would not forget what I saw—if there was ever any possibility of it—because it was just a small concentration camp that we liberated, but as I said to someone today, the bodies were just as dead and they were piled just as high—four and five feet high. A gentleman pointed out the bodies to us as we were going through the camp, and here they are in the washroom all across the floor.

I was with the 82nd Airborne Division. I had been with the division for my entire war experience. I was overseas two years and eight months. We met the Russians 50 miles beyond the Elbe River at Lugwigslust[3] on May 2. On May 3, point teams were sent out in the area to ensure security, and reports came back of the concentration camp at Woebbelin[4] four miles north of Lugwigslust.

The commanding general went out and saw it, and on the morning of the fourth he turned the responsibility for the camp over to me and said, "I want you to carry out General Eisenhower's directive and all that that implies."

First, of course, I had to go to the camp and see what I was involved with. Remember, the camp had been free now for 24 hours. We found a man whom we could quickly make contact with—a Frenchman who could speak English—and he acted as our guide. He was 67. He was a Paris factory manager. He had made the mistake of questioning Nazi politics, and for two years he had been in concentration camps.

This particular one at Woebbelin was a transit camp. It had been in existence for six months and, during that six-month period, 6,000 people had passed through it as the armies were coming closer and closer together. The Germans would bring the people out of concentration camps as quickly as possible, and so they set up these transit camps. There were 4,000 in the camp at the time we liberated it. One-quarter of them were dead, and all but 200, and those whose bodies were too rotten to bury, had been buried.

Peter Martin [the Frenchman] took us into the first barrack, and that barrack was filled with Jews. They were too weak to get up and go outside even though they had been liberated for 24 hours. This particular picture here shows the three-tiered bunks that we found there. The living and the dead are together here. These were dead on the floor, dying on the upper levels of the bunk. The starving men were lying in their own fecal matter, breathing the nauseating stench of chronic dysentery and rotting flesh.

We saw two living skeletons among this group of boys, and we found out their names were Robert and Paul, from Budapest. One was 23, the other 16. Their crime was the unpardonable one of being Jewish. Their fathers and mothers had been killed, and for three years they had been in concentration camps.

The next barrack we were taken into was a long washroom with wash troughs along each side and dead bodies underneath the wash troughs. At each end of the washroom the bodies were piled four and five feet high. This picture here that I showed you shows the body along the wash trough which is here, and the gentleman is pointing to it.

An English-speaking Dutchman contacted us. He was walking around, and he made an interesting comment. He said that the deaths had been heaviest among his people. He said that the reason for that was their bodies were the first to disintegrate because the Dutch people were used to rich foods. I always remember that comment that he made.

When the first Allied wagon of food came in, and we got the food from German stores of food in the area, the people acted like cattle. They fought savagely with each other. One frenzied man, a madman, dropped dead in convulsions. One man crawled on the ground and picked up with his mouth the crumbs from off the ground. Perhaps you cannot quite understand the condition of these people unless I make the point that there was evidence of cannibalism there.

The Jews were in the minority in this camp. This Holocaust camp contained Poles and Czechs and French and Dutch and Danes and Norwegians and Belgians, and even some Spanish Republicans. I have been reading lately Herman Wouk's book *The Winds of War*, and in this book a foreign service officer makes the comment that the concentration camps were for anybody who still wanted the socialist part of national socialism. I think those comments are appropriate to mention at this point.

As I said, 200 of the dead bodies had not yet rotted, and it was my responsibility to see that these people were given a decent and proper burial according to General Eisenhower's directive. There was a large public square in front of the palace of the Archduke of Mecklenburg in Ludwigslust. So I had the citizenry of Ludwigslust come to the camp with all sorts of wagons and what not and load the bodies on the wagons and bring them into Ludwigslust.

I had the Bürgermeister pick up 200 sheets. I asked for 400 men to dig 200 regulation-size graves, and here in this particular picture you see the dead laid out in honor and the German citizenry going around observing them. We also had the staff of the German 21st Field Army, which had surrendered to the 82nd Airborne Division, take in those who were laid out in honor.

We had a service with three chaplains—myself, a Roman Catholic chaplain who translated and used my homily in German, and a Baptist chaplain who said Jewish prayers. The band was there. Afterwards, the bodies were reverently lowered into the graves, the dirt was thrown upon them, and they were buried. On each grave there was a cross and on every fourth cross a Star of David.

I'd like to read to you a letter that I wrote to a former parishioner on the 14th of May [1945]. She died just a few weeks ago and sent me this before she died. She was 83 years old. I said:

"You have read about it in the papers, but I have seen it. It is indeed a horrible sight—bodies piled in one building like disordered cordwood, in other buildings the sick and dying lying with the dead in their own feces and vomit. Everywhere such filth that it is indescribable. Gaunt, emaciated, half-crazed men would cry out for chocolate and sugar.

"For three weeks, these men died at the

rate of 50 a day, and even now many of the hundreds whom we removed to hospitals are dying because they are too exhausted to take nourishment. A Dutchman of the Amsterdam underground was picked up on January 3 of this year, and in these few months he had lost 75 pounds.

"Across the way was a Polish women's camp of 600 where the conditions were better because they were worked 20 hours—12 in a factory, eight in the field. They cried with joy when they learned they were to have a mass which they had been denied for six years. Their heads were shaved if they were discovered with even a homemade rosary.

"The enclosed tells of the ceremony we had for the mass burial of these 200 victims of atrocity. The civilians were made to file by the bodies laid out in state beside the graves they had dug. A band played softly while the bodies were lowered into the graves, and then the pro-Nazi Bürgermeister spoke to his people to the effect that they were being given an opportunity to right a wrong committed by the German nation. Even the German officers stood at "present arms" for the national anthem which followed the services.

"Among the civilians there was much weeping, and one woman was overheard to say, 'It's a disgrace to be a German.' It was impossible to identify any of these dead, but it was estimated that a fourth of them were Jews. So on every fourth cross is the imprint of the Star of David. It was a scene I shall never forget."

I'd like to read the homily, which was very short, to you because it shows the effort of a man 35 years ago trying to remain Christian in his interpretation of an event which was so cruelly harrowing and so thoroughly pagan:

"We are assembled here today before God and the sight of man to give proper and reverent burial to the victims of atrocities committed by armed forces in the name and by the order of the German government. These 200 bodies were found by the American army in a concentration camp four miles north of the city of Ludwigslust.

"The crimes here commited in the name of the German people and by their acquiescence were minor compared to those to be found in concentration camps elsewhere in Germany. Here there were no gas chambers, no crematoria. These men of Holland, Russia, Poland, Czechoslovakia, and France were simply allowed to starve to death. Within four miles of your comfortable homes, 4,000 men were forced to live like animals, deprived even of the food you would give to your dogs. In three weeks, 1,000 of these men were starved to death. Eight hundred of them were buried in pits in the nearby woods. These 200 who lie before us in these graves were found piled four and five feet high in one building and lying with the sick and dying in other buildings.

"The world has long been horrified at the crimes of the German nation. These crimes were never clearly brought to light until the armies of the United Nations overran Germany. This is not war as conducted by the international rules of warfare. This is murder such as is not even known among savages.

"Though you claim no knowledge of these acts, you are still individually and collectively responsible for these atrocities, for they were committed by a government elected[5] to office by yourselves in 1933 and continued in office by your indifference to organized brutality. It should be the firm resolve of the German people that never again should any leader or party bring them to such moral degradation as is exhibited here.

"It is the custom of the United States army through its Chaplains Corps to ensure a proper and decent burial to any deceased person whether he be civilian or soldier, friend or foe, according to religious preference. The Supreme Commander of the Allied forces has ordered that all atrocity victims be buried in a public place and that the cemetery be given the same perpetual care that is given to all military cemeteries. Crosses will be placed at the head of the graves of Christians and Stars of David at the head of the graves of Jews.

"A stone monument will be set up in memory of these deceased. Protestant, Catholic, and Jewish prayers will be said by chaplains Wood, Hannan, and Wall of the 82nd Airborne Division for these victims as we lay them to rest and commit them into the hands of our Heavenly Father in the hope that the world will not again be faced with such barbarity."

RABBI HERSCHEL SCHACTER

I do not know how many of you were present this morning in the session in the larger auditorium when it was my privilege to speak and describe in some detail some of the scenes that met my eyes on the most unforgettable day in my life, which was April 11, 1945.

I think that from all that we have heard and seen, from all that we have read and thought, there emerges a fact—a fact that seems to be a paradox.

If ever there was a generation that was cursed—cursed with unspeakable, indescribable pain and torture and barbarism and bestiality and martyrdom, it is, of course, our generation.

Yet, if ever there was a generation that was blessed—blessed with unprecedented and unparalleled opportunity and privilege and insight and understanding, it is again our generation.

I served as a chaplain in the American army for over three years. I consider it a privilege—a privilege that brought with it much pain and grief and heartache—and yet I truly consider it a privilege to have witnessed, to have participated in the ravages of war, to have seen the curse of war, of cities laid waste and homes destroyed and human beings crushed. I especially consider it a privilege, tragic and grievous though it was, to have come face to face with the stark, bitter, sordid reality of Jewish tragedy.

Yes, I was in that hellhole called Buchenwald within a matter of hours after the first columns of American tanks rolled through and liberated that dungeon on the face of this earth.[6] As I said a moment ago, this morning I spoke in detail. I clearly do not want to. I do not think I would have the strength to repeat all that I said this morning. But we—certainly those of us around this table, and I am sure our friends in the rest of this room—are people who believe, and the experience of this cursed and blessed generation has sorely tried our faith.

If I may, brothers, I would like to convey a thought precisely in terms of Scripture. This is hardly the time or the place to deliver a sermon, and yet I think that I can best express the thoughts that come to my mind if I resort to a verse from our Bible that was read in the synagogues throughout the world just this past Sabbath.

For us in the synagogue, this last Sabbath was known as Shabbat Bereschit. It was the Sabbath day on which we began once again to read from the very beginning of our Torah, our Bible.

Against the background of the tremendous story of creation, a cosmic story of the creation of heaven and earth, we come upon the story of two brothers—two brothers who were alone—the only two brothers on the face of the earth. Each brought an offering to God. One was accepted; the other was rejected. When Cain's offer was rejected, he was sorely depressed. He was angry. His face fell in chagrin and remorse. When he was alone with his brother in the field, he rose up and killed him, and I often wondered why, as so many of us do when we think of the Holocaust: Why was Cain angry at Abel? Why was it Abel's fault? If God rejected the offering of Cain, Cain should have railed in anger against God. Why did he kill Abel?

What was Abel's sin? I submit, dear friends, if I may, that Abel acted in a very strange manner. Abel could not help but see that his brother's offering was rejected. He saw the pain, the agony, the grief that Cain was suffering, but we find nowhere any reaction. Abel said nothing. He lifted not a finger. He did not come to his brother when he saw how dejected his brother was. He did not come and put his hand around his shoulder and say, "Brother, what is ailing you? What is bothering you? Can I help you?" Not a word of comfort, of concern. Abel was startlingly silent, apathetic, indifferent. It was only the Lord who spoke to Cain.

The very next verse, after the Torah describes how dejected and hurt Cain was, tells us that God spoke to Cain and asked him, "Why? Why are you so wrought? Why are you so angry? Why has your face fallen?"

That was Abel's great sin—his callous indifference to the plight of his brother.

When we face the tragedy of the Holocaust in our generation, there are those who rail out against the Lord—where was God and how could God have allowed this to happen? It is not God who is to blame. It is man. It is the callous indifference of a world that sat silently by when innocent men, women, and children were being tortured and martyred and murdered.

Why? There is an old statement in the Talmud: "Vehaney Kovshe Derachmana Lama Lach." "We cannot penetrate the secrets of the Divine." We believe that there is a reason. The fact that you and I cannot fathom the reason, the fact that the reason defies our finite understanding cannot mean that there is just a wanton, reckless, meaningless, purposeless slaughter.

Our faith is tried, of course, but we remain men and women of faith. We believe in the ultimate triumph. We must believe or Hitler will have won the war. If, indeed, we can be driven to a negation of our faith in God, in man, in the essential goodness of humanity, we will have handed Hitler a posthumous victory.

We believe, and we will continue to believe and to hope and to pray.

FATHER EDWARD P. DOYLE

I was there. I was present. I saw the sights. I will never forget.

You have heard the story many times before. On the night of April 11, 1945, my division, of which I was the Catholic chaplain, took the town of Nordhausen. The following morning, with the dawn, we discovered a concentration camp. Immediately the call went out for all the medics possible, for all personnel that could be spared, to be present. It was my want as a Catholic priest to serve my regiment during combat at the medical center. Having heard this, I immediately went and of course saw the sights that very morning of our capturing and taking over this place.

We are told there were 6,000 political prisoners, 5,000 of whom were emaciated corpses, scattered, mutilated, starved, and dead. But among those we found approximately 1,000 who were alive, and they were our first order of concern. Everybody went to work, if at all possible, to assist and to help. The doctors came with us, of course, and they indeed told us what to do because you cannot feed a person that far gone—I say living—without the proper prescription.

I would like to pay tribute to the medical profession. This was not my first experience with death, for having gone through combat in France, Belgium, Holland, and Germany, I spent all my time in a medical clinic giving consolation, giving the sacraments, consoling, but at the same time physically helping the doctors. This could be cutting off the uniform where the wound was, cutting shoelaces off the shoes, preparing for the doctors, and being there to assist and to help.

The doctors were with us then. Immediately we offered our help. They told us what to do and what we could do to assist them. We took care of the survivors in every way we possibly could. Of course, as a Catholic priest, I gave absolution conditionally.

But that would be my theme as I go on for a few moments. My theme is this: I have not forgotten. As a priest at the altar of God, I will not forget. You've heard the description so many times that personally it is very difficult for me to recall and to express with such eloquence around me what to me was a softer voice, I think, but deeper in my soul than all. It is difficult for me to tell you as a Catholic priest.

Only last Sunday, our Scripture was from the Apostle Matthew. Christ was asked, "What is the greatest commandment?" And He said, "The greatest commandment is you will love the Lord your God with your whole mind, your whole soul, and with all your strength. And the second is like unto this. You shall love your neighbor as yourself." If we abided by that second part of the first commandment, there would be no need for any other law.

I agree with my colleagues, my brothers here in the clergy, that we must love one another, and we did in taking care of the living. Then we came to the dead. The job was overwhelming. Thousands and thousands.

Then our group went into the town of Nordhausen, and we commandeered all the elderly German men to come to the camp and bury the dead. Particularly, we utilized every possible thing. I recall vividly—and I reflected upon it this past week or so—we took pieces of carpet, and they became a litter, if you will, or a sheet or a door, any way by which we could carry these bodies and lay them out and find any living among them before we prepared for the mass grave. I saw men and women—some deny it—but I saw for myself women, and somewhere in my mind there is always a picture of a child, a bloated child, which has lived with me all these years.

Again, my privilege was at the altar of God to remember the unknown, and that indeed, as I say, is my function—to remember those who are unknown because, on that day, and days to follow, with the use of the trenches—and you know what a trench of course is—six foot wide, six foot deep—long trenches to bury all those people.

One German man said to me through an interpreter, "I am ashamed to be German." I heard these very words here today, whether or not we have believed them fully.

I just finished a year of research fellowship at Yale in psychology, and sometimes we talk about believing 50 percent or 75 percent, but take it for what it is worth. They were ashamed that day, but it was their work to bring themselves to assist in every way possible to bring those people to restful peace. I'm sure in my day I did my part as a priest. I absolved them. I gave them all that I possibly could.

This brings me to the reason. I was a young priest. I have been ordained 42 years by the grace of God. I came out of the university to Providence College, and Pearl Harbor came with me. As a young priest, I volunteered, but I was told by my superiors, "You're too young. Go back to your classroom." I asked the following year again, and I was told "Not yet." In 1943 I was granted a commission and I was in uniform. I might ask, why did I go into the service?

I believe, as all of us believe, that patriotism and religion are from the same parent virtue of justice. General Pershing told us that religion and patriotism go together—to love God, you love your country—and they belong indeed together. So I left my classroom, put on the uniform of the United States Army as a chaplain, and went through France and Belgium and Holland.

On that morning in Nordhausen, I knew why I was there. I found the reason for it—man's inhumanity to man. What has happened to that beautiful commandment of the Decalogue, the commandment of God to love one another? Ten years after the war, I went back to the cemeteries of Belgium and Holland, there being at that time no troops buried in Germany. Every sixth cross had the words, "Unknown but to God." I took that upon myself, and from that time on, all these 36 years, I have never forgotten because, again, I had the privilege of the altar of God. Particularly on holy days when we remember all those who have gone before us, my mind is very keenly centered on the obligation to remember what has gone before us.

As a result, I adapted a beautiful poem which contains my sentiments. As you might recall, "In Flanders Fields" was written by a Canadian colonel and talks about the poppies growing row on row in the Flanders field. My little verse which I adapted from "In Flanders Fields" is rather crude poetically, but it has my thoughts, and I call it, "In a Foreign Field."

In a foreign field we now repose.
Who we are nobody knows!
God knows we suffered at the hand of man.
Now we rest in another land.

We are the dead: short years of life
We lived, felt hope and saw human strife
Loved and in turn were loved and now
We lie in a foreign field.

Take up our quarrel with the foe!
To you from failing hands we throw
THE TORCH. 'Tis yours to hold high!
If ye break faith with us who die
We shall not sleep, for we lie
In a foreign field.

FATHER JOHN PAWLIKOWSKI

Of course I comment on this from a somewhat different perspective from the other people on this panel. I was a child during the Holocaust. I do remember my grandmother speaking about some of the atrocities that her own family was suffering in Poland, but I essentially have come to the Holocaust as a part of the second generation or of the new generation that is now charged with—and I take that very seriously—keeping alive the memory and the testimonies that we have heard presented so eloquently in the conference so far. If we are to profit ultimately from this conference, from the experiences that the speakers on this panel and other panels have narrated, as well as the testimonies of so many others who are not here, it is up to us, the younger generation of theologians and educators, to try to interpret this to people of our generation and to the people who are following us as students.

I myself do not think—and in a decade of studying the Holocaust, I have become more and more convinced of this—that the Holocaust is simply a kind of irrational happening in human history. We have many examples of irrational behavior by dictators of various types, and in those instances many people's lives were lost. At one level, the loss of any life by whatever means is to be mourned. Every human life is precious, whether it is lost as a result of irrationality or whether it is lost through the development of a highly rational system of terror.

At one level, it does not matter, but at another level it does matter very much because I think what we learned from Nazi Germany, and what I have learned in a decade of study and from trying to put together the testimony of so many people, is that Auschwitz did truly represent the beginning of the new era: an era in which the development of bureaucracy, the development of technology, and the growing loss of what I would call a transcendent or traditional morality came together to make possible a whole system of mass murder and mass extermination that was deprived of a good deal of emotion and which was so highly systematized that, in the last analysis, it became as routine as putting automobiles together in a Detroit assembly line. It represented the development of a whole language of extermination in which the human component had been driven out.

So I think we are faced with new possibilities in our age, possibilities that no generation has faced before. We have the possibilities of mass extermination, and we also, perhaps, have a situation where much of the moral values that put some kind of check in the past on immoral human behavior have begun to vanish. It seems to me the challenge before us, as many have already said around the table, is to harness technology, to make sure that we do not become so bureaucratic that the human component is lost.

On this score, for example, I know of the work of Professor Henry Friedlander[7] who made comparisons of how the language employed during the Viet Nam period by our own government in reporting the death statistics day by day bears some of the same kind of dehumanized tones that marked the Nazi reports of what went on day by day in the extermination camps. Certainly we need bureaucracy in a mass society, but can we have bureaucracy that does not lose the preciousness of human life and that does not lose the sense that ultimately bureaucracy is for the people, not to dominate people? Those of us who are church people or religious people have to deal very seriously with the moral crisis of our age. We have to recognize that in very important ways, our society has become much more one-dimensional, very, very secular.

I am not sure that we can simply solve this dilemma by returning to the old pious platitudes of the past. I agree with many of the observations made. I myself have said that to blame God for the Holocaust is in many ways a cop-out, and I believe that very strongly. I believe very strongly the remark that Elie Wiesel made at a lecture some years ago in the Chicago area when a rather young Jewish scholar, who obviously was very upset by the Holocaust and at God's lack of compassion in the Holocaust, challenged Wiesel and asked, "How can you tell us to continue to believe in God after Auschwitz?" Elie, in his quite dramatic fashion, turned to this young Jewish scholar and said, "My friend, I think the question after Auschwitz is not how we can believe in God but how can we believe in man."

However, I believe something else. I believe that perhaps our understanding of the God/human community relationship has been altered by Auschwitz. God has a very important place, but perhaps we have to examine much more closely our role, and perhaps new responsibility has been thrust into our hands. Professor Hans Jonas,[8] a Jewish philosopher, described very well the post-Auschwitz state of things when he remarked some time ago that we have come to live in the generation in which near omnipotence is paired with near emptiness, greatest capacity with knowing least what for. It seems to me that is the challenge before us.

What is the purpose of society? How can we take the new forces of bureaucracy and technology and harvest them once again for the service of humankind? How can we, as religious people, as religious communities, provide the moral tone that will in fact prevent bureaucracy and technology from creating future nightmares like those that we have learned about from Auschwitz and, in turn, create a new world in which brothers and sisters can live in freedom, peace, and justice?

Auschwitz is not over. It was the beginning of a new era. As a younger theologian, I do feel the responsibility of challenging myself and my church because Auschwitz was not simply the final stage in the history of anti-Semitism, as many have said here. It was due to racial theories which come from outside Christianity which represented a kind of paganism. That doesn't excuse the Christian churches, however, because there is no doubt in my mind that traditional Christian anti-Semitism provided an indispensable seedbed for Auschwitz. We must confront that in the churches, but we must also move on to confront the even greater problem of providing some kind of moral ethos in concert with our brothers and sisters in the Jewish community, in other religious communities, and also with those who might describe themselves as humanists so that our world can love instead of hate in the future.

own flocks who simply haven't been able to go back. Do you have reflections on that particular problem?

DISCUSSION

REV. FRANKLIN LITTELL: I think we all feel a very strong commitment to the dead and to the living as we make our testimonies, if I may use a Wesleyan word, of what we have learned. As we think back upon crucial experiences in our own lives and think about our responsibilities as those who are alive, we are blessed to be alive today and to preach and to teach.

I would like to ask one or two questions of panelists to bring out a point or so. I was struck by the fact that the Reverend Wood and Rabbi Nadich both reported the way in which our forces brought the German civilian population into the moment of accountability, particularly in the handling of the bodies. Both Father Doyle and Father Wood mentioned the shame that was expressed by Germans.

One thing which has struck me about our conference here is that we have a session on resistance, but we don't have anything on German resistance. There was German resistance.

We have examined each other as to how much we have learned and how much we have not learned in the decades. One of the problems in our international community today—in the North Atlantic community particularly—is how much have the Germans learned in both East Germany and West Germany?

What do you think to be the genuine effect as nearly as you can tell? Do you think it was just a fleeting moment in which somebody felt shame or do you think there's evidence that we have had a new day in terms of our relationship to the German people?

It is a very sensitive question. I'm sure our rabbis have pastored members of their

RABBI JUDAH NADICH: I have had two different kinds of experience with Germans. I think I can divide them into the older generation and the younger generation. The experiences I refer to that fall into the first category are meetings with Germans in the village of Dachau, which was not very far from the concentration camp.

I am certain that there were many days when the winds must have carried the stench from the chimneys of the crematoria to the village of Dachau. Certainly, trucks went back and forth through the village streets daily. Yet, when I spoke to Germans in the village of Dachau, they said they were completely unaware of the fact that there was a concentration camp a couple of miles away.

"My friend and colleague Rabbi Schacter shares with me the experience of having gone back to Germany to lead retreats, religious retreats, for our American troops of the Jewish faith in the postwar years. I was there in 1974 at Berchtesgaden[9] and it was a strange phenomenon that all the Germans spoken to by any of our troops always said—and I'm speaking about the older generation—that they were in the German army but that none of them ever fought against Americans, that they fought only against Russians. I see in both of these experiences a defensive attitude or an attitude of trying to deny the truth.

On the other hand, I have met young Germans on their way to Israel to work in Israeli kibbutzim [collective farms] for, as they said, a kind of repentance for what their parents did. My wife and I were in Poland in August of 1980, and in one of the two still existing synagogues in Cracow we met a group of about 25 or 30 young Germans on their way to Israel to atone, as they said, for the sins of their parents.

So I think you see two different kinds of reactions on the part of Germans.

RABBI HERSCHEL SCHACTER: I was in Germany less than two months ago on the mission that Rabbi Nadich described. I have the distinct pleasure of being Rabbi Nadich's successor as the chairman of the Commission on Jewish Chaplaincy of the National Jewish Welfare Board. In that capacity, I conducted a retreat for all chaplains of our faith who are currently serving in the American forces in Europe.

I inquired about precisely this question that you raised, Dr. Littell, and I think that it would be fair and intelligent to react and say that all generalizations are irrational. It is just as difficult—and impossible—as it would be to try to ascertain what is the attitude of the American people toward any given issue, past or present.

It is a fact that there are many Germans who deny. It is a fact that the few Jews who still live in Germany outside of the military communities encounter various covert and occasionally overt expressions of rank anti-Semitism.

On the other hand, I do not know whether we should necessarily speak of the older versus the younger German. There may be older who have genuine remorse and younger who would just as soon wipe this experience away from their consciousness. There is good and bad in every people, and it is the degree to which we can maintain a measure of faith in the ultimate goodness of humanity that we can retain our sanity.

REV. FRANKLIN LITTELL: Another question which was a bit blurred in some of our discussion—it comes up all the time in these public education conferences—is, were there 11 million victims of the Holocaust or were there six million victims of the Holocaust? Is the Holocaust a term which is to be used interchangeably with genocide in World War II? How do you see this particular issue?

FATHER EDWARD DOYLE: Well, just the other day I consulted *Webster's Collegiate Dictionary*. Number One, the Holocaust has reference to the massacre of the Jews. Secondly, it is genocide for all nations. So, I think that answers your question. I would like to ask a question of the rabbis who are present. How about the question of a person with hatred? What do we do to eradicate that hatred? Hatred, you know, naturally came forth with all this here, but hatred is sort of a cancer that works in your own disposition. How do you dispose of that or how do you eliminate that from people?

UNIDENTIFIED VOICE: That is a long, long educational process, together with much prayer and with the invocation of divine help. It depends in many cases upon the cause for the hatred. All of us who saw the concentration camps can well understand the hatred of the victims for the persecutors, and I would be loathe to ask them to erase their hatred. I was not in their position.

UNIDENTIFIED VOICE: I live in a community that has a considerable number of Germans in it. There are two reactions. I will state them simply and quickly. Those Germans who have come recently from Germany—I mean, since World War II—just resent any mention of the Holocaust, concentration camps, etc. They do not want to be disturbed by it. The Germans who are of three generations can justify it by remarks bordering on hatred in their attitude toward Jews.

REV. FRANKLIN LITTELL: I would like to throw a curve into the discussion by saying that although it comes naturally to us, the terms "sadism," "cruelty," "bestiality," "lust," "anger," and "hatred" do not really exhaust the problem of the Holocaust. After all, these are all human emotions or feelings.

I was impressed, reading again Thomas Mann's *Dr. Faustus,* by an exchange between Leverkühn and his purported biographer. Leverkühn asks, "Do you know anything stronger than love?" and his friend said, "Is there anything stronger than love?" Leverkühn replies, "Yes, curiosity," which is to say there is a demonic note there that anything which can be done will be done.

The question in my mind is whether the Holocaust is really—except for cases of abuse and brutal guards and so forth—to be subsumed under cruelty and anger and bigotry and hatred and so forth, or whether it represents a massive running-wild of technological capacity. After all, these camps were built, supervised, rationalized, and excused by Ph.D's. They were products of some of the best universities in the world—not Nazi universities, but universities of the Weimar Republic and the late German Empire.

What does that say? I would think it would say to us that the problem has to be dealt with also in terms of scientific technological capacity which has a demonic thrust to do whatever can be done, which has lost ethics, which has lost commitment to life. To treat it as though it is cruelty like some savage torturing of a defeated foe or something like that does not really handle it, does it?

FATHER EDWARD DOYLE: I would say that theologically there are more vices than virtues. In other words, man has the capacity of doing more wrong than he does right. You can enumerate the natural virtues—prudence, justice, temperance, fortitude—but man has that demonic aspect within him, so there are more vices than there are virtues.

UNIDENTIFIED VOICE: I would add that I think we learned from this that it is not sufficient to cultivate the mind. As you indicated, the mind can be used to create the most diabolical evils. In addition to cultivating the mind, there must be the cultivation of the soul or of the spirit. If you do not have both of them going together at the same time, you may very well destroy civilization.

I think that is a lesson not only learned from the past. It is something that we have to be very much aware of here in the United States and indeed throughout the entire contemporary world. It is not enough to depend upon science and upon technology. They can lead us to the death camps.

FATHER EDWARD DOYLE: Man has a free will. The intellect and the will correspond back and forth. The intellect proposes something, and the will carries it out. The longer you keep things in your mind, the more attractive they become.

No one commits a sin to be unhappy. For example, if I am going to steal an automobile, I think to myself, "Should I do what I want?" The more I think of it, the more my will is propelled toward it, and I go for it, but my idea was based in the mind. Therefore, morally you have got a will so the will must also be educated. That is where the morality comes in. I may know it is wrong, but the more I dwell on it—instead of just dissipating it from my mind—the more I tend to follow it, and then I am wrong. That is where the will comes in.

RABBI HERSCHEL SCHACTER: I think that this provides us with the only intelligent rationale that we can bring to bear in groping and struggling with the fundamental theological problem that I posed earlier. I think that those quasi-theologians who came forth with the concepts, "God is dead," and, "There is no God after Auschwitz," and all of these other notions, have simply thrown up their hands in despair and blamed God for what was clearly the failing of man.

As Dr. Littell and Judah Nadich pointed

out, and as we all say, it is precisely those who pursued the technological advances of modern science, without any regard to the moral implications of their work, who are responsible for the tragedies that befell us. We cannot blame God. We must blame ourselves.

REV. FRANKLIN LITTELL: This suggests, perhaps, to pin it down, that the people of the universities—and that is most of us in this room, I'm sure—and the people in our congregations, Jewish and Christian, have to take seriously lessons of the Holocaust in the law schools, medical schools, teachers, colleges, theological faculties, engineering schools, and the like.

Notes

[1] Harrison's official position in 1945 was that of U.S. Representative to the Intergovernmental Committee on Refugees. From 1946 to 1947 he served as Chairman of the National Citizens Committee on Displaced Persons Legislation, and from 1945 to 1948 as Chairman of the National Committee on Post-War Immigration Policy.

[2] It should be noted again here that the gas chamber at Dachau was never operational.

[3] Ludwigslust is about 90 miles northwest of Berlin.

[4] Woebbelin was a satellite of Neuengamme.

[5] This is not strictly correct. On January 30, 1933, the President of Germany appointed Hitler as chancellor to form a coalition government. The Nazi Party by itself never received a majority vote in a national election.

[6] In fact, the inmates of Buchenwald, organized by the illegal International Camp Committee, liberated the camp themselves shortly before the first U.S. troops arrived at the camp. See Walter Bartel, et al., *Buchenwald. Mahnung and Verpflichtung* (Berlin [East], 1983), pp. 610–616 and 750–751.

[7] Henry Friedlander, "The Manipulation of Language," in Henry Friedlander and Sybil Milton, eds., *The Holocaust: Ideology, Bureaucracy, and Genocide* (Milwood, New York, 1980), pp. 103–13.

[8] Hans Jonas, philosopher and educator, author of numerous books on religion, freedom, and ethics.

[9] Berchtesgaden, in the Alps on the Bavarian-Austrian border, was the location of Hitler's mountain retreat.

CHAPTER VIII

THE WAR CRIMES TRIBUNALS

Moderator: Bernard Fischman, Esq. (USA): Attorney, Shea & Gould.

Dr. Czeslaw Pilichowski (Poland): Professor of political science; Director, Main Commission for the Investigation of Nazi Crimes in Poland.

Prof. G.I.A.D. Draper (UK): International lawyer; participated in trials of German war criminals before British military tribunals.

Col. (Ret.) Nikolai Mikhailovich Kotlyar (USSR): Participated in prosecution of Nazi war criminals; author, *Under the Name of Law*.

Delphin Debenest (France): Member of French resistance; survivor of Buchenwald; adjunct prosecutor, Nuremberg trials.

Gideon Hausner (Israel): Jurist and statesman; prosecuted Nazi war criminal Adolf Eichmann.

Adrian Fisher, Esq. (USA): Former Dean of Georgetown University Law School; participated in prosecution of Nazi war criminals.

Institutional identifications are those at the time of the Conference.

DR. CZESLAW PILICHOWSKI*

I am deeply moved that I have the opportunity to speak to you at an international conference dedicated to the problems of liberation from Hitler's concentration camps and the consequences stemming from it. The subject of my presentation today is the problem of persecuting and punishing war crimes.

Poland suffered heavy losses—biological, material, and cultural. In September of 1939, it was the first country to offer resistance to Hitler's aggression. It lost over six million of its citizens, including Polish Jews. At the beginning, I would like to stress that this tragedy and these murders of Polish Jews are an integral part of the history of our country and of our peoples. Starting in December of 1939, Poland presented the world the problem of Hitler's crimes and terror which were spread by Hitler's henchmen on Polish soil.

After many discussions, a charter for an International Military Tribunal in Nuremberg was finally approved in 1945. The principles of Nuremberg, the principles of international law, which were formulated concerning genocide by Hitler, unfortunately are not recognized by all countries at this time, particularly by the Federal Republic of Germany where Hitler's crimes of genocide are still treated as common crimes, as simple crimes. This has resulted, on a global scale, in the punishment of only 50,000 of Hitler's criminals by the entire anti-Hitler coalition tribunals, Polish courts, and courts of countries occupied by the Third Reich.

[Unfortunately, the tape recording of the proceedings is garbled at this point. Among other things, Dr. Pilichowski expressed his concern that two of the German officials who participated in the Wannsee Conference were living in freedom in the Federal Republic of Germany in 1980. See Gideon Hausner's presentation below.]

I would like to say that as far as Poland is concerned, we represent the position that Hitler's crimes can never be subject to limits; any statute of limitations cannot apply from the point of view of Poland. With the support of Israel and the support of many other countries, on November 26, 1968, we confirmed a convention.[1] Unfortunately, this convention was signed by only 21 countries. Fifty countries voted for this convention out of the more than 100 members of the UN. Today in international law we are dealing with the fact that only 21 countries have signed it.

What does it mean? It means that the main condition has not been satisfied which emanates from Hitler's crimes, that is, genocide and all the consequences stemming from it. In other words, it is our duty to undertake such actions—to develop human rights, general morality, and the respect of law in international relations. Therefore, Poland has always demanded, since December of 1949, a just trial of Hitler's criminals and their war crimes against humanity.

Finally, I would like to draw your attention to this problem: It would seem at first that Poland pursues a certain vengeance against the Germans. I would like to assure you, ladies and gentlemen, that this feeling of revenge against the German people is very foreign to us Poles. We put the problem this way: The problem of Hitler's crimes—the problem of pursuing and punishing the criminals—is not only a problem of truth; it is also a political and a moral problem. I would like to state very clearly that we in Poland will never forget Hitler's crimes and we will never stop pursuing the perpetrators of these crimes.

I would like to say that here we deal in accordance with international law, with the norms of the Nuremberg trials, and that is what we will do as long as anywhere in the world one of Hitler's criminals is still free. We have prepared a report about the state of pursuing and studying these crimes which we have submitted to the United Nations organization. Here I have the pleasure of presenting it to the chairman of today's meeting, and I hope

*Dr. Pilichowski made his remarks in Polish; this is the simultaneous translation.

that all countries will support us in that we feel that we have to do it from the legal point of view, from the political point of view, and from the moral point of view. We owe that to the victims of Hitler, be it six million or three million. It is difficult to imagine. What is three million? What is six million? What is 18 million? Let us not delude ourselves that our imagination should fail because then we will not be able to deal with the real problem of showing Hitler's crimes in their whole dimension and of dealing in international law, which we wanted to do at Nuremberg, to punish Hitler's criminals wherever they may be.

G.I.A.D. DRAPER

The whole question of the trial of war criminals is voluminous, difficult, highly technical, and in stark contrast to the overt brutality and horror of the crimes with which it is concerned.

When a government decides that it will take upon itself the responsibility for conducting war crimes trials within the competence of its jurisdictions, believe me, ladies and gentlemen, it takes upon itself a formidable legal, logistical, political, and indeed a moral task.

I think few governments in 1945, at the close of the war under the cover of which the grossest crimes had been committed, these governments had little idea of what this task entailed. Speaking, if I may be so bold, on behalf of the government of the United Kingdom, it was a novel experience in which all persons concerned, from ministers down to humble war crimes prosecutors such as myself, were singularly unversed, untutored, and, if I may say so, naive. Of course, now, standing before you today, I speak in the light of hindsight. Had we but known much that we know now, perhaps many of our mistakes would have been avoided.

The first thing with which we were confronted was the sheer volume of criminality, the overwhelming tidal wave of evidence that flowed into our offices, almost inundating us. One felt like a man fighting to keep his head above water in a strong running sea, and that sea was evidence upon evidence upon evidence of the grossest criminality which our minds had yet experienced. Even staring at the documents, looking at the photographs, and perusing captured German documents, of which we were not in short supply, the sheer horror of the thing weighed upon us day and—in my case, I can tell you—night.

The only thing to do was to try and keep calm. It was a form of therapeutic, stabilizing, and leveling exercise to endeavor to concentrate upon what I might call the "technicalities of the exercise." When you are dealing with the prosecution of war crimes, you are moving in three main areas of law. And I do not wish to give you a law lecture, because otherwise you will be shaking your watches to see if they are going.

You are first concerned with the jurisdiction. By that we mean the competence of the tribunals before which you, a prosecutor, are going to appear, the legal competence of handling a case of the accused who is being brought to trial on that occasion. Under the system of the prosecution of war criminals, the provision of adequate defense facilities is part of the necessary process of doing justice, and that was what we were trying to do. Our court of law does not apply justice; it applies something more difficult—justice according to law. That was the novel part of the exercise in the area of war criminality.

It is true, we had some isolated precedents of war crimes trials. One of the most notorious is in the 15th century in central Europe, but for the types of crimes that we were dealing with and the type of jurisdiction and the type of problem with getting the accused before the court and finding the evidence to link him to the crimes with which he was charged, I can assure you it was a task that would break the backs of most lawyers.

The British work on a doctrine of maximum effort and economy of personnel. There were not many of us. At the peak of our war crimes prosecutions in western Europe—I speak not of the Far East, which was a separate exercise—we had not more than 12 prosecutors, of which two were very young lawyers, almost under instruction.

We had teams of investigators, men who had performed many diverse roles in the army and were used to what is called "getting around on their own." Then we had to have technicians—people such as documentary research analysts, people who knew German and were knowledgeable about the German military, SS, SD, and Gestapo etc. organizations. You have to have people who know about orders of battle. If you are going to prosecute a German field marshal for campaigns in eastern Europe, you have to have a great deal of what I might call military expertise at your elbow.

The prosecutor goes to a podium with captured documents on one side, research analysts on the other, technicians sitting around him. It is really almost like being equipped to fight a war. We had none of these things; it all had to be gathered together slowly and bit by bit. The evidence came in faster than we had facilities to deal with it.

It is the normal practice of a war criminal to try to get into a country where the evidence against him does not exist. The war criminals could learn very early on that there were multiple different jurisdictions in different countries, and by going from one country to another, he might elude not only capture, but the technical process of bringing him to justice.

The getting of an accused from one state to another caused endless troubles. There was no international machinery dealing with extradition or the handing over of war criminals. There was no court for extradition. It was made by desk decision. We not only had to go into court and prosecute cases, we had to make desk decisions on countless cases of whether Accused "X" was to be handed over to State "Y" and whether the evidence presented by State "Y" was adequate to make such a delivery. None of these things had been thought of at the time the prosecutions were first entertained by our Cabinet.

Let me tell you one thing. The ordinary criminal jurisdiction of the United Kingdom was never, never invoked at any time for the prosecution of one single German war criminal. Our domestic, ordinary penal courts were never invoked; it was all done in the British Zone of occupied Germany under what we would call a Royal Warrant which is a decree of the executive arm of government. Military tribunals were set up within the organization of the military, and the nearest analogy to these courts would be the type of military court that tries a prisoner of war who commits a crime while a prisoner of war.

There was also the parallel jurisdiction, less invoked, of the Allied Control Council, British Element.[2] This applied quite a different law than that which we were applying.

The military courts before which I prosecuted applied the traditional, classical law of war; a war crime was a violation of the existing law of war. It followed that the British military had no jurisdiction whatsoever over crimes committed before the war. Crimes against humanity and crimes against peace were two of the three main war crimes tried before the Nuremberg International Military Tribunal that were not within the competence of the British military courts.[3]

Moreover, owing to our difficulties of our own home law and the relationship of international law to domestic law, these military tribunals had to bear the whole load of what I might call the "war crimes exercise in occupied Germany." This was at a time—1945 and 1946—when the lawyers who were already in the armed forces were flowing back into civilian life where they belonged, so that the numbers of British lawyers left in the armed forces to handle this extensive commitment was dwindling every day.

In the very early days, such as for the Belsen trial which was the second trial we conducted, the defense lawyers were British military officers serving in the ordinary course of their military duties who happened to be qualified lawyers in peacetime.[4] These men, normally a little older, very swiftly left the armed forces, and then we had recourse to the use of German professional advocates, ordinary German practitioners. The system of denazification eliminated a very large number of the German bar, and those German lawyers who were cleared for appearing on behalf of the accused had, by the definition of the Nazi state, normally been out of practice for the whole period of the war. They were singularly out of touch, out of date with recent developments. Therefore, one had this perennial criticism coming in that the defense of these war criminals had burdens which were not on the backs of the prosecution.

We have a great saying in my country, "It is not only important that justice be done, but it is equally important that justice be seen openly and manifestly to be done." Equality of competence of the defense counsel is part of that exercise.

There was also the next question of what law was to be applied. Before the military tribunals we used the ordinary, customary, and conventional law of war, which forms part of what was generally known as international law. The jurisdiction we gave ourselves had one very sharp provision in it—no plea or attack may be made by the defense upon the jurisdiction. That is a very tough provision. I know of one case only where such an attack was launched, and it was launched for the defense of Field Marshal von Manstein who was tried very late on by the British authorities, as late as 1949.[5]

I would like to pay a tribute in passing, in reference to that event, to the Polish government of the day for assisting us in providing a great deal of evidence about war crimes that had taken place in 1939 and 1940 in Poland.

Detachment was, I am convinced, a very important quality to retain as a prosecutor at such war crimes trials. There was a body of law, of long history, to be applied. There was a court by which it was to be brought to bear, impartially and justly, and there were rules that governed the evidence and the procedures that had to be followed. Any attempt to ignore such law had to be firmly rejected, unless such courts were to become a charade of justice and an insult to the memory of the victims of the accused. That more could have been done by way of such trials, is true. Within the resources and time provided by the government, and the personnel and skills available, such trials are not a discredit to the history and doing of justice in circumstances that were as unique as the crimes. There is something to be said for the aphorism expressed by the late Mr. Justice Jackson, the architect of the Nuremburg Four-Power trial: "Better the worst sort of justice than the best sort of violence."[6] The proposal to shoot, summarily, a hundred or so major German war criminals would without doubt have been a crime. It had to be rejected if man was to preserve his decency at a time when it was more needed than at any other time in the sad history of this world. Let us be thankful for that and never forget it.

*NIKOLAI M. KOTLYAR**

Even if I wanted to, I could not hide the emotions with which I approach this opportunity to speak to such an illustrious international gathering. On June 22 of this year, my people and we war veterans, with great emotion and pain, celebrated the anniversary of fascist Germany's attack on our country in the beginning of the Great Patriotic War.

*Mr. Kotlyar made his remarks in Russian; this is the simultaneous translation.

This war lasted 1,014 days; over 20 million Soviet citizens were killed and nearly 50 million wounded. Whole economic regions of my country were destroyed. There is hardly a single family that has not suffered in that war and to this day does not feel this painful loss. This explains the caution and the trepidation with which my nation and we war veterans approach the slightest threat of a new war or any efforts to start a new arms race.

These two days of this conference, in which participants in the war and inmates of fascist camps again have shown Hitler's monstrous acts, have been fruitful and useful. Indeed, we remember these horrors, the laws with which we punished them, and the initiators of this aggressive war, not so that our hearts would bleed again, but so that with the mutual effort of all honest people of the world, all nations, and all peoples, they will remember what a policy will inadvertently lead to when people attack other nations and want to be masters there. That is what the fascists of Hitler's Germany wanted to do.

It was a long and painful road. I started it in 1941, at a place between the cities of Minsk and Smolensk as a private, and finished it as a colonel and military prosecutor in Berlin of this very same Fifth Shock Army which stormed the last fascist stronghold, the Reichskanzlei [Reich Chancellery]. I was the first military prosecutor of captured Berlin. I was present at the Nuremberg trials. I represented the Soviet Union in Sachsenhausen and was also the Soviet representative as an observer, as they say, at a very interesting trial at Dachau.

As a soldier and a military prosecutor I have seen so much evil at the Nuremberg trials, which is impossible to contain in the heart of one human being. In Nuremberg it was clearly demonstrated that fascist Germany had been preparing for this war of aggression for a long time. The plan was to create a fascist world empire by adding such countries as France, Britain, and practically all other states in central and southeast Europe and the territories of the Near and Middle East to the fascist Reich, with the subsequent occupation of the United States of America. I have cited these facts.

No, gentlemen, no separate monsters of fascism dealt with all the territories occupied by Hitler's army. Hitler's fascists introduced a ruthless policy and executed it with the power of their own forces, but Hitler's plan of world domination—as was shown at the Nuremberg trials—saw its biggest obstacle in the existence of the Soviet Union. Therefore, after the liquidation of Poland had to come the liquidation of the Soviet state.

As can be seen from the Barbarossa Plan,[7] which was demonstrated at Nuremberg, Germany wanted simply to destroy the Soviet Union. There was never such a state, according to them, as the Union of Soviet Socialist Republics on the political map of their world, and it was the aim to destroy everything, to depopulate it, to bleed it to death.

It is with pain and sorrow that I recollect the crimes against my people who were subjected especially to hard torture and humiliation. The Soviet soldier protected the freedom and independence of his country and, with other nations of the anti-Hitlerite coalition, saved mankind from the threat of fascist slavery.

The British Prime Minister at that time, Mr. Winston Churchill, said that future generations will recognize their tribute to the Red Army just as irrevocably as we are doing it now.[8]

Today as we pay our respects to the victims of fascism and of war, when the international situation is unfortunately much more complicated, we must remember that not only our laws must punish the evil deeds, but there must be some laws which once and for all will preclude new aggression and new wars.

In our constitution, we have a provision against war propaganda. It would seem to me that all countries of the world must have such a law and apply it to those who are warmongers. We veterans of that war remind you to show how the road leading to World

The International Liberators Conference Washington, D.C., 1981

Opposite page:

Above, *Miles Lerman, Chairman, International Relations Committee of the U.S. Holocaust Memorial Council; John Eisenhower, U.S. Delegation.*

Below, *Mark Talisman, Vice-chairman, U.S. Holocaust Memorial Council (1980-1986); Alexander M. Haig, U.S. Secretary of State (1980-1982); Elie Wiesel, Chairman U.S. Holocaust Memorial Council (1980-1986).*

This page:

Above, *Elie Wiesel*

Below, *Lt. Col. (Res.) Arieh Pinchuk, Jewish Brigade; Miles Lerman; Elie Wiesel.*

This page:

Above, *Sigmund Strochlitz, U.S. Holocaust Memorial Council.*
Below, *Alexander M. Haig and Miles Lerman.*

Opposite page:

Above, *Sam Block, Special Advisor to the Chairman, U.S. Holocaust Memorial Council; Kalman Sultanik, U.S. Holocaust Memorial Council.*
Below, left, *Benjamin Meed, U.S. Holocaust Memorial Council.*
Below, right, *Lt. Gen. (Res.) Vassily Yakovlevich Petrenko, U.S.S.R. Delegation.*

Col. Branko Pavlo
YUGOSLAVIA

Opposite page:
Above, left, *Esther Raab (USA).*
Above, right, *Col. Branko Pavlovic, Yugoslavian Delegation.*
Below, left, *Siggi B. Wilzig, U.S. Holocaust Memorial Council.*
Below, right, *Leon Bass, U.S. Delegation.*

This page:
Above, *Fred W. Friendly, U.S. Delegation.*
Below, *Adolf L. Fedetov and Lt. Gen. Pavel Danilovich Gudz, U.S.S.R. Delegation; Jean Laurain, French Delegation.*

This page:

Above, *Marie Ellifritz (USA) and Rev. George B. Wood, U.S. Delegation.*
Below, *Guy Fassina, French Delegation.*

Opposite page:

Above, left, *Richard Glazer (Switzerland).*
Above, right, *Michal Chilczuk, Polish Delegation.*
Below, *Col. Guy Hinterlang, French Delegation.*

Col. Guy Hinterlang
FRANCE

Opposite page:

Above, *Trygve Bratteli, Norwegian Delegation; Cantor Isaac Goodfriend, U.S. Holocaust Memorial Council.*
Below, *The Canadian Delegation.*

This page:

Above, *Trygve Bratteli and Leo Eitinger, Norwegian Delegation.*
Below, *Brig. Michael S. Gray, British Delegation.*

This page:

Above, *Menachim Rosensaft, Second Generation Advisor to the Chairman, U.S. Holocaust Memorial Council; Dr. Hadassah Rosensaft, U.S. Holocaust Memorial Council.*
Below, *Lt. Gen. William W. Quinn, U.S. Delegation.*

Opposite page:

Above, *Jan Karski (USA), Vladka Meed (USA), Benjamin Meed, Yitzhak Arad (Israel), and Gideon Hausner (Israel).*
Below, left, *Frode Jakobsen, Danish Delegation.*
Below, middle, *Alexander Donat (USA).*
Below, right, *Rabbi Herschel Schacter (USA).*

Rabbi Herschel Schacter
USA

Opposite page:
Above, *Brig. Gen. James L. Collins and Father Edward P. Doyle, U.S. Delegation.*
Below, *Lewis Weinstein (USA).*

This page:
Above, *Marvin Kalb (USA); Elie Wiesel; John W. Pehle, U.S. Delegation; Jan Karski; V.Y. Petrenko; and Robert Wolfe (USA).*
Middle, *Louis de Jong, Netherlands Delegation; Renee Aubrey, French Delegation.*
Below, *Raul Hilberg, U.S. Holocaust Memorial Council.*

Above, *Father John T. Pawlikowski, U.S. Holocaust Memorial Council.* **Below,** *Eduard Kukan, Czechoslovakian Delegation; Miles Lerman; Elie Wiesel.*

War II was built. Sometimes we did not bc lieve that the war would come, but we see that the same road is being built right now. This is why we must not only have some laws, but all the criminals that fled our country must be returned to us, even though some countries are against it.

I would like, in conclusion, to remind you that not so long ago at the UN General Assembly there was a new proposal to regard as criminals, real criminals, those who try in any form whatsoever to apply nuclear arms, because otherwise there will never be another conference, because there will be nobody there to attend such a conference, or to pray to remember those who have perished. Now we have to devote all our efforts to prevent this monstrous possibility.

*DELPHIN DEBENEST**

I have been asked to talk on the subject of war crimes and the judicial organizations which heard those trials. It is not my intention to explain to you in technical and juridical detail what was involved, because we have been asked here to bear witness. I feel that it is on the basis of such bearing of witness that it will be possible to study and draw up proposals on a judicial organization and rules that should be used for the functioning of such a judicial body.

The witness that I am going to bring to bear I will give you in two separate categories: as someone who for four years lived under the German occupation, as a member of the underground, of the resistance, and also as an inmate in Buchenwald concentration camp. Thereafter, I will talk to you as a General Advocate of France, one of the judges at the Nuremberg trials.[9]

I will be relating to you facts that I knew and lived through personally or facts that I read in the authentic documents at Nuremberg. All of these facts have been proven, unquestionably, without doubt, without challenge. These are German documents that were collected during the advance of the Allied armies, especially by the United States forces. I know how fragile human testimony and witness is, and I know how easy it is to cast doubt on it, so I am only going to talk about things that are based on written proof and documents.

The speaker from Great Britain, who preceded me here, told you of the jurisdictional aspects of the courts that heard these crimes. These jurisdictions took place in Germany or in the occupied territories. These courts were the same in France as in Great Britain, so I will not dwell on this point so as not to go on any longer than I need to.

Judge Robert Jackson, who was the chief prosecutor for the United States in the Nuremberg trials and to whom we owe the organization of the International Military Tribunals, defined war crimes in accordance with the norms of all civilized countries. In other words, these are acts contrary to the custom and usage and traditions of war as customarily practiced. A few examples would be acts of violence against persons and property which do not aim at a military purpose, including the massacre of the wounded, mistreatment of war prisoners, pillage, systematic destruction, mistreatment of persons in occupied territories, persecution for racial or religious reasons, and following a general and systematic policy of terrorism and repression in the occupied countries.

The Second World War started by a true war crime, the air bombing of Poland on September 1, 1939, without any declaration of war.

There were many acts of terrorism in occupied France: the taking of hostages; the terrorizing and hanging of peasants working in their fields; and arrests of members of the

*Mr. Debenest made his remarks in French; this is the simultaneous translation.

underground and, their execution without trial in Paris and in Vercors.[10] The Germans found wounded people whom they summarily executed, and they also killed the people who were taking care of them.

There were also things that were done to the members of the resistance to make them confess. There were atrocities, for example, against members of the resistance, even greater atrocities in Tulle, and in Oradour-sur-Glans, where healthy men were found, put together, and executed together with women and children. They were closed into churches, and the Panzer divisions of the Germans, after barricading the doors of these churches, burned them. One single woman escaped death on this occasion. In another place, hostages were taken. These are just a few examples among many. And the place where they were imprisoned was set fire to. All perished.

There were commissions of crimes with no reason, no purpose, because they just confused Oradour-sur-Glans with another town named Oradour in another place.[11] The pretext was that nearby there were members of the underground. But even if there were some, they didn't find them. There were many acts of terrorism. I could name many whole towns and villages burned, Haute-Ubaye in the Alps, for instance. And there were many members of the Resistance who were arrested and underwent terrible tortures in prison when they were not executed before firing squads.

I must say that in France—here I am only talking about France because I know the case better, but the same thing could be said of other countries, especially Belgium and Denmark—there were people who underwent terrible tortures even after General Eisenhower made it possible to shut off the advance of the German troops coming up from the south.

I won't talk about the documents because time has caught up with me, but I would like to mention as war crimes what was committed in Bastogne[12] where people were chained and run over by tanks. I won't mention either, because of time restraints, the medical experiments which were found in the concentration camps, but there is a lot to say about that because these were done on the orders of the high command of the air force and the army of Germany, and there is voluminous proof of these crimes in Nuremberg. I participated in trials on this, and all of this evidence is very sound.

We finally were able to find a jurisdiction that could hear these crimes, and that jurisdiction of course, as you have already been told, is Nuremberg. Nuremberg was a jurisdiction that needed to be modified, perhaps, but in any case it was essential that these states, given the validity of the facts and the events, were able to pass judgment on these people. Nuremberg is not just the justice of the victors against the vanquished; it makes it possible to bring to our young people, who are unaware, the facts they need to know, and it gives us an opportunity to extend the knowledge of these war crimes to the coming generations.

GIDEON HAUSNER

The capture of Adolf Eichmann in Argentina and his transfer to Israel in 1960 provided an occasion for one of the most dramatic trials of our times, for the accused had been handpicked at the time by the supreme leadership of Nazi Germany to implement what they had called the Final Solution of the Jewish question in Europe which, as we all know, had involved the physical destruction of all Jews within the German sphere of influence. Wherever a victorious swastika flag was hoisted, from the icy waters of the Arctic Ocean in the north to the sun-baked sands of the Sahara Desert in the south, from the peaks of the Pyrenees in the West to the rugged hills of the Caucasus in the East, within this vast continent the Jew was doomed. He had to be extirpated, by definition.

This was the decision of a conference convened at Wannsee[13] on January 20, 1942, chaired by Reinhard Heydrich, attended by 13 members of the highest hierarchy of the Third Reich, and very carefully prepared by Adolf Eichmann.

I listened with great interest to your observations, Dr. Pilichowski. Our two countries are among those who took the resolution never to forget. I also fully endorse your regret that some of the participants in the Wannsee Conference and other war criminals have not yet been brought to the bar of justice. Eichmann's examination, both before his trial and in the courtroom, had offered us an opportunity for a closer look at this assemblage of dignitaries which sealed the fate of European Jewry.

In your kit, you will find one page of the protocol of this conference where all European countries were listed, one by one, with the number of Jews to be destroyed. This staggering total figure, according to this Nazi document, exceeds the astronomical sum of 11 million. Some places like Estonia, then under Soviet sovereignty, are already listed as free of Jews — judenfrei.

But the Wannsee people, ladies and gentlemen, were not a bunch of aborigines of the jungle, nor were they escapees from lunatic asylums, nor murderous sadists. They all held university degrees; they were steeped in European culture; they belonged to the intellectual elite of their country, for in Germany one could have been a rabid Nazi, a fiery racist, and still be considered a Kulturmensch, a man of culture. You could be a university professor or a Nobel Prize winner like the physicist Philipp Lenard of Heidelberg or Johannes Stark who undertook to write a new German physics book omitting Einstein.[14] In Germany, you could have been an acclaimed intellectual and at the same time a fanatic Nazi.

This is the frightening element, for this is also a lesson for the world today. Professor Hilberg yesterday spoke of the warning omens of genocide, the red lights which, when they start blinking, should put us on our guard. Yet on the human side there are no such red lights. High education, accomplishments in the field of science, and academic careers are no warranty. Often, on the contrary, some of the people who did the dirtiest job in the field, some of the leaders of Einsatzgruppen, who murdered millions of Jews and Soviet prisoners of war, were university professors. To mention just two, there were Ohlendorf and Six.[15]

This 20th century of ours, which Churchill called "the terrible 20th," began with anarchism, went over to Nazism, and is finishing with terrorism. Even today you can be an intellectual; you can be considered a progressive man; you can be a writer, journalist, or actor, and yet also be an adherent of unbridled terror aimed at synagogues, schoolchildren, or innocent people. We say, Never Again, but, ladies and gentlemen, it is already happening again.

In the course of the Eichmann trial, I tried to find out what made the Nazis break the barrier, "Thou shalt not kill." Wars have been with mankind since the dawn of history. Unfortunately, they have not ceased, and I share all appeals made from this rostrum that there should be no more wars.

When going deeper into this at the trial, we discovered that the pernicious teachings of the 19th century philosophers, theologians, social scientists, and even Social Darwinists had all contributed to this terrible sewer of fatality. Eichmann was not an intellectual; still he claimed that he wished all his life to be guided by the categorical imperative of behavior laid down by Immanuel Kant.[16] Just for the fun of it, he was asked what that imperative was. To the astonishment of everybody in the courtroom, he came out with a more or less correct definition that one's behavior should be such that you would want it to be a model for general legislation.

None of the assembled dignitaries of Wannsee raised the slightest objection to the mass murder of the Jews. Heydrich, by the way, did not bring Hitler's order; he brought Hitler's suggestion only, for he [Hitler] had wanted all of the leadership of Nazi Germany to be implicated in the crimes.

We have the protocol of this meeting.[17] Nobody had any observations, either on the account of morality or even for such pragmatic reasons as what the people would say outside of Germany about this terrible mass murder. But it was possible to discuss the issue and to consider it, as was evidenced by the lively dispute which took place not on the killing of 11 million Jews, but what would be the fate of the Mischlinge, the offspring of mixed marriages who had some good blood in their veins and some "polluted" blood. They had disputed which mixture would seal the fate of an individual and which would still be tolerable.

I asked Eichmann whether he had met any objection from the leaders of the Church. He said no. This brought about today the reaction of some great Christian theologians, some present here with us, who decided that they must find what they call "a Christian answer to Auschwitz."

We tried to find out when it all began, when Hitler really made up his mind. We found a document dated September 1939, when the fighting was still going on in Poland and when the heroes of the Polish army were still defending the Westerplatte[18] in Danzig, which revealed that he had already summoned his Einsatzgruppen leaders and had given them their secret directions for the Final Solution to come.

At the Eichmann trial we also had to record perhaps the saddest point of all—the complete indifference of the free world. The world had closed its gates to Jewish refugees and had bolted its hearts. We were left in a no man's land of humanity. Measures were taken to avoid, to frustrate, to make it impossible for the frantic stampede of Jews across Europe to find asylum anywhere.

Conferences were convened, only to cover up the inactivity. Maybe that is why today, at least, when the boat-people of Southeast Asia are sailing the seven seas, they were offered asylum in many places. Maybe part of the lesson went home. I am happy that my country did its share.

Permit me to make a personal observation. I am sorry that my country, Israel, had to be brought to this place through the back door and that there is no official delegation of Israel for the very strange argument that Israel did not exist at the time of these crimes. Israel is the country of the saved remnant. It existed in the hearts of all of our martyrs.

I am sorry that in the material produced here there is not one word of Hebrew or Yiddish. These were their languages. I am happy that at least Secretary Haig referred to Yad Vashem[19] as the important central institution of commemoration.

In Jerusalem we established a precedent—Eichmann was hiding beyond the seas, and he thought he would find shelter behind the passage of time. Well, neither helped him. He was rooted out; he was found; he was brought to court, and sentenced before the whole world. Even his attorney had to say it was a fair trial, and it is the only case in which Israel has ever put into effect the death sentence.

At the time of the trial we were thinking of a very Biblical prophecy, "Saviors shall come up on the Mount of Zion to judge the Mount of Esau and the kingdom shall be the Lord's." It is very fitting to speak to you liberators as the saviors. We have climbed and scaled many mountains and overcome many obstacles to save the remnants of a nation. It is our duty, yours and ours, to band together in order to secure the future of the world. We owe it as a reverence to our dead and as a debt of duty to our children, for, verily, we are our brothers' keepers.

ADRIAN FISHER

One of the greatest affectations of Washington is you supply the introducer with your title and then look embarrassed. The fact is, I was a technical advisor. It is another good way of saying "law clerk," except they had people like Quincy Wright[20] and others who had rather prestigious jobs. I had been a law clerk, too. I had been a law clerk for [Supreme Court] Justices Brandeis and Frankfurter, so calling me a "law clerk" didn't bother me, but it sort of bothered them. So we got the fancy title of "technical adviser," and I got a free ride along with them.

We don't have much time. I would like to deal with just about three things: one is, what did Nuremberg do on this issue of "let's not forget" and what did it leave undone? The first thing that this international trial did was to lay a foundation, without the doubt of any reasonable man of the true enormity of what had happened.

You listen to a person describe how an outfit comes into a town, rounds up all the people, makes them dig mass graves, strips them, and then shoots them. . . .I know that some of the U.S. judges for whom I worked, particularly Judge Parker,[21] just could not believe it until he believed it, and then he went into almost a funk as a result of it because he just could not accept that people could be that evil. So it established without any doubt, notwithstanding some rather kooky voices from the extreme right, that this thing in fact happened.

It also established without much doubt, as General Hausner said, that there was not a great deal of opposition to it in Germany at that point and the whole notion of superior orders was a fake. He mentioned Ohlendorf who led one of the Einsatzgruppen. He was asked if his estimate of 100,000 as the number killed on a particular mission wasn't a little low, because one of the other groups had said they had killed 150,000. He said no and that the other group was just bragging. That will just give you some idea of the value judgment.

You have laid a theoretical basis for dealing with this problem in the past. It has a gap; there is no question about that. The gap is that it didn't deal with prewar issues.

As my distinguished colleague has said, there are a lot of things that were left undone. The first is, the whole Nuremberg trials and the subsequent proceedings were based on occupation powers. No serious difficulty; all of this argument against the Nuremberg trials was ex post facto—nonsense as applied to this. The Geneva and Hague Conventions were there, and they made it clear it was a crime to mistreat people of occupied territory. It was very clear. But this was an occupation problem, and it is also a whole group of other problems that have been dealt with, such as: How do you get these guys? What do you do when the occupation is over? Are you going to delay the occupation of what is now the Federal Republic of Germany until the entire war crime problem has been settled? It has not been settled yet, and would we want to delay it that much further? Was that within the political capability of any of our countries? I have some doubt if it was within the political capability of the United States.

What, then, are we saying? One obvious answer is that there is a convention that deals with this, that carries these modalities lying around loose. It is the Genocide Convention. It deals with such matters as extradition. I do not think right now the problem of pre-1939 crimes is the thing that worries us the most. What worries us the most is whether or not the post-1939 crimes are really cleared up. There is going to be a statute of limitations on that—not a legal statute of limitations, but a limitation of death, where people may avoid one punishment to perhaps go to a somewhat more serious one.

We really ought to get cracking to ratify the Genocide Convention,[22] so we won't have all of these technical arguments on these kinds of things. We have to recognize that the juridical tools are with us for dealing with this problem. The problem is purely one of will, "political will," to use a phrase I heard very often in arms control negotiations. If the term is "political will," it is up to us to tell our respective governments not to get cracking, but to keep cracking, and that is the only way we can keep this thing in its proper role.

Notes

1 The reference is to the Convention on Non-Applicability of Statutory Limitation to War Crimes and Crimes Against Humanity, which was opened for ratification in the United Nations General Assembly on December 16, 1968. Twenty-nine nations, mostly from eastern Europe and the non-aligned movement, had ratified it by the end of 1984. The United States, the nations of the North Atlantic Treaty Organization, and Israel had not ratified the convention by the end of 1984.

2 The Allied Control Council was established in 1945 by joint agreement of the United States, the Soviet Union, Great Britain, and France. Its purpose was to coordinate and administer all aspects of occupation government in Germany. The Control Council ceased to be meaningful in March 1948, when the Soviet representative withdrew from the body.

3 The third category was "war crimes." Whereas the concept of "crimes against humanity" was an innovation of the International Military Tribunal designed to deal with the unprecedented scope and nature of Nazi atrocities, the concept of "war crimes" was already well-grounded in international law.

4 Forty-four officers, guards, and other personnel associated with Bergen-Belsen were tried before a British military tribunal beginning in September 1945. Eleven, including one-time camp commandment Josef Kramer, were sentenced to death and executed.

5 A British military tribunal sentenced Field Marshall Erich von Manstein to 18 years imprisonment. The sentence was subsequently reduced to 12 years, but Manstein was released in 1952.

6 Robert H. Jackson was the chief American prosecutor at the International Military Tribunal. He had previously served as Attorney General and as a Justice on the U.S. Supreme Court.

7 Barbarossa was the German code name for the invasion of the Soviet Union. It took its name from the medieval German emperor Friedrich Barbarossa.

8 The source in Churchill's works has not been located.

9 A general advocate is an assistant public prosecutor in the French judicial system.

10 Vercors is a region in southeastern France.

11 The massacre in Oradour-sur-Glans, located in western France in the department of Deux-Sevres, took place on June 10, 1944. Troops of the Waffen SS shot all of the males living in the village, and then collected the women and children into the church, which they then burned to the ground. Only a handful of the 800 or so residents of the village managed to escape.

12 Bastogne is in the southern tip of Belgium, near the border with Luxembourg.

13 Wannsee was, and remains, a recreational and luxury residential district in the western part of Berlin.

14 On the "Aryan physics" of Philipp Lenard and Johannes Stark, see Alan Beyerchen, *Scientists under Hitler* (New Haven, 1977), chaps. 5-6.

15 Franz Six, leader of the Vorkommando Moskau of Einsatzgruppe B, had been a professor of Foreign Studies at the University of Berlin. After the war, he was sentenced to 20 years imprisonment by a U.S. tribunal. His sentence was subsequently reduced, and Six was released in 1952.

Otto Ohlendorf, commander of Einsatzgruppe D, held a doctorate in jurisprudence. After the war he was condemned to death by an American tribunal, and was executed in 1951.

16 The Categorical Imperative, a concept introduced by the 18th century German philospher Immanuel Kant, is commonly understood as an absolute moral law, valid for all individuals in all situations. Thus the commandment, "Thou shalt not kill," may be considered a categorical imperative, for it is universal and unconditional.

17 For a reproduction and translation of the Protocol, as well as a number of related documents, see John Mendelsohn, ed. *The Holocaust: Selected Documents in Eighteen Volumes* (New York, 1982), vol. 11.

18 A Polish fortress on a peninsula near Danzig

(Gdansk), the Westerplatte was captured by the Germans in September 1939. The courage of the outnumbered defenders of the fortress became an important symbol of resistance for the Poles.

[19] Yad Vashem in Jerusalem, The Holocaust Martyrs' and Heroes' Remembrance Authority, is Israel's most important institution devoted to the Holocaust.

[20] Quincy Wright, author, professor, and authority in the field of international law, served as an American technical adviser at the International Military Tribunal.

[21] John J. Parker was the alternate U.S. judge on the International Military Tribunal.

[22] A United Nations "Convention on the Prevention and Punishment of the Crime of Genocide" was passed in 1946. The U.S. Senate ratified this convention on February 18, 1986.

CHAPTER IX

THE RESISTANCE

Moderator: Frank R. Lautenberg (USA): Businessman; member, U.S. Holocaust Memorial Council. (Elected to U.S. Senate 1982.)

Louis de Jong (Netherlands): Historian; former director of the Netherlands State Institute for War Documentation.

Renée Aubry (France): Chief of Cabinet in Ministry of Veterans; widow of resistance fighter.

Frode Jakobsen (Denmark): Former resistance fighter; member of first postoccupation cabinet; member of the Danish parliament.

Branko Lakic (Yugoslavia): Counsel General in Washington; partisan fighter.

Samuel Gruber (USA): Survivor of Majdanek; partisan fighter.

Benjamin Meed (USA): Businessman; president, Warsaw Ghetto Resistance Organization; member, U.S. Holocaust Memorial Council.

Institutional identifications are those at the time of the Conference.

LOUIS DE JONG

First of all, as to my personal involvement, I am Jewish, and this was one of the factors which made me decide in May 1940, when the German army attacked the Netherlands, to try and escape to Britain. I was one of the very few people who succeeded in doing so.

In Britain, I worked for five years broadcasting in Dutch to the people of occupied Holland, and after the war in 1945, I was given the task of organizing and directing a state institute of war documentation. I did so until 1979 when I retired. The main part of my work over the past 20 years, has been to prepare an overall history of the Netherlands in World War II in which inevitably much attention is paid both to Jewish persecution and to the resistance.

You might like to know that these books attract tremendous notice in my country, testifying to the strong interest among the Dutch people for what happened in World War II. We generally start with the first printing of 100,000 copies, which would mean a million-and-a-half when it would come to the size of the United States. They are usually very quickly sold out.

You will understand also that given the fact that my books—at least the ones that have been published so far—total some 10,000 pages, it is fairly difficult to compress them into 10 minutes.

I would like to stress first of all the country is as flat as a pancake. It was and is very densely populated and has an area the size of about 12,000 to 13,000 square miles or 30,000 square kilometers. It is inhabited by nine million people. There are no impenetrable swamps. There are no mountains. There are no deep forests.

So, forms of resistance that were possible elsewhere in Europe, particularly in Eastern Europe, Poland, the Soviet Union, Yugoslavia, Greece, and some parts of Italy and France, were out of the question in a country like Holland with its excellent road and communication system. If you had to carry out resistance and save people, you could only hide them, so to speak, within the folds of society as it was, and this is what happened.

It is not so easy to give a proper definition of what resistance is. In my opinion, one should ask first of all what were, with regard to Holland, the aims which the Nazi occupier had in mind?

I would be able to indicate four of these aims.

First of all, he intended to Nazify Holland, that is to change the existing Dutch institutions into Nazi institutions, and this was completely unsuccessful.

Most people—I would say 95 to 98 percent—said no to the German occupation right from the start, and I would like to remind you that Holland is perhaps the only country in world history where an impressive and tremendous strike movement took place to protest against what was happening to the Dutch Jews. I am referring to the strike movement in February of 1941 in Amsterdam—a strike which lasted for two days, which one might say had no material effect, but which clearly proved to the German occupier that his political aim, the attempt to Nazify the Netherlands, was not to be attained.

A second aim was the economic exploitation of Holland, and in this the occupier largely succeeded. That is to say that Dutch industry was forced to work as part of the German war machine, and some hundreds of thousands of Dutch workers were forced to work in Germany.

A third aim—I will be coming back to that—was the deportation of virtually all Jews and of another group which should not be forgotten—the Gypsies.

A fourth aim was to counteract all forms of resistance. He wanted a passive nation, but this passive nation he never got.

First of all, I would like to inform you that out of a total population of about nine million, the number of Jews living in Holland was 140,000, 20,000 of them being Jewish refugees from Germany and Austria.

Resistance started right from the beginning in the form of the publication of underground papers of which some 2,000 were produced during the occupation. I mean 2,000 separate titles. The most important underground papers were printed every week or every two weeks in editions of 60,000 to 100,000 copies.

Secondly, there was an important element of sabotage of war factories and the like.

In the third place, help was given to people who wanted to go into hiding—not only Jews, but also members of resistance groups.

And in the fourth place, there were intelligence groups which were active in collecting military intelligence which was passed on either to London or to Moscow.

An important fact which I would like to bring to your notice is that proportionally the number of Jews taking part in the Dutch resistance was higher, albeit only slightly higher, than the proportion of non-Jews.

With regard to the reactions of the Jews themselves, I would submit that those Jews who decided to go into hiding committed an act of resistance. The Germans wanted to deport them, and the German intention of destroying them after deportation was completely unknown to virtually all people concerned. Therefore, going into hiding was, as I see it, an act of resistance, but I would like to underline that there were many, perhaps even tens of thousands, among the Dutch Jews who were given the opportunity to go into hiding but who refused to do so for various reasons.

One reason is that they had no idea whatsoever what was in store for them in the extermination camps in eastern Europe.

The second is that they wanted to carry the burden of their fate themselves and not impose certain risks on non-Jewish Dutchmen who were willing to help them.

In order to go into hiding, you needed an address, people who were willing to give you shelter. In many cases, you needed money. If you had found that address where people were willing to give you shelter, you had to get your weekly or monthly food coupons. So, an entire operation was needed to keep a Jewish family, or members of a Jewish family who were sheltered at a certain address, alive.

There were many members of what one might call the resistance movement who specialized in organizing help for Jews who wanted to go into hiding. I estimate the number of people whose resistance work wholly or mainly consisted of organizing help for Jews who wanted to go into hiding at between 1,000 and 2,000.

Earlier I told you that the number of Jews living in Holland and who were intended to be deported was about 140,000. Of these 140,000, 25,000 were able to find shelter in the Netherlands, among them between 6,000 and 7,000 children who were usually separated from their parents. In addition to these 25,000 Jews who accepted the risk of going into hiding, there were about 4,000 Jews who managed to escape, usually with the help of non-Jewish Dutchmen, to countries like Spain, Switzerland, and some of them to Sweden.

It is hard to estimate how many families were in a position where they accepted Jews as people whom they would like to save. I know of many cases of Jews who, when they went into hiding in 1942, were still living at the same hiding address in 1944 or in 1945 when liberation came. I say 1944 because, as you probably know, the southern part of the Netherlands was liberated in the autumn of 1944 and the remainder of the Netherlands not until April and May 1945.

I know of many other cases where Jews had to change their address time and time again, so that they perhaps found shelter with 10 or 20 different families, often living in different towns and villages. The total number of foster families, as I call them, may also be estimated at 25,000. On the other hand, of these 25,000 Jews, some 8,000 were detected while they were being cared for by Dutch families and were, unfortunately, also deported.

I have done my best to give some of the main facts, both on the Dutch resistance and on the part of Jews in the Dutch resistance and the help that was given to them by people.

I am sure that all of you have read Anne Frank's diary. This merely gives you the story of one single girl. I think that if you remember that there were 25,000 people who were in the same position as Anne with regard to the help they received from the Dutch nation, this will give you some idea of the risks many Dutchmen took in order to protect their Jewish co-citizens.

*RENÉE AUBRY**

The goal of our conference was primarily to get to know better the entire subject of concentration camps. It was, of course, difficult to speak about concentration camps without speaking about the resistance movements. We are grateful that you included this subject on your agenda.

The resistance movement we are discussing this afternoon is a very special kind of awareness that came about in a lot of countries—to strive towards liberation, first of all, and to take up the defense of those who were threatened.

It would take a lot of time to discuss this resistance which began nationally and became international, and I believe that no country was immune. No country failed to rise against the dictatorship of National Socialism. It was a worldwide movement that invaded populations still waiting for the help of major nations, waiting impatiently to be saved because they were being decimated. They undertook to maintain and to free themselves, when they could.

I believe that we must pay tribute to Great Britain, to the United States, and to the Soviet Union because these are the countries which permitted the resistance movements to fight strenuously and to work in cooperation, particularly with London, as far as the French were concerned.

There was another phenomenon that we must stress in this kind of struggle. Up to now, wars were the monopoly of men, but in France many women went in the underground and played an important role either as liaison agents or as parachute drop assistants, and sometimes in the underground-proper they held a rifle together with their comrades. They were also war correspondents. I was thinking of my many friends who were in Bergen-Belsen, in particular at Majdanek, who took pictures which were stirring in the horror they depicted.

The importance of the resistance must be stressed in particular because if it had not been useful, there would have been no point. As far as France is concerned, you asked me how resistance was structured in France. Well, we had the underground units which were members of networks of different movements, and then there were the individuals acting alone who received parachute drops. Our friends who are here today know that these were experiences that we shared in all nations.

But I would like to say that this resistance, since we are talking directly about what happened in the camps, permitted us to speed up the process of liberation. I remember that I was waiting for my husband who had been deported to a camp little mentioned, Lerbeck.[1] When the British troops arrived, the camp had been evacuated, but evacuated under tragic circumstances. Little is said about that particular camp which was liberated late, and when the Allied troops arrived, no one was left in the camp.

What matters is that the resistance from within—and we felt this deeply in

*Madame Aubry made her remarks in French; this is the simultaneous translation.

France—which was designed to harass the enemy, forced the Nazi troops to resort to tactics which were an impediment to them.

As we know, there were landings in France, such as the landing at Toulon[2] and the landing in Normandy. You should have seen what the landing in Normandy entailed to understand the bravery and the daring of the underground fighters. The French from London landed as did the Americans, and we do not forget when we are on our own shores how much we owe to them.

The time we have is very limited, and I am trying to be effective. For us, this conference has an extraordinary significance. We would like that this should not just end today. We hope that we have established contact with all the other countries, that each of us knows what everybody else was doing. Each of us did the utmost of what he or she could do, and there is great hope for us to think that people who were in such small numbers, who were so limited in their means of waging war, in the final analysis are those who won because they were on the side of freedom and on the side of hope.

Today we spoke. I listened very carefully to a subject which is very dear to me since I am the president of the International Association of Survivors of Neuengamme. Neuengamme and its satellites were the camps of the Final Solution. They were the camps for underground fighters—Jewish or non-Jewish—because they had stood up and they were treated differently.

There were also underground fighters within the camps. Resistance within the camps was not useless. We are studying that particular subject very closely, and I believe that all countries gathered here today will help us study deeper and know better what was going on within the camps in terms of resistance.

What we must do is to bear witness while we are still alive. At the same time, we must give the younger generation an opportunity to project back to us what their perception of us is rather than projecting our own perceptions upon them.

That is how we shall win them over to our side. Along those lines, in France and within the framework of the Department of Veterans Affairs, we have set up a special section—we call it a special commission—which will study the history of wars, and, through the knowledge thus acquired, it will help promote peace. All men of good will want peace, and if I dare, I would like to ask that all women join them more firmly, more steadfastly to ensure that their children will never be killed.

There is no time to speak of the children. There is no time to speak really of what resistance was in France—the parachute drops, missions of information, hiding those that were sent to us from London or elsewhere, the reception organized for those American flyers we loved so much because they were the symbol of the liberation.

So, to be here today is extremely important for all of us. It is deeply moving, but it is not enough to be moved. You must also be useful. I believe that that's what we are going to be able to do all together.

FRODE JAKOBSEN

May I first say that it is a good feeling for me to be here among people whom, in most cases, I have never met before, but with whom I was united, in those days so long ago, in a great cause which perhaps meant the survival or the downfall of civilization.

Denmark's contribution to the downfall of Nazism was not big, but it was our contribution, and therefore, right or wrong, we can never forget it. For how was the situation in Denmark until the Danish people really stood up to fight? Before that, we had felt the anguish in our hearts, not only the anxiety that all that we believed in was about to perish, but also the fear that our people, the Danish people, should fail in what we felt was our duty.

You must understand what a shocking experience it was to awake in the morning and to be informed that during the night your country had been occupied by the Nazis. This capitulation, however, was never the main criticism of the Danish resistance. Denmark had been told beforehand, even by Churchill, that nobody could come to our rescue.

We were told by our political leaders that now we were in the cage with the tiger and that we were like prisoners of war; therefore nobody could expect anything from us. We had to leave all the fighting to those who were still free, but this fight was also a fight for our freedom.

So the Danish resistance grew up as a fight on two fronts: directly against the German occupation and indirectly against an official policy which we held to be wrong, but of which we knew had only one object—the saving of the Danish people from the horrors of war. Therefore, in Denmark it is not so difficult to tell what resistance is.

For some of us, the resistance was not wanting to be spared; we did not want to be the canary bird of Hitler. We had to stand up and fight, fight with fear in our hearts, fear that we would be too weak, and that something dreadful was about to conquer the world. We could not help it. We had to fight no matter what our government told us. It is a mockery to speak about a democratic government which you have to obey in a country occupied by the enemy.

The final break between official Denmark and the Germans came. It came when the Germans demanded that death sentences against saboteurs from then on be carried out not by the Germans, but by Danish authorities. No Danish politician could ever accept that and still hope to be a Danish politician after the war.

From then on, there was no Danish government, and soon there was no Danish police either. That meant no suffrage, but we were happier. Our political freedom we won later. Our moral freedom we won on that day. Now we could concentrate all our energies directly against the enemy.

I have chosen not to speak about details but about what I would call the spirit of resistance. What is that spirit? To keep the sense of human dignity unimpaired was still more important than military effects.

I am not a young man any longer. You may be able to see that. I remember the resistance we were so sure of in 1932 and 1933—the German Social Democrats and Communists who would overthrow Hitler after a short period. I have seen how that collapsed like a soap bubble.

There we stood dejected. Was the revolt of the human spirit against degradation only a naive illusion after all?

One year later, however, they fought in Vienna. An unequal fight, a foolish fight—artillery against the workers' buildings. It was another defeat, but before that, a heroic battle. It was a defeat, but a defeat which raised our courage again—we who had despaired in 1933.[3]

About 10 years later there was a fight in Warsaw. That fight was also doomed to defeat, but if I were a Jew, I would be proud that my people rose in the last desperate, uncalculating defiance.[4]

As for Danish resistance, it was sabotage and the organizing of an underground army of 55,000 people armed with weapons dropped down by the British. The sabotage was mainly against factories working for the Germans. How could we contribute war materials to kill those who were fighting for the cause which was also ours?

It was also sabotage against railways carrying German troops through Denmark, which became important after the invasion in Normandy. The Nazis had to move badly needed troops through Denmark to the front in France. We could delay them sometimes for a week in Jutland.[5]

The rescue of the Jews to Sweden is a different category. It was not a special contribution of those active in the resistance but of the whole Danish population. After 40 years, there is a tendency to stress the unity of all Danes during the war, and I believe that unity was greater than in most countries. But the truth is that we were not completely united until the Germans started to persecute the Jews.

Speaking of resistance, I sometimes make a distinction between two different ways to love one's nation, or another human being, for that matter. You may be more preoccupied with the well-being of those you love, or you may be more concerned that those you love behave well.

This was the difference between the political parties and the resistance, but there were ideals neither of the two would think of compromising. One of these ideals was equal treatment of the Jews and the rest of Danes. There the resistance and what we call the "old politicians" met in a united Denmark in a fight for humanity, for the dignity of man.

BRANKO LAKIC

During the war I was young, but in the second part of 1943, I left to participate in the liberation. I hope that many of you know that Yugoslavia is a small country in the southeastern part of Europe. I am going to describe the situation in Yugoslavia during the war.

Its contribution to the Allied forces was substantial: 1.7 million people, or 11.2 percent of the total population, were killed in combat, in concentration camps and in prisons. For example, in the notorious concentration camp at Jasenovac[6] about 700,000 patriots of all nationalities including Jews and Gypsies, were put to death, many of them women and children. (Last year [1980], a new charnel house was discovered in the area of Jasenovac, which is estimated to have been the common tomb for another 40,000.)

Yugoslavia's uprising in 1941 caused a major delay in the Nazi invasion of the Soviet Union which eventually changed the course of the war. The Yugoslav forces, though significantly outnumbered by the enemy, managed to tie down about 30 divisions of the Axis powers at any given time during the war. In April 1941, there were 520,000 Germans, 350,000 Italians, 100,000 Hungarians, and 30,000 Bulgarians, or a total of one million enemy troops, in Yugoslavia. On the other hand, there were 80,000 troops fighting in the National Liberation Army in the autumn and winter of 1941.

Yugoslavia was the first country to liberate a part of its territory in 1941 when the Nazis were on the offensive on every front line in Europe.

For example, I have to use a few details. The National Liberation Army had 305,000 dead and 425,000 wounded. The greatest casualties were among the youth between the ages of 16 and 21. There were about 100,000 women fighting in the ranks of the National Liberation Army.

As the Yugoslavian theater of war began to acquire glory and importance, in 1943, Hitler decided to launch a massive offensive against the main operative group of the Supreme Headquarters and the First Croatian and the First Bosnian Army Corps which operated in Bosnia and Herzegovina. He deployed over 104,000 German, Italian, and quisling[7] troops with air support from 150 planes in January 1943.

As of late 1944, the National Liberation Army of Yugoslavia numbered over 500,000 troops, 17 army corps, 53 divisions (two air force divisions), a navy, a river flotilla, and a large number of smaller partisan detachments. The Yugoslav Army and all armed members of the national liberation struggle fought to the death with a total of over 800,000 persons in May 1945.

The Yugoslavians suffered terrible devastation. The statistics are staggering: 289,000 farms were ruined; 822,000 buildings, of which 65,000 were town dwellings, were bombed and reduced to rubble; 137 power plants were put out of commission; 28,000 railway cargo wagons and 3,000 passenger carriages were destroyed. At least one-fourth of all Yugoslav citizens were left homeless. As a result, the Yugoslav national income was reduced by $9 billion, and war damages were estimated at $46.9 billion at 1939 prices.

The price was high, but the prize was supreme—freedom. One million seven hundred thousand women, men, and children laid down their lives for these causes. In other words, every tenth Yugoslav was killed in the war.

In 1943 these contributions were recognized by the Allies. Missions of Great Britain, the USSR, and the USA were parachuted into Yugoslavia to keep their commands informed of the true sources of resistance. The difficulty the Allied Command attributed to these missions is best illustrated by the fact that Sir Winston Churchill assigned his son Randolph to this important task.

Of about 75,000 Jews living in Yugoslavia in 1941, only 15,000 lived to see the dawn of May 1945.

This extreme suffering cannot and should never be wiped from the memory of mankind.

As a conclusion, let me repeat a beautiful thought Senator McGovern expressed on one of his visits to Yugoslavia in the postwar years. Landing at the military airport of Vis where he had landed once before during the war, and stunned by the change, he exclaimed that he wished all the military airports of the world were bordered by vineyards like this one was.[8]

SAMUEL GRUBER

My name is Samuel Gruber. In the wartime it was Mietek.

In September 1939 in Poland, when the war broke out, I found myself drafted into the Polish army. After eight days of fighting, I was wounded in my right shoulder and taken prisoner by the Germans. After a short stay in a hospital, I was sent out with other Polish prisoners of war to Stalag 13A near Nuremberg, Germany. There they selected all Jewish prisoners and put us in separate barracks and sent us out for all kinds of manual work.

In February 1941, the Germans decided to send all Jewish prisoners of war back to Poland, stating, "You are no more prisoners of war. You are plain Jews." And as such, they sent me and about 2,000 others to a camp near Lublin. Here, they gave us over to the SS. Before we were under the Wehrmacht. They put us to work all over the town of Lublin and then to build the known concentration camp Majdanek. Every day there were beatings, hangings, and shootings. When we saw this, we started to organize. Then we started talking to people about what to do and how to plan to escape.

I think I live today because I was a believer. I believed when Hitler said that he would kill all the Jews. I believed when Himmler and Goebbels and others wrote in their books and their theory that they would kill us all. I believed it, but a lot of us did not. When I came over to my people and asked them to run away with me, a lot of them said, "No. Why should we? We don't know what will happen there. And here we have a place to sleep. They give us food. All right, they are beating some of us, they are killing some of us, but they wouldn't kill everybody."

But I believed that they would do it. Realizing that the whole camp of 2,000 people couldn't escape, I organized a group of 22 Jews. In October 1942, I ran away to the woods around Lublin. In the beginning, we had a very hard time adjusting to our new life. We had no guns, no weapons to defend ourselves, and food was also a problem.

In a short while, we found some connections with other Jewish boys and girls who had run away from concentration camps and other ghettos and also with some Polish groups. Together we organized a partisan unit ready to fight the Germans. We started to sabotage the links of communication and the railway train, stop trucks, cut telephone wires, ambush German soldiers, and kill spies and collaborators. After a time, our Jewish group was singled out by the leader as the best organized fighting men in the woods.

I want to recall here one episode of our actions. I recall the first train derailment we engineered and the excitement of it. We prepared for this moment for three days ahead, finding out the right spot, timing, and also where the military installation and placement of German soldiers were. The night was dark, and we took positions on the embankment around a railroad line going from Lublin to Warsaw.

Our bomb expert put his bomb under the train rail, and we were all waiting with nervous tension for the train to come. After half an hour, we heard a locomotive hissing. Our explosion erupted, and the train turned on its back. The train carried oil, war materials, tanks, and parts for the military machinery. There were interruptions for two to three days in the military communications.

This was a very big accomplishment for us and made us very proud and gave us the courage to fight more.

All over Poland, Jews seeing their plight, started to organize and fight back. There were revolts in the ghettos of Warsaw, Vilna, Grodno, Bialystok[9] and others, and in the concentration camps of Sobibor and Treblinka, but the remnants from those fights and from the revolts came to us, to the partisan sector. It is estimated that 50,000 Jews fought in the partisans.

I wrote a book about my experience. The name is *I Chose Life*. I am glad that I was able to write that for what I and my fellow fighters went through. Too many comrades perished in the struggle, and by writing this story in detail I believe I fulfilled their dying last wish that their sufferings should not be forgotten.

BENJAMIN MEED

I am a survivor of the Warsaw Ghetto. I was a member of the underground in the Warsaw Ghetto since 1940. I have been living here in the United States for the past 35 years. A year after the liberation by the Russian army I arrived in the United States, and here, together with my wife, Vladka, we established our home and raised our family with deep roots in this new homeland.

Thirty-six years have gone by since the liberation—of tension, uncertainty, constant crises, and distress and years of rebuilding our life here after the Holocaust. Nothing however, can erase from our minds the impact and the significance of our survival from the Nazi era, especially our life in the Warsaw Ghetto, our involvement in the underground activities, and the witnessing of the heroic Warsaw Ghetto uprising—the symbol of Jewish resistance during the Nazi occupation.

But I choose to speak today not about the uprising, which will be tomorrow's topic, but about the people of the Warsaw Ghetto. For many years, historians have seemed to focus on the nature of Jewish resistance. How many fought and why and when, and why did they wait so long? These questions are for us survivors the height of disrespect for our martyrs.

I find it difficult to separate the Warsaw Ghetto uprising from all other events that preceded it. We must first understand that the dramatic climax of the organized Jewish resistance of the Warsaw Ghetto was not the only such occurrence and it certainly was not an act of sudden impulse. Neither were any of the uprisings in other ghettos and camps of the partisans. They should not be seen as isolated acts of glory with which to ransom the honor of those who perished.

Yes, in those times, under the constant threat of death in the Warsaw Ghetto, a network of illegal schools was organized—Yeshivas,[10] libraries, lectures. In addition there was a clandestine net of political activities, although under different circumstances than in the countries like Denmark, Holland, and France.

I doubt that there were ever other circumstances in Jewish history in which the ordinary Jew had been so involved and enveloped in communal experience as he was during the ghetto period.

There were over half-a-million people in the Warsaw Ghetto. If the Ghetto did not commit acts of violence against the Germans in those days, it was not because of lack of courage or organized leadership, but because the Jews felt that their purpose would not be served.

The underground movement was hampered by the murderous German practice of applying collective responsibility which we understand so well today. For every one German killed, hundreds of Jews were killed. The aim and the goal of the Ghetto and the people of the Ghetto was to survive, to remain with human dignity or to outwit the enemy and to live for the day to be the witness of his destruction. Every effort which lent strength to this purpose was an act of resistance.

But then the Final Solution started. The final deportations, the sudden German round-ups, and the continued shootings stunned and immobilized the entire Ghetto population and kept even the most courageous from direct counteraction. And this was in every ghetto in Poland.

Very little has been written about the moral dilemmas, which were so important, facing the ordinary Jew in the ghetto during those days of deportations. For instance, when Jews were being rounded up, some factories issued permits to workers allowing them for the time being to remain with their families—up to four people in the family was the limit. A worker who was employed in such a factory who had three children had to decide which two to keep and which one to send away—to death, he knew—or whether the whole family should allow themselves to be taken away. What about a mother? Should an unmarried worker claim her as his wife or would it be more safe for him to abandon her? Should one stay with his family, risking deportation, or escape to try to join the partisans in the forest?

An abyss of temptation to live, of self-preservation, yawned before each, but only a tiny, tiny minority sank into it. Only a few betrayed their families or bought their lives at the price of another's. The majority of the Jews maintained their humanity and their integrity and their Jewish consciences.

I can still remember thousands of us forced to line up in the narrow streets of the Warsaw Ghetto and the German officer at the head of the line pointing with a stick, "Left, right, left, right." I can still feel the dread as we stood in that line. Left—to the death camps. Right—a few more days of survival in the Ghetto. And the world let it happen.

I can still feel the dread today because I fear that it could happen again.

Do not forget, the Germans were the masters of technology. They used their scientific and psychological knowledge to murder innocent men, women, and children. Their engineers designed the crematoria. Their psychologists devised the techniques of mass murder.

And we were chosen as the people to be completely destroyed—the Jews.

Jewish struggle in the Warsaw Ghetto and other cities assumed various forms throughout the occupation years, and they all were intertwined and related with each other. The form which the resistance took always depended on the particular time and circumstances.

One of the great failures of the research and the literature of our destruction is that it has not produced a clear picture of the day-to-day life of the ordinary Jew in the ghetto in that time.

Each individual was a universe unto himself, making his way from hour to hour, from day to day, seeking to survive with his self-respect. He was abandoned and forgotten as an individual within the turmoil around him. He was concealed and overshadowed by the dramatic happenings of that time.

It is only when one sees all the circumstances of Jewish behavior leading up to the epic act of physical defiance that one can better understand what took place behind the blood-stained Ghetto walls. It was an existence burning with determination to thwart the enemy's design, which was to break and destroy the race both physically and spiritually, and to do this even before we were brought to the gas chambers.

Let me for a moment recall the Warsaw Ghetto where I lived as a young man, where in 1941 half-a-million people lived: the crowded street that I hid on behind the high Ghetto walls, the starvation, the corpses lying unclaimed on the sidewalks, the typhoid epidemic. Death pursued us at every side. Merely to stay alive amidst all this—every day, every hour—was in itself a real struggle.

But survival was not the one dominating impulse of the Ghetto. I remember seeing the streets of the Ghetto and the little display carts laden with books—yes, books, emaciated Jews hovering over them, looking for a bargain, even starving for a bargain, in literature, and literature not only about Jews but of the whole world. I can still see my neighbors standing in the doorway of our house, watching for the approaching Germans or policeman while in our basement, teachers—I was one of them—held secret classes for young children. I recall the seminars of the young people, held in the hidden places.

We cannot simply console ourselves by saying it cannot happen again, for if our tragic past teaches us anything, it teaches us that the impossible is indeed possible, that the unbelievable can indeed, God forbid, happen once more.

Yes, we the survivors—and there are many in this room now—remember, and we will remember.

We will try to teach the next generation also to remember, for our task of reminding the world will never be finished, and we must be sure that there are others like you people here to carry on the message that another Holocaust should and must never be permitted again.

DISCUSSION

FRANK LAUTENBERG: Professor Yehuda Bauer, whom you've either met or heard at this conference or whose material you have read, defines resistance as any group action taken in opposition to known or surmised laws, actions, or intentions directed against the Jews by the Germans and their collaborators.

Mr. Jakobsen said that the thing that seemed to unite the Danish people more than anything else was the German action against the Jews. That's a particularly important statement. The fact that General Eisenhower, the Supreme Allied Commander, said that resistance was worth six divisions is quite a statement. Helen Fein, in her work *Accounting for Genocide*[11] argues that there is a direct relationship between the degree to which a country resisted Nazism and the murder of Jews.

I would like to pose this to you as a question in the few minutes remaining to see how it corresponds to your own views. Was that, in fact, the case? Was the resistance to the murder of Jews something that enabled the countries that you represent—that you lived in—to struggle harder against the Nazis and to keep them from achieving their objectives?

FRODE JAKOBSEN: I said that the Danish people were united when the Germans made this distinction between Danish Jews and other Danish people, but that did not mean that resistance did not exist before. Resistance existed at once, but we had a government which was more interested in having good economic conditions in the country. It was really two fights—a fight against what we call the wrong policy, and a fight against the Germans.

And this resistance grew so strong that, even before the persecution of the Jews, the government was overthrown. The turning point for us was the decree that the death sentences to saboteurs were to be executed by the Danes themselves. Nobody could accept that. But this difference between what we called "old politicians" and resistance fighters diminished completely when the persecution of the Jews started because even those very wise politicians could not accept that. Then we were united.

It was not the element of resistance but it was the uniting of the people who were for resistance and the people who until then were against resistance.

FRANK LAUTENBERG: We have a question from the floor: Did any members of this panel have any links with German resistance? What are those links? What was the extent of the German underground? Is anybody aware of that?

FRODE JAKOBSEN: Yes. I think I said I have been in this for 50 years. In 1933 I went on a bicycle as a courier between emigré groups in Copenhagen and underground resistance groups in Hamburg and Berlin. I was a young student, and when all the emigrés came to Denmark, their greatest problem was to know what was happening in Germany. You could never know what was true and what were lies in German newspapers. And in the same way, the emigrés who wanted to cooperate with the resistance couldn't know anything of what happened in Germany.

But when we speak of German resistance, that has nothing to do with what happened during the war. We are speaking of the revolt of the officers—the Social Democratic opposition, the Communist opposition, etc.—which had already been crushed by 1933.[12]

LOUIS DE JONG: German resistance had to be carried out under circumstances even more difficult than the resistance on the part of other people. It is hard to fight for the liberation of your country. It is even harder to fight for the defeat of your country, and that's what inevitably the members of the German resistance had to do.

There have been various forms of German resistance organized by political parties, the Communist Party in the first place and the Socialist Party, too. Later on, in the 1941–1943 period, we have the attempts on Hitler's life, which unfortunately failed, by certain German officers who also had important links from the end of 1943 with the Dutch underground and who were completely trusted. These links, of course, were broken off after the Stauffenberg attempt on Hitler on July 20, 1944.[13]

But I think that, although it is accepted by everyone here present, and there is no official German delegation present here, we should all understand that the first people who entered the Nazi concentration camps were Germans.

Secondly, we must realize that in Germany there were not hundreds but thousands of people who were willing to risk their lives in order to give help to their German co-citizens.

I am sorry that I, as a Dutchman, have to produce these facts, but I am profoundly convinced that a wrong impression would be left on this meeting—particularly on those who are not historians—if these simple facts were not brought to the fore.

UNIDENTIFIED SPEAKER: You are right, and what you are saying is that there could be German resistance against the government or one taking over the government. But here we are just interested in the genocide of the Jewish people and other peoples, and I have never, in the 40 years since the war ended, come across any document or any notion of German resistance against the Nazi atrocities. Today I even heard another speaker say that five days after Hitler was already dead the gas chambers were active in the death camps.

I never heard of a revolt to do something about stopping the killing of the Jews. I have heard the revolt about taking over the German government, but I never heard from any underground of the German people about their coming out against the killing.

FRODE JAKOBSEN: I am not saying that, and everything you have said I can agree with, but it does not invalidate the factual statements I have made.

RENÉE AUBRY: I wanted to say that where France is concerned, the relations with Hitler's Germany were extremely difficult, and in spite of everything, there were some German underground agents who came into France. In our own underground units, we had a few Germans who either left very early or succeeded in fleeing Germany. It's a very special area relative to what you have been talking about.

May I come back to your first question? When you asked if the atrocities against the Jewish race were a decisive factor for resistance, that's not quite the way it happened, but we were struggling also against our own domestic government of Marshal Pétain[14].

When the Jews were gathered by the thousands in Paris, the French nation arose in anger, and people who did not feel involved began at that point to understand what this could mean in real terms. That is the witness I wish to present on behalf of France.

SAMUEL GRUBER: We had at least five or six German officers in the partisans who had run away from the Army and who came to us and fought with us. For example, one was from the SS in Czechoslovakia and one was from Stuttgart.

They fought with us until the end, but this wasn't organized. They just felt that the Germans had perhaps lost the war or something. They came to us, and they fought with us.

UNIDENTIFIED SPEAKER: There are people like that, we know, and from those people they organized a special German unit. They fought together with us.

FRANK LAUTENBERG: I have a last question from the floor. It's addressed to the Polish resistance fighters, two of whom are represented here.

The question asks for comment on the safety of Jewish fugitives and resistance fighters who fled to the woods in Poland. They often found that circumstances could be as dangerous for them from some of the population surrounding that area, even as bad as those they already faced, and that Jews were killed as they fell into local hands.

SAMUEL GRUBER: It is true, and we can talk about this a lot, but we have to underline that many Polish people had helped us. Otherwise, we would not have lived. A partisan in any place had to have a backer. He had to have some people helping him or he could not exist. We came to the population. They had to give us food. They had to give us help and they gave us information on how to work against the Germans.

But there were a lot of Polish people who surrendered the Jews and even the partisans when they caught them; they killed them, themselves, without the Germans. This was true, but I cannot say the whole population was against us. There is a story in my book about a man who kept us, a group of about 20 people, and everybody was wounded. I, myself, was wounded twice. He gave us food and he kept about 20 people at one time, but there were also a lot of people against us.

BENJAMIN MEED: I must say that it is difficult for you to comprehend. Our situation was much different. You are coming from a country, Denmark, where 90 percent of the Jewish population survived. You are coming from Holland where 50 or 60 percent—I don't know exactly the numbers. I'm coming and my colleague is coming from a country where the majority of our people perished. Ninety percent of our people. We lost the majority of our people. I don't want to get into numbers, but it is important.[15]

Without good people, without even the Poles—I would not be sitting here. Without good people in any country, we wouldn't be here, but when I think about Denmark and I compare it to Poland, I feel terrible. I feel terrible that I had to be born in Poland and somebody else had to be born in Denmark or vice versa.

I think there is a tremendous lesson to be learned from this. I was also in the Polish uprising as a Gentile. I went through 1943, and a year later I was in the Polish uprising. I cannot forget the time during the Warsaw Ghetto uprising when people did not have any interest in helping us. They just kept looking at the burning Ghetto and performing their daily life like this was just a routine day in the street.

When I was in the Polish uprising, I could not forget what happened to us there together that day. I was not happy at what happened, but I was just sorry for not having enough understanding for each other to realize that what happened to Jews at that time could happen tomorrow to Frenchmen or to Dutchmen, or Poles, or anybody else.

The Holocaust—which was directed against us—is not only for us, and if we don't learn the lesson, there could be a holocaust of other people tomorrow. That's why it's so important that we should teach and go on remembering and not let the world forget.

Notes

1 Lerbeck was a satellite of Neuengamme.

2 American and Free French forces landed near Toulon on the French Mediterranean coast on August 15, 1944.

3 In March 1933, Austria's Christian-Socialist Chancellor, Engelbert Dollfuss, suspended the Austrian parliament and began to rule the country as a dictator. Determined to crush not only the Austrian Nazis, but also the Communists and Socialists, in February 1934, he banned all political parties except his own and those allied with it. The Socialists, in retaliation, called a general strike. Dollfuss then ordered the arrest of many Socialist leaders, precipitating a virtual civil war in Vienna and other cities. In the end Dollfuss called in the army, which brutally suppressed the Socialists.

4 Presumably a reference to the Warsaw Ghetto uprising in 1943.

5 Jutland is the Danish peninsula.

6 Jasenovac is approximately 120 miles north of Sarajevo.

7 Vidkun Quisling was a Norwegian Fascist installed by the Nazis as puppet ruler of German-occupied Norway in 1940. After the war he was executed for betraying his country. Ever since, the word *quisling* has been identified with treason and collaboration with an enemy.

8 As a pilot in the U.S. Army Air Force (15th Air Force, 455th Bombardment Group, 741st Squadron), George McGovern was forced to crashland his B-24 at Vis in 1943. He returned to the site in 1977.

9 Vilna, Grodno, and Bialystok lie 250 miles, 110 miles, and 160 miles northeast of Warsaw, respectively.

10 Yeshivas are Jewish schools for both religious and secular education.

[11] Helen Fein, *Accounting for Genocide: National Responses and Jewish Victimization during the Holocaust* (New York, 1979).

[12] The nature and extent of German resistance to Nazi rule has long been a controversial issue. There is no doubt, however, that pockets of resistance did indeed exist in various sectors of German society throughout the Nazi period. Communists and Socialists attempted secretly to organize factory workers against the regime; university students distributed illegal pamphlets; Protestant and Catholic clergymen delivered sermons critical of Nazi policies; and, prior to 1939, military officers conspired to overthrow the Nazi regime. Although resistance conspiracies included a number of attempts on Hitler's life, the possibility of armed rebellion was ruled out by the effectiveness of the Gestapo, as well as by the overwhelming support of the German people for Hitler. For an authoritative examination see Peter Hoffmann, *The History of the German Resistance, 1933–1945* (Cambridge, Mass., 1977).

[13] Colonel Claus Schenk von Stauffenburg, conspiring with several other German officers to assassinate Hitler, planted a bomb at Hitler's "Wolf's Lair" military headquarters in East Prussia on July 20, 1944. The bomb went off, killing several of those present, but only injuring Hitler. Stauffenburg was arrested and shot, and many of his co-conspirators were convicted at a show trial and executed.

[14] Henri Philippe Pétain, a French military hero in World War I, was head of state in the collaborationist Vichy government in France during World War II.

[15] Raul Hilberg, *The Destruction of the European Jews*, 2nd ed. (New York, 1985), III, 1048, estimates that about 14 percent of Holland's Jewish population of 1939 survived the war, whereas the figure for Denmark is about 85 percent.

CHAPTER X

THE SURVIVORS

Moderator: Prof. Yaffa Eliach (USA): Survivor; Director, Center for Holocaust Studies, Brooklyn, NY.

Esther Cohen (USA): Member, Board of Trustees, Simon Wiesenthal Center for Holocaust Studies; trustee, Yeshiva University; Holocaust survivor; member, U.S. Holocaust Memorial Council.

Trygve Bratteli (Norway): Concentration camp survivor and former Prime Minister of Norway.

Isaac Goodfriend (USA): Cantor of Ahavath Achim Congregation, Atlanta; Holocaust survivor; member, U.S. Holocaust Memorial Council.

Guy Hinterlang (France): Military historian; survivor of Buchenwald.

A.F. van Velsen (Netherlands): Survivor of Auschwitz and Sachsenhausen.

Benjamin Meed (USA): Businessman; president, Warsaw Ghetto Resistance Organization; member, U.S. Holocaust Memorial Council.

Dr. Hadassah Rosensaft (USA): Survivor of Auschwitz and Bergen-Belsen; lecturer and author on the Holocaust; member, U.S. Holocaust Memorial Council.

Sigmund Strochlitz (USA): Businessman; Holocaust survivor; president, American Friends of Haifa University, where he endowed a chair in Holocaust Studies; member, U.S. Holocaust Memorial Council.

Kalman Sultanik (USA): Vice President, World Jewish Congress; Holocaust survivor; member, U.S. Holocaust Memorial Council.

Siggi B. Wilzig (USA): Businessman; Holocaust survivor; member, U.S. Holocaust Memorial Council.

Eli Zborowski (USA): Businessman; Holocaust survivor; honorary president, American Federation of Jewish Fighters, Camp Inmates, and Nazi Victims; member, U.S. Holocaust Memorial Council.

Institutional identifications are those at the time of the Conference.

YAFFA ELIACH

I was liberated by the Russian Army at the age of seven, and I was one of the first people in the United States to include the liberation of the concentration camp as a discipline of Holocaust studies. Therefore, I am especially privileged that I was asked to chair this distinguished panel.

This is an historic moment. Liberators and survivors meet once more, some 30 years later. This time we are all equals. We are all free men and women, branded by the agony of memories and the compulsion to tell them and record them so the events of the Holocaust will be known by the next generation, so they may learn and, we hope, be spared the suffering and death all of us in this room knew first hand.

Once more, we would like to bear witness and give an eyewitness account of the days when the gates of hell were opened, to paraphrase Colonel Fellenz, a liberator of Dachau. We are going to recall the events when the gates of hell were opened, not only of concentration camps but of hiding places, death marches, forests, partisans, and every place in the occupied countries where Jews and other oppressed and suffering people were suffering from German tyranny.

It was a long-awaited moment, and the price for liberation was a great one. What did it mean to us around this table to return to a civilization branded forever with the mark of Cain and the ashes of Auschwitz? This is what we came to tell here this morning.

ESTHER COHEN

To speak of liberation and what it means to me is to speak from the heart and the soul, and probably for hours. But in respect to the time element, I have taken the privilege of just writing out a few notes and giving you one feeling that I have.

At the actual time of liberation, I do not think I truly believed it was over. Certainly, hard as I tried, I could never begin to understand the madness, the blackness, and the brutality of the years past that were now over. What I did know was that for the first time in what seemed like an eternity, people had smiles on their faces, even if those smiles lasted only a moment, as their minds flashed back to those lost, to a world gone mad, to acts and events that were beyond human comprehension.

What I remember best is my father taking me in his arms and saying to me, "My dear child. Our family, once a strong beautiful tree, is no more. They have chopped it in pieces and cast those pieces in the inferno. But a branch has survived, and now that branch must grow, and from it must come new life." Those words and my mother's eyes when she looked at me have remained in my heart and my soul as a reminder that somehow I lived when so many others did not.

But it was some time later that I began to feel free and secure. It was in the United States, in New York, at our first apartment—a small room with two cots and a small bathroom down the hall shared with many families. It was and is to this day the best place I have ever lived in, for in that small room I could read, I could dream, I could do whatever my heart desired, and no one could come to harm me. I was free—free at last. I could go to school, walk the streets, I could go to the synagogue with my family on the Sabbath. I could even have friends with whom I could argue about different issues, and they would still be my friends. I could no longer be hurt because I was born a Jew.

As the years went on, the meaning of being free took on much deeper feelings. There was the inevitable question of "Why me? Why did I survive?" Eventually I gave up on that question, for I knew that I would never have the answer.

But yet, some answers did come to other questions. Yes, there were people out there who cared, who were willing to give their lives so that we could live and maybe, more importantly, so that mankind might have a just reason to go on. For as our brothers and sisters were dying, with them was vanishing any and all reason for the human race to continue.

It is today in this room that I feel the meaning of liberation. It is at the polling booths in my city when I am free to follow my conscience that I know the full meaning of my liberation. It is when I watch the sun rise in Jerusalem that I joyfully cry for being free.

I thank God, and I thank the men and women who fought so valiantly to free me and to restore justice and reason. I will never forget.

TRYGVE BRATTELI

May I say this about Norway: there were thousands of political prisoners during the war and the occupation. Norway was occupied by the Germans in 1940, as certainly most people know, and for many reasons big groups, not the least of whom were leading people in Norwegian society, went abroad or were sent abroad. One of the groups that left were the political prisoners who had been taken by Germans and sent to German concentration camps. The Germans also organized camps in Norway.

However, the prisoners were not the biggest group of people who had to leave the country during the war. There were groups of seamen on board the Norwegian merchant fleet who participated in the war as much as the military forces did.[1]

The leadership of all political parties, so to speak, also left. They went to Great Britain in June 1940, when the German occupation became a fact which could not be changed for a very long time. The people from the administration and organizations of the Norwegian government settled down in London where a Norwegian exile government was formed.

What was important, both in war time and the time afterwards, was that all the important social and economic groups in Norway had representation in all these various groups. When we went back after the war ended, these people met in Denmark and Sweden and within a rather short time in Norway, and they could discuss both their experiences and the future of the country from a different perspective which the war had given the various groups.

I came back, as you understand, as a political prisoner after more than three years in a camp in Germany. I was very lucky personally because I had not been totally destroyed. My normal weight was about 72 kilos, and I came back to Norway with a weight of 45 kilos, but I was not medically destroyed. I went back to Oslo May 15, 1945, and went straight to my office where I had my work, and I continued my work there.

Among these different groups of Norwegians which spent up to several years abroad, there was one common attitude I noticed when I went back. They were, above all, interested in the reconstruction and to a large extent in the reformation of all generations of society. When we met in Norway again in 1945, the whole Norwegian population was united in a way which had not been experienced before the war.

But we largely avoided the difficulties of the occupation because the main groups had the same intention. They wanted to cooperate in their big task of reconstructing the country and building it up better than it was before, which indeed we succeeded in doing in the first 10 to 15 years after the war ended.

My group was one of the last which was discovered in southwestern Germany, although I was the first to leave Germany and go back to Sweden, even before the occupation of Norway had ended. Most of the Norwegian prisoners—all kinds of prisoners—were taken care of by a special arrangement organized by Sweden and by Norwegian authorities in London. We were taken care of by what in the Nordic countries was called the "White Buses," which were organized by the Red Cross. They got permission from the German authorities in the last months of the war to work within Germany, and they got most of the Norwegian political prisoners out of Germany just in the days before the end of the war.

May I just add that in the time afterward we certainly had a lot of very difficult problems connected with these various groups of Norwegians who spent a long time outside. I think it is right to say that the worst-struck people from the merchant fleet were, generally speaking, even weaker than many of the prisoners who went back to Norway at that time. During the occupation, a common attitude was formed that the various groups should not be isolated when they came back to Norway. It was decided that they would not isolate themselves into groups of former German prisoners, or of former seamen, etc., although certainly all of us had some tendencies in that direction.

Mainly because the leadership of most important organizations in Norway had been abroad, they also succeeded in uniting all these forces with regard to the reconstruction of Norway after the occupation.

In conclusion, let me report that when we heard the thundering of the Allied armies not far from Alsace where we were in a camp, we were very happy to see them.

We met people from all western Europe, Soviet Russia, and all of these countries. We tried to prepare ourselves for a big meeting with the Allied forces when they came to our camp. We trained up on what we could of the English language. We were especially interested in informing each other in English of the names of our favorite dishes which we were going to ask of the first people who came from the Allies.

But before that happened, and I think just a few days before the Allied forces moved into that part of Germany, we were removed by the Swedish Red Cross White Busses and came over the border to Denmark and Sweden before the very last days. There were a lot of exceptions. We have long, long lists of political prisoners and other prisoners who were taken to Germany about whom we have never heard anything.

ISAAC GOODFRIEND

We have heard in the last two days that time will never heal our wounds and our pains and our suffering. I feel that this conference and meeting again the liberators did help to soothe my wounds and to alleviate some of my pain, for I did not have a chance on January 18, 1945, to personally go out and shake the hands of the soldiers who liberated my home town, Piotrkow.[2]

I was liberated a few times, saved a few times, by the grace of Polish people. I was separated from my family on October 10, 1942, when I said the last good-bye to my mother, my brothers and sisters, and my grandparents. The last act that my grandfather did was to walk over to the bookcase, pull out a tiny little book, and say to me, "Let this tiny little book guard you." I remember the book. I have a book by the same author, the same book, in my library now, because the original was taken away from me.

I was saved in 1943 by a Polish engineer who was hired by the German factory of my slave labor camp where I worked. I was prepared—the guards prepared me—to be sent to the Gestapo for a minor accident that I caused in the factory. If it had not been for the intervention of this Polish engineer, I would not be sitting here and telling you this story. He simply threatened the authority of this particular camp that if I were sent away, he would not finish the job. And I was saved.

One day a non-Jewish neighbor who lived with my grandparents in the same house slipped a note under the fence of this labor camp from my contact on the outside that said the house was open at any time when I felt that there was danger ahead. It said I could come and spend time with them.

So one early morning in 1944—I believe it was the beginning of 1944—I escaped from the labor camp and made my way to this farmer's house on the outskirts of the city where this farmer saved nine Jewish lives. There were nine of us. It was, of course, a liberation of a dream, a liberation that was not reality because we knew from experience that we lived from hour to hour, from minute to minute, not knowing what the next day would bring. This, too, was like living in a dream world.

However, since I was brought up in a very orthodox Jewish home, we managed to do our prayers every morning, even putting on the Tefillin [phylacteries][3] without having a prayer book. We prayed by heart. How can I forget the last High Holy Day while in hiding? There were four men trying to help one another to do our services by heart. Those who are familiar with the liturgy of the High Holy Day services would understand how difficult it is to say those prayers by heart, but we did.

Until January 17, 1945, we lived in fear because we knew we could not go out and walk among people. Everything we did was in hiding. We whispered—we didn't talk, even though there were no neighbors around. We whispered even after the war. After I was liberated, I could not get back to normal; I kept on whispering for two months after the war. We couldn't sneeze or cough. There was a little girl with us, my cousin, who was at that time four years old. We were afraid that she might cry and a neighbor from far away or a field worker might hear her.

The night of January the 17th we said to one another, "Let's sit down and talk seriously. What will happen if the Germans come and they discover us? Who will ever know that here, in this place, in a far remote place in central Poland there were nine Jews hidden and saved by the grace of this family?"

So we sat down and we said to one another, "Let's write a legacy, and we'll bury it in the ground in some sort of a bottle or a glass jar. Maybe somehow in the future some people will come and find it." We knew that there were no remnants of our families. I was the only one who survived my family, as it was with the others.

So we started to write, and everybody had something to say. It took about 15 minutes until we could not write anymore because of our emotions. I recently found out from one of my friends who was with me that he does have this testimony in his possession. This man lives in Pittsburgh.

About a half-hour later the same evening, we saw suddenly the sky lighting up. We could not make out what it was. As the hours and the time moved on, we heard something like thundering. We connected thunder with lightning and thought we might have rain. But we knew there could be no rain in January in Poland, and certainly no lightning.

Then the sounds of the cannons came closer. We realized that perhaps someone was approaching to liberate us, or maybe it was the other way around. Maybe the Germans were going to destroy the city before they left. Maybe they were burning some houses with people in them because this is what we were used to since 1939.

Sure enough, the Russians were approaching. The next morning while I was standing in the field and preparing some ground for growing vegetables and grain, we saw the Russian planes come down and drop some bombs. I remember I started to dance for joy, whereby my landlord, the farmer, knelt down in prayer. With two different feelings, I thought, "Let it fall, let it come."

We heard that the first two Russian tanks were in the city. We wanted to greet them. We came out. We were the first two Jewish young men visible in a city of 28,000 in which only about 1,000 had survived.

But there is one thing I would like to share with you, and they are the final words that my friend the Polish farmer said to us when we were about to leave his house. He called us together and asked us to sit down because he wanted to talk to us. These are the words he said to us, looking down on the little girl: "You are free. You can go, but where? There is nobody waiting for you out there. This little child—I don't know how, how a little child would survive. The men? You work, maybe. But now you're free. But where will you go?"

*GUY HINTERLANG**

For the past two days, I have been hearing so many eloquent statements made here at this conference of the liberators that it seems very difficult for me really to hold your attention, because everything has already been said, and so well said, about the liberation of the camps.

So, I shall simply give you a very quick glimpse of the personal experience that I lived through at that time. I think it will be necessary, first of all, to say that if the French Minister of Defense assigned two officers to represent him here at this conference in the French delegation led by the Minister of Veterans Affairs himself, Mr. Jean Laurain, I think you can conclude that this was due to the role played by the French army in the liberation of Europe and of the camps. This French army had many of its members both on the side of the liberators and those who were liberated—and I am one of those who was liberated.

During the campaigns that they carried out in southern Germany and in Austria, the French troops did not have, as did the other three Allied armies, an opportunity to liberate any of the large concentration camps; only Kommandos were involved. But we did play a sufficiently large part in the victory over the Third Reich so that we can testify to their efficiency in participating in the liberation of all of those who were held in the chains of the enemy.

Obviously, the army contributed also to the repatriation of the deportees which, as you know, was absolutely essential in order to restore and, indeed, even save the lives of these deportees.

We wanted to make sure that the greatest number of our members were informed of the living conditions in the concentration camps; therefore, General Leclerc,[4] who was commanding the famous Second French Armored Division that was operating in Bavaria with the U.S. Army, gave orders that the maximum number of officers and men from his division, despite the concern to carry on the offensive, be given the opportunity to see for themselves the horror of the camp at Dachau immediately after it was liberated by the U.S. forces.

But the French army also expected a great deal from the liberation of the camps. There were elements of the French internal resistance, the military resistance in particular, that paid a very heavy price for the struggle which they waged against the enemy. Along with the 100,000 racial deportees who did not come back from deportation, the overall number of dead French resistance fighters was 60,000. Among these, we had 400 officers and 350 career NCOs, in other words, about one-tenth of our officers and NCOs who were still present on occupied territory and able to participate in the resistance.

As for those who were able to escape death in the camps, they provided an absolutely remarkable number of officers who had held very high responsibilities since the end of the war. I am thinking particularly of the officers who, prior to the current army chief, of staff, held that post, the highest rank in the army.

*Mr. Hinterlang made his remarks in French; this is the simultaneous translation.

Now let us come to the experience that I had in the camps. This deeply affected my life, even though I was only 19 years old. Incidentally, this almost marked the opening of my military career at that time. In only a brief time, I went from a very lowly officer and—at the time of the Normandy landing, the school of officers of gendarmerie in Guéret, which is a prefecture in the central part of France—took up arms and with the assistance of the local maquis,[5] we took over the town. But on the sixth of June, 1944, it was still too early for this to be a lasting undertaking, and the enemy then arrived with the SS Reich Division. This totally cleaned out the whole area with the cruelty that made this notorious, particularly because of the massacre of Oradour-sur-Glâns, which you all remember. During this combat, in the area of Guéret, I was taken prisoner with some 30 other military men. We were transferred to the great internment camp of Compiégne, some 50 kilometers north of Paris.

This camp was the place where the SS drew their men to send to concentration camps in Germany. In August of 1944, before the Allies advanced, this camp was emptied out for the last time because the SS did not care to carry out the agreement that had been concluded between the Consul General of Sweden in Paris, Mr. Nordling, and the German military high command in Paris, which was to have prevented any further deportations. However, the head of the SS troops decided that he had received an order and that he had to execute it.

After this dreadful trip in cattle cars, I was sent to Buchenwald and later to two successive Kommandos located at Niedersachswerfen and the Leau[6] salt mines, where we worked 450 meters under the surface building underground plants.

I shall stop here just for a moment to bring out one point that seems to me to be particularly important. In this Compiègne camp, many people—these are people who had occupied important roles in the resistance when they were arrested, and they had some idea, presumably, of what was going on in Germany in the camps—simply were not aware of what was at the other end of this long trip.

There were internees who had been held for many months who were packing their baggage and opening their bags just as though they were changing residences. They said, "We may not see this baggage," but the SS let them pack because there is always a bit of comedy, even a bit of humor, in these blackest situations.

In the car where I was packed in with some 80 other comrades, one of them knew what we could expect because he had already been in Germany. He had already been interned and had been able to escape, and he told us exactly what to expect. Nobody wanted to believe him, of course. Some even wanted to try to correct him and argue with his account. This incident shows how difficult it was to determine the truth about what these concentration camps were really like—those who created these camps took such great care to cover them up in great secrecy.

In any case, you know very well that one rarely believes witnesses and eyewitnesses. In fact, we have a proverb in French that says, "There is no one that is deafer than someone who doesn't want to hear, and there is no one blinder than one who does not wish to see."

A second glimpse or highlight that I would like to bring out about our life as "Häftlinge" [prisoners] was the spectacle that one saw every three or four days at the Kommando of Lauenburg.[7] This was the sight of a cart filled high with naked bodies, with numbers painted on their chests. The whole contents of this cart served to fuel an open charnel house near the little town where we were located. It's obviously very difficult to imagine that those people in that village didn't know what was going on. Once again, as I say, there are people who refuse to see and believe their own eyes.

Of my deportation, I would wish to say no more because it is really not even comparable to the experience of my other colleagues and companions here; but I nonetheless would like to talk about the end of my experience.

When Buchenwald was liberated, our Kommando was set out on the road. This was the solution that was arrived at by the Lagerführer [camp commander] to avoid the total liquidation that he had been ordered to carry out and which he did not wish to carry out. After three days of an absolutely exhausting march, we were to be liberated totally by chance on the road from Dessau to Leipzig. Our encounter with our American saviors almost didn't take place, but chance often works in our favor, and Providence was on our side for one time that day.

I can still remember when we came out of the woods that we were crossing through, we ran into these few American tanks that had just cleaned out the edge of the forest. They saw our column approaching along the road, and they started to aim at us, it looked like. But then, all of a sudden, they came toward us and things sorted themselves out very quickly.

There were only about 5,000-6,000 of us left on the road by that time, because obviously the invalids and the ill had been left in the camps. Of the 1,500 in the Kommando when I arrived, some 600 were left in the charnel house when we left.

You asked us, Madame Chairman, what were our feelings after the liberation. Well, there were two feelings, I think. First of all, I thought that nothing like this could ever happen to me again. Everything in my life in the future would be perfect, and I would never live through such dreadful experiences again like those that I had lived through during the 11 months.

And the second feeling? It was that of some pessimism, that is, that there is no man, no people, that can claim to be the Herrenvolk [master race]. But there is no race that is free of malice and evil because I feel that this is in the heart of man, if you allow your instincts to have free reign. I think that these feelings are the expression of what may truly happen. I have a lot of comrades, colleagues, and officers who some years later in a distant theater of operations underwent an entirely comparable experience in the physical destruction of the type that we experienced. I am talking also about brainwashing, something that the Nazis had avoided imposing on us. But you can also push things a bit further, and beyond, indeed. Beyond physical destruction you can also add the destruction of the human spirit, and that is extremely grave.

You can see that one cannot think, as our fathers and grandfathers said after World War I, that we had come to the last of the wars, the "war to end all wars," to be specific in the term they used. You have to be watchful from every angle. You have to keep on the alert because the danger of totalitarian destruction can come at you from any direction.

What is the remedy for this? Our Minister [Laurain] talked in his statement of the trust that one had to repose in the teachings of history. In France, this is something that we are thinking very seriously about, because obviously you can't be sure of the future without knowing exactly what your past has been.

I would like to add—this is a personal view here—that there is capital importance to be given to moral rehabilitation. All these fine and beautiful speeches will serve for naught if you cannot—perhaps not change man—but at least make man a better person, and make man more conscious of what his fate must be.

You have your love of your neighbor. That is the second great commandment; it is as important as the first commandment, as you know. That is the commandment that we ought to teach our young people and our children, because it is not in just seeking the easy way out—perversions and vices, and so forth—that we can find the solution to our life's problems. Otherwise, we are going to fall forever into the pit.

ANTHONY F. VAN VELSEN

We survivors are asked to tell you, and by you the world, what we felt at the moment of liberation.

We heard a row of speakers during this conference giving their impression of what they felt at the time of liberation and now so many years after the liberation. We all heard of gratitude, because they, the survivors, and what was left of their relatives could go on at that time after the liberation to take part in that great adventure that is free life. This picture, however, is somewhat oversimplified. I was in Birkenau where the actual gassing took place for more than two years, and few persons stayed as long as I did in Birkenau. I know exactly what took place, and I gained an insight into the feelings of quite a lot of companions in the camps. I can speak, therefore, with some authority about matters of life and death in Hitler's man-destructing machinery.

I am still with the former inmates, for I am a lawyer nowadays. I represent them in courts when their rights as men who came out of the camps are at stake. I know for that reason that quite a lot of the survivors who are not present here are not happy. They lead a life that is full of frustration in which the "KZ syndrome" [8] makes them prisoners again every night and tortures them anew. Their liberation was only a physical one. In the psychological sense, they were not liberated and will never be liberated. The end of their anguish can only come when they shall die one day.

We should bear that clearly in mind. For them, Auschwitz is still there, and they are still in the psychological grip of the horrors of yesterday. For them is not the peace they longed for. Quite a lot of them have the additional drawback of the so-called "survivor syndrome," that is, the constant self-accusation that they, in one way or another, did not manage to bring with them out of this inferno a beloved friend or relative. I said "inferno," but I should like to speak of a state of anti-life.

They are under the never-ending reproach that they themselves think they failed. We know from undeniable medical evidence that there are serious problems in the second generation; failures in life are connected with the mental wounds of the parents.

Of course, they are thankful for their liberation, but their sorrow still exists. There needs to be an all-out effort to come to the help of these men and women who are still battling with the Holocaust. I bring here to you their screams for help and for your understanding. They still are not dead, and this road to their world end is a terrible, awesome path.

Other voices also cannot be heard in this conference. I am convinced that my experience in the camp gives me the right, the duty, to translate in front of you what they felt when they were on the threshhold of death.

I should like to have at this very moment the strength of voice to reach the ears of all the inhabitants of our world to tell you and them that there was no gratitude when they had to bid farewell to their lives. No. No. No. They felt utterly desolate and lonesome. They felt that their living contemporaries in and outside the camp—the politicians, the armies, and the whole population of their respective countries had let them down. They felt not only hatred for the Nazi extermination machinery, but also a reproach to the free world that no direct action was taken to save their lives.

I, as a Christian, living in the midst of the Holocaust with the Jews, from almost the beginning of the organized gassing and extermination in Auschwitz-Birkenau, was ashamed of what the Christian world as a whole had failed to do to help the Jewish and Gypsy people, because the Gypsies—and I was in the Gypsy camp, too, there—were also gassed.

Of course, lots of individuals helped the Jews go in hiding, but the fact cannot be denied that this failed for six million Jews.

As a matter of fact, only a handful of non-Jewish people fought the battle against the Holocaust in Auschwitz-Birkenau.

As a survivor of this unbelievable fight with almost insurmountable odds and barriers, I have the right, even the duty, to bring to you these complaints that left the lips of six million children, men, and women on the threshhold of death. We, the non-Jewish people, were utterly too late.

Please don't misunderstand me. I don't want to suggest that it was a fault on the side of the liberators. It was due to the circumstances. No, the reproach goes to the community as a whole—the hesitation of people to accept the intrinsic evil of Nazism and the lack of foresight on the side of politicians to prepare the community as a whole to counteract. Six million people fell out of Europe and my hands because they were not in the hearts and the souls of the community as a whole.

Realizing that gave me the extra strength in the struggle with my comrades against the Holocaust. We were so determined that we dared to set up an underground movement in Birkenau under the very eyes of the SS and their constant surveillance, and we succeeded by our own hands to blow up a gas chamber and a crematorium.

The political weakness that paved the way for Nazism and, therefore, for the Holocaust is still there in our world of today. Nazism is not a way of political thinking but a criminal attitude towards mankind and should therefore be destroyed at the very beginning. That means that there is not in this world a political force that can kill attempts for a new Holocaust.

We have heard in the speeches that we should not forget about the Holocaust and that we, the survivors and the liberators, should speak out and give eyewitness accounts. But my dear friends, do you realize that within a short time we shall not live anymore. Who will give the eyewitness account then? Nobody.

Giving eyewitness accounts is not bad, but it is only the beginning. It is not enough. What we need is an international instrument to stop the onslaught from the beginning, something that with the establishment of the Jewish State is an ultimate answer for the problems of the Jews. Perhaps that is true in a certain way for Jews, but who stopped the recent holocaust in Vietnam after the United States of America left that country, and in Cambodia? No one.

Even at this moment the holocaust goes on, without anyone to do something to stop it. Red Cross activities can't stop a holocaust; only an active attack, and if needed with weapons. I am speaking as a retired colonel of the Royal Netherlands Marines.

You, the ones who were not in the Holocaust, and you, the youth of the world, should realize this. If not, then at some time in the future there will be a new holocaust, and the survivors will have to go their terrible, awesome way again.

This is not a friendly and soothing statement, but please understand that it is the meaning of a total complaint of six million people who are not here anymore and in whose name I wanted to speak.

BENJAMIN MEED

Mr. van Velsen, the proper thing for us to do after your speech would be to stand up in silence. Your remarks covered so much, and I hope that these remarks will be published as soon as possible and brought to the whole world.

Two days ago, I was asked to participate in this panel. Yesterday I started to write down a few points, but after a few seconds I stopped writing because what I would like to say would probably not be possible to say in public. I do it every night to my pillow. I still keep that dialogue. I am a survivor from the Warsaw Ghetto, and you are right. I am still in the Warsaw Ghetto, 38 years later—and I don't think I ever left the Ghetto.

How does one answer today how he felt the day after the liberation? As far as I can remember, this was not a day of joy. Maybe it should have been a day of joy, but it was not.

When liberation came, I remember feeling and thinking that the whole world was destroyed, not only our loved ones, but the whole world, a whole civilization had been lost. I felt then, and I'm feeling today, that something we left had been taken out of us and that the wounds will never heal.

I was liberated on January 16 by the Russian army. Together with my wife, Vladka, who took part with me in the Polish uprising in Warsaw, I was living 35 miles from Warsaw in a small village. The whole village had only 30 families, and we were living there in that village as Gentiles, as good, practicing Catholics. We never missed a Sunday in the church while living there.

When the first tanks arrived, we came out to look at the Russian tanks, and both of us looked at each other. I don't remember even talking to each other on that day of liberation.

After a while I remembered that I had made a promise which I had to fulfill. My promise was to my comrades in the Polish uprising, the Jews who took part in the Polish uprising. When I left Warsaw in October 1944, I was not sure that I would survive. I had left 11 people in a bunker in a house when the whole city had to leave. I promised them something.

All of them were Jewish people, but they couldn't pass as Poles; therefore, they decided to remain in Warsaw in the empty city. I remembered that I had sworn to them that if I survived, I would come back one day to that bunker. I would take them out from that bunker and bring them to the Jewish cemetery. This was my promise when I left them. I survived with that knowledge of that promise, and that same day Vladka and I got on two bicycles and went to Warsaw.

I arrived in Warsaw January 17 and went to where my friends supposedly were buried in that bunker. I came to the house. Nobody was living there, but there was already movement in the city. I found that bunker untouched, the way I left it, the way I covered it before I left. I was sure I had found them, but I was also afraid they were dead.

I knew I must continue with my promise. I started to dig, and I dug for a few hours, but unfortunately, with a small tool I could not reach the bunker that evening. It became dark, and I was afraid to remain and dig. I decided to stop digging and went to Cracow to spend the night because there was no place in Warsaw to stay; everything was destroyed.

The next morning at eight o'clock, I came back to dig again. When I opened that bunker, I found nobody there. I found out later that my friends thought that they had been discovered. Fortunately, they all were alive, and that night they decided to leave the bunker and to get into the sewers. Three days later, I found them in Warsaw, but for three days they did not know that they had been liberated. This was my first day of liberation.

Each one of us survivors has a different story to tell, but each one of us has a collective message—a message not from us, but a collective message of those whom we left behind. The Holocaust, the Nazi experience, was just a trial of how to destroy the world in the 20th century. It seemed to work. They picked the weakest of all. They picked the Jewish people. But later, as I told you, I was in the uprising of the Polish people. They were the next in line.

Our message to the world is that the Holocaust was distinctly a Jewish catastrophe of our people. We lost a third of our people, but I'm afraid that the next Holocaust will be the holocaust of the world. Maybe we with our testimony, we can help avoid it; we can teach the people to be aware. You are right, Mr. van Velsen. We have to do it now by looking at the first symptoms.

DR. HADASSAH ROSENSAFT

My name is Hadassah Bimko-Rosensaft. I am a Jew, born in Sosnowiec,[9] Poland. My parents, my first husband, and my six-year-old son were gassed by the Germans in the extermination camp of Auschwitz-Birkenau. My entire family perished during the Holocaust, gassed by the Germans in Treblinka and Auschwitz. I was in Auschwitz-Birkenau more than a year, and thereafter I was in the concentration camp of Bergen-Belsen where I was liberated by the British army on April 15, 1945.

I arrived in Bergen-Belsen from Auschwitz on November 23, 1944, together with eight other Jewish women. We were two doctors and six nurses, and had been sent as a medical team, supposedly to work in the camp's hospital. Conditions in Bergen-Belsen were terrible. The camp was filthy beyond anyone's imagination. There was no place for the inmates to wash. Everybody was hungry. It was a cold winter, and we were all freezing. Diseases were rampant. Conditions in the hospital were no better, and, in addition, there was no medication for the sick. We were desperate.

There were no gas chambers in Bergen-Belsen, nor did the doctors conduct terminal medical experiments on human beings as they did in other camps. Rather, it was the place to which thousands of inmates from other camps were sent in 1944 and 1945 as the Germans were forced to retreat from Poland and eastern Germany before the onslaught of the Allied armies.

On January 18, 1945, the Germans liquidated Auschwitz, and again transports with thousands of inmates arrived at Bergen-Belsen. They were exhausted from the long journey, starving, sick with innumerable diseases, and many were literally frozen to death. With these transports from Auschwitz came also the monstrous SS guards and SS doctors whom many of us already knew, and they turned Belsen into an indescribable hell.

Conditions in Bergen-Belsen were at their worst three weeks before the liberation. Typhus, tuberculosis and other epidemics were raging through the camp simultaneously. In the barracks and in the hospital people were lying on the floor, starving and dying. About 1,000 perished each day. Only a small group, which had already had the diseases in Auschwitz, were immune and could resist. The small crematorium could not cope with all the corpses even though it was burning day and night. The unburied corpses were strewn all over the camp. The SS, who felt that their own end was near, cut off the water supply, and we were given one piece of bread per person only three times a week, and a half a pint of so-called turnip soup a day. On top of it all, the Germans kept us in mortal fear by telling us that the camp was mined and that we would all be blown up. Such was our situation on the eve of liberation: disease, starvation, despair, fear, and not a single ray of hope from anywhere.

On April 12, 1945, we saw in the distance that the SS were burning papers, but we didn't know why. The following day, we saw many SS men and women leaving the camp, and the few who remained wore white armbands on their left sleeves. Rumors started to spread that the camp was about to be declared "neutral" as the result of negotiations between the Germans and the British. Nobody knew what this meant, or where the news came from, and in any event we didn't believe it. However, on Saturday, April 14, we received Red Cross food parcels, one for four people, and we began to believe that something was happening.

And then came April 15, 1945. I will never forget that day. It was Sunday, a very hot day; it was quiet; nobody was to be seen outside the barracks; the camp seemed to have become abandoned, almost like a cemetery. I was sitting with the children with whom I lived in the same barrack.

Suddenly we felt the tremors of the earth—something was moving—and then we heard the sound of rolling tanks. We were convinced that the Germans were about to blow up the camp. But then—it was 3 o'clock in the afternoon—we heard a loud voice say in German: "Hello, hello, you are free! We are British soldiers, and we came to liberate you!"

We ran out of the barracks and saw in the middle of the road a British army car with a loudspeaker on top going through the camp and repeating the same message over and over again. Within minutes, hundreds of women stopped the car, screaming, laughing, and crying, and the British soldier inside was crying with us. (The soldier was the late Captain Derek Sington.) It seemed a dream which soon turned into reality. How tragic it was that the great majority did not even realize that we were free, because they were unconscious or too sick to understand what was happening.

The British tanks rolled on in pursuit of the German army, and for one day the camp remained in the charge of a group of Hungarian SS guards who, in this one day, killed 72 Jews and 11 non-Jews. The British came back to us on April 17, this time to stay. They found 58,000 inmates, both men and women, 90 percent of whom were Jews. The vast majority were living skeletons; most of them were too ill and too weak even to walk. Within the following eight weeks, 13,944 more died. In addition, there were more than 10,000 unburied corpses lying around the camp. The late Brigadier General H.L. Glyn Hughes, as the Chief Medical Officer of the British Army of the Rhine, came to see the camp. I was asked to take him around. What he saw was a sea of crying, screaming bones. At the sight of the huts with their dead and near-dead, General Glyn Hughes, a medical officer hardened to human suffering, cried unashamedly. He decided on the spot to try to save as many sick as possible in spite of the conflicting needs of the military casualties for whom he was responsible.

Not far from the concentration camp were German army barracks, strong brick buildings with all necessary amenities. General Glyn Hughes decided to transform these barracks into a hospital for some 17,000 patients—the more desperately ill among the survivors. I was asked to help, and was appointed administrator of the hospital for the survivors. I was honored and privileged to work with him and the other British medical personnel. My first task was to issue a call to the doctors and nurses among the survivors to come forward. Twenty-eight doctors and 590 female and 30 male nurses reported immediately. Not all the nurses were qualified, and most of them were still extremely weak, but they all worked with great devotion. General Glyn Hughes said about them, and I quote: "I would like to pay a special tribute to those who, although inmates for a long period, had survived and retained their moral standards and sense of responsibility. By their unselfish devotion to others, they must themselves have saved countless lives. After the liberation, they continued their excellent work and were invaluable to the helpers who came in."

We started to work immediately. It took several weeks to evacuate the concentration camp. Once this process was completed, and all the survivors had been relocated in the former German military barracks, the British on May 21 burned down the barracks of the concentration camp in order to contain the spread of the epidemics.

The burning down of the old camp also marked the beginning of regular medical attention for the sick of Belsen, instead of the emergency measures of the past month.

As far as our own feelings are concerned, it is hard for me to put them into words. At first, we paid our respects to the tens of thousands of our dead brothers and sisters for whom the help came too late, and who were buried in mass grave after mass grave.

For the greatest part of the liberated Jews of Bergen-Belsen, there was no ecstasy, no joy at our liberation. We had lost our families, our homes. We had no place to go to, nobody to hug. Nobody was waiting for us anywhere. We had been liberated from death and the fear of death, but not from the fear of life.

SIGMUND STROCHLITZ

It is with a sense of obligation and humility that I will share with you the grim realities the survivors faced immediately after being liberated from the Nazi inferno.

Having forgotten how people live, only knowing how people die—not how they die in real life, in normal life, but how they die in flames—we survivors reentered this world, accepted leadership positions, and became a source of vitality and a testimony to the indestructible spirit of the Jewish people.

Let me turn the clock back to those days when the gates of hell were shut and the chimneys of concentration camps stopped vomiting black clouds of human flesh, and we were told we are free.

It was April 15, 1945—liberation day. It is anchored in my mind and even compared by some survivors with the stories of Biblical salvations. Our prayers for liberation that we uttered in silence, in desperation, and perhaps more in defiance, and our hopes to survive that we nourished for such a long time became on that sunny, bright Sunday morning a reality. Yet, there was no joy or any sense of happiness among survivors of Hitler's Final Solution. We felt strangely empty, with a submerged sense of guilt for having survived.

The western world was celebrating victory and rightfully and properly so. We were the remnants of once-flourishing Jewish communities, broken physically and mentally, and confused on our liberation day by the sheepish and cowardly behavior of the Nazi murderers and bewildered by the actions and reactions of our liberators. We suspected that the Germans, the perpetrators of the greatest crimes against the Jewish people and mankind, even though badly defeated and living in abject poverty, would be able in time on their own soil to rebuild their lives and their homes.

Only we alone were facing an uncertain future. We alone could not go back. There were no homes anywhere. Where once our ancestors lived for generations, there were no families waiting for us. Only stones, stinking of indignity and humiliation, were there to greet us. This was not a happy ending. It was the beginning of something unknown, disturbing. An empty victory.

Furthermore, the hostile or, at best, indifferent behavior of the local population during the war gave us good reason to believe that we would not be received with open arms by those who took over our homes and our possessions.

The cries were loud, and yet mute. We only sensed freedom in solitude, reading on one another's despairing faces the knowledge that tomorrow would bring no one else back to share the burden of facing a new reality alone.

The natural instinctive reaction during those first weeks of liberation—as I so well remember— was to look for somebody to lean on. We were yearning for something to hold onto, to have faith in, to draw us forward, to bring us back into the mainstream of life. But we were looking in vain.

Our liberators to whom our gratitude was boundless, the victors for whom our admiration was limitless, traumatized by the experiences of a horrible war and shocked by what they had encountered in the liberated camps, were eager to return to civilian life and be reunited with their families. For the Allied governments, after years of exhausting fighting, the monumental problems of postwar awakening were their first priority and, again, rightfully so.

So, with every passing day, it became more evident to us that we must not appear before the world as separate individuals, but that we were a community, a family united by what we had lived through together, by what we had felt together, and that we were no more the Jews that once lived in Poland, France, Hungary, or in any other part of Europe.

We were the Jews, the survivors, who could and must find comfort and meaning in supporting each other and only hoping that in time the world would recognize the need to resettle us.

Accepting that premise was difficult for those few who were arguing that if they had known what the outside world was going to be like, they would have given in long ago. We understood them even if we disagreed. We lived for many years in liberated camps or in cities among the murderers.

The gates of Palestine were shut. Nobody really wanted us. We finally became an embarrassment, and with the help of President Truman, those armed with courage went to Israel to build a Jewish homeland.

Some attracted by the vision of a comfortable and easy life landed in the United States, while others scattered and dispersed all over the world—not bitter, not sinking into a paralyzing sadness, somber and riddled with doubts, but determined not to become prisoners of yesterday, victims unable to meet new challenges.

Grief did not become our master. We chose to rebuild our shattered lives, raising families in strange cultures, coping with unknown behavior patterns, making contributions to our adopted countries, and helping to build societies based on freedom and justice for all. The pain, however, was constant, residing silently in the private places of the heart.

The wounds opened, however hidden in the innermost recesses of our minds. The past was shared in the privacy of our homes only with those who survived the cataclysm, even though the desire to bear witness, to tell the world what happened, was essentially what kept many of us alive.

Today it is with pride and perhaps a sense of accomplishment that I whisper, mindful of our irreplaceable losses: We survivors did not waste our lives.

KALMAN SULTANIK

May 12, early in the morning, 1942. A beautiful day, and I had slept in quietness. The ghetto was surrounded, and we were asked to get together all belongings in 10 minutes. My two brothers were already in the labor camp in Plaszow.[10] My mother, father, two children, and myself gathered with the rest of the ghetto of the Jewish community.

We were taken to the station where we were separated—children, women, and the old on one side; young men, able to work, on the other side.

The Germans behaved this day, contrary to the previous days where no day had gone by without a shooting, a killing. Nevertheless, they gave away their behavior. They told my father, who was on the border between being old or being able to go to work, to go on the right side with the young and able. My father refused. He said, "I cannot leave my wife and my two daughters."

He pushed me to the other side. He knew he was going to death because before going out, we divided our valuable things. He took the valuable things from my mother and two sisters and gave them to me with the hope that I, together with my younger brothers, would survive. He told me I had to take care of them in the labor camp to be able to survive.

A few days later, after I was already in Plaszow, I decided to go back to Miechow.[11]

I could leave the camp because I was connected with a Zionist youth group which took me out of the camp. On my initiative, we decided to send someone to follow the train and find out where it was going.

In a few days, a Gentile woman whom we hired came back and told us the train had gone to Belzec and that there was no sign of life. I communicated this message, which brings me to a bitter conclusion. If we could find out under these circumstances what happened to the trains, how could the Allies, the democratic world, not have known? This has been very disappointing to me.

After I was freed by the Russian army on May 10 and on the march from Dresden to Theresienstadt, my first thought was to go back to Miechow, my home town. As I approached Miechow, which seemed like a ghost town, the first news I received was that my uncle had been killed by some Polish pro-Nazi hooligans. My mind went blank and I could not comprehend this tragedy.

Although warned by several people that my uncle's fate could befall me as well, I decided to approach the Russian officers stationed in Miechow and ask for protection, since I wanted to stay on in Miechow for a few more days to see if anyone from my family might still return. The captain in charge happened to be Jewish from Minsk. He told me his story—how his family had been killed when the Nazis had invaded his town, and we both cried.

After the trauma of World War II, we Holocaust survivors could not help but accuse the forces not directly involved in the Holocaust. Why could those forces not have foreseen the horrendous proportion the Holocaust was fated to take on? We were deeply perplexed, and we remain perplexed.

I was doing some research on this period, and I found out that there was only one Jewish organization that attempted to save the death marchers. In Geneva, in the beginning of 1945, Gerhardt Riegner of the World Jewish Congress appealed to the Red Cross to save the people from the marches—not only Jews but Gypsies and anyone who was on the marches. However, it was to no avail.[12]

Yet, the extermination of six million Jews took place in the heart of Christian Europe, in the citadel of western culture and learning. Churchgoing Christians, devotees of literature, art, and philosophy, participated in these crimes, apparently with good conscience. The crisis that had begun with the Jews required a coalition of major powers and tens of millions of non-Jewish victims to defeat the Nazi regime.

After World War II, we survivors had a right to believe we would have a world in which the unparalleled atrocities of the Holocaust could never again be repeated. I was convinced that the Jews—the number one victims of Nazism—and mankind in general would never again be subjected to the suffering undergone during World War II and that anti-Semitism would never dare rise again.

Only 27 years after the establishment of the State of Israel, which arose from the ashes of the six million Jews, the United Nations Assembly—the very body which had made the existence of Israel possible—adopted a resolution condemning Zionism as a form of racism. This is anti-Semitism.

The rest of the world which was concerned with West Germany's economic recovery after the war has done little or nothing to encourage that country to enlighten German youth on the Nazi crimes committed during the Holocaust and to consider what must be done to avoid another catastrophe.

Over the centuries, Jews have been confronted with the forces of evil and of benevolence. The forces of evil have often prevailed. The survivors' disappointment, after their liberation, in the attitude of the world—not losing the sense of historical proportion—can be compared with the situation of the Jews in the latter part of the 19th century when, in 1866, Bismarck brought about the last phase in obtaining equal status for Jews which had begun with the French Revolution.[13] But, 10 to 15 years later, the forces of evil reappeared.

Politicians, writers, and intellectuals once again began to heed fanatics. A whole movement was created to oppose the Jews. After a 15-year hiatus, this movement came as a great shock; it frightened the enlightened 19th century community, and the Jews more than ever before.

While Jews were in the ghettos, voices had been raised against the religious minorities that did not have equal status. But now, at the end of the 19th century, a movement came out against citizens with equal rights, maintaining that Jews were not worthy of equality.

It was not so simple to turn the clock back. New slogans had to be found to undermine the Jews. The reemergence of the modern term "anti-Semitism" and not "anti-Jewishness" indicated that it was not Judaism nor the Jewish religion that worked against the Jews. Instead, their behavior and their personality traits were stereotyped. This was a movement that began in Germany at the end of the 1870s, found disciples in other European countries for a different reason, and with the chain of events that followed, brought Hitler to power.

Neo-Nazi groups at the present time neither enjoy large-scale public support nor do they pose a direct threat to the established democratic order in western Europe or in the United States. It is still too early to predict the effects of terrorists on democracy in Germany, Italy, France, and Belgium where the most recent outbreaks have just occurred.

In conclusion, my dear friends, it is bitter to have to say this, but pro-Jewish voices raised on behalf of the Jews are no more than voices crying out in the wilderness. Precious as those voices are, the world as a whole—even after the extermination of the six million Jews—remains a wilderness for the Jews—a silent wilderness.

In my opinion, this is a problem we must address ourselves to.

SIGGI WILZIG

I had thought that I would be the only angry man, but I found a companion in addition to companionships. This gathering has had an extraordinary effect on me. I don't believe it was a coincidence that Mr. van Velsen is sitting next to me because of our alphabet or that I was chosen to be the host for the Dutch delegation. It wasn't a coincidence; it was one of those acts that just happened, just as some of us survived and some didn't.

When I was asked to talk about the liberation, I told you I couldn't do that. That would be an injustice to the six million Jews, particularly my generation—the children, the million children, under 15, since I was 14—and an injustice to the Christians, the noble Gentiles, who suffered with us and died with us.

I didn't know where God was when I was in Auschwitz at the age of 16. While in my religion we do not have a son of God, I believe he had his angels in the form of our friend sitting next to me. There is a special place in heaven for people like you, sir.

We all have the same story—the facts. Who really knows what happened on the day of liberation? Who of us had the strength at 70 and 80 pounds to know?

I started out saying that I'm angry. I have been angry since I was 12 years old. It's one thing to talk about it in a lecture at West Point and Brown University and the University of Pennsylvania, and for Elie Wiesel, at Boston University. It is one thing to hear yourself and try to avoid the emotions when it touches your heart, but it brings tears to your eyes. You zig-zag and talk about personalities until you get back your composure and you go on talking. But liberation didn't come easy, and we paid a high price.

How does it feel for someone whose family—a German-Jewish orthodox family—lived and died for the country, whose uncles volunteered at the ages of 18 and 19 for the First World War? How does it feel for someone to remember the day after Hitler was appointed. How does it feel to go through Auschwitz and lose 59 of your relatives? How does it feel to remember whether there were 18 or 19 selections—half of them before Mengele? How does it feel to remember the pinching of your cheeks and the sticking out of your stomach that was blown up from the rotten soup we ate?

How do you want to remember being in Block 9 and being with a young man who saw his mother by coincidence being brought into Block 10, the experimental block?

He looked out in the month of April in 1943, and he saw less and less of his mother's face until it vanished. Who knows that it wasn't just the SS? I, having been born in Germany, saw the emblems of the German Luftwaffe [air force]. Yes, the doctors of the army and the Luftwaffe came to the block. How do you tell a young man of 15½ that the mother was transferred, we saw it, when indeed she was carried out as a corpse to the crematorium?

So why talk about the liberation? Who talks about the fact that 11 days before the liberation two of my brothers were murdered in cold blood? Eleven days before.

Who talks about the seven-year-old nephew—oh, he wasn't dark-haired or Jewish looking, no, blond and blue-eyed. And if Hitler would be alive today, he would die 16 times over seeing that maybe a third of Israel's children are indeed blond and blue-eyed.

I was angry at 12 because half of my family was already in concentration camps.

Shortly after the conference in Evian where 37 nations gathered and one by one got up and said they couldn't take in the handful of Jews, everyone had excuses.[14] One country even got up to say that it would be bad for us if they took us in. It would bring out anti-Semitism. That is all recorded. The seven Gestapo agents in the back in civilian clothes couldn't control their laughter.

Without diminishing the crime of the Nazis, let us not forget that the western world stood idly by. They said business is business. Sure, they were fooled in 1935 and 1936 during the Olympics, but they knew quite well what was going on.

Let's talk about the nuns and the priests who died with us. But the Holy Father, Pope Pius, kept quiet and said he prayed. He prayed while my nephew at seven and my niece at two went to the gas chambers, and not a single word, not a single broadcast, came out.

I live in Auschwitz every day today. I am not liberated yet. I am fortunate to have a family, and it is possibly helpful that I'm married to an American-born woman. My children live it; how can I have forgotten it?

The liberation that we hoped would be the end is not the end at all. My nightmares that went away for years came back. They came back when the books were published that the Holocaust never happened. That indeed is the cruelest crime for the last few years.

Hitler didn't start just with the Jews. You know how he ended up. So, therefore, our Christian colleagues should remember. When 90 books are published in 16 languages telling us that the Holocaust didn't exist and that my number on the arm doesn't exist and that my parents and brothers and sisters and 59 relatives didn't die, I have to continue living in Auschwitz every day.

A funeral reminds me of Auschwitz. When there's too much food, I'm reminded of Auschwitz because there was none. When there was too little food, it reminds me. Yesterday at lunchtime I wanted to take the sherbet and move it over to my colleague to give him a second portion. I told him so. That was a natural way of looking at it.

In closing: A conspiracy has taken place, but nobody talks about it. You wouldn't have had an Auschwitz if there had been an Israel. You had Auschwitz because there was no Israel. The western world, their conscience bothered, gave us Israel as we deserved. How do you destroy Israel?—for the sake of oil and the PLO, by denying that there was an Auschwitz, by denying that there was a Holocaust.

We had Auschwitz. We got Israel. Deny that there was an Auschwitz, and then you can get rid of Israel. So, I appeal to you not just to care for ourselves and for the survivors. I disagree with those who want me to help about Cambodia. Ask for money, and I will help you.

We need to fight the pests, the disease that old Nazis and new Nazis are spreading with the help of oil money to destroy the freedom and the existence of Israel. If they destroy the truth about the Holocaust, then Israel, God forbid, is to follow. That is our duty as survivors.

ELI ZBOROWSKI

When the day of liberation came, I was in a group of 10 Jews hiding in a chicken coop on a very poor Polish farm. I had joined this group only in the last six months before liberation.

I will not speak of my long journey of living in a ghetto, working in an underground Zionist youth organization, later a member and liaison for the United Jewish Resistance Organization, living later on Aryan papers, and hiding and changing places. All these experiences of that period belong to another place to speak of.

I want to share with you my simple loneliness in the experience of being liberated and the immediate weeks, months following the events that meant so much for us, who became known under the word and name, survivors.

It was on January 17. We were living in a cellar with no windows in darkness—10 Jews. We were told that a Russian soldier was there on the premises, and I, having Aryan papers, was allowed to go out from the cellar to join and speak with the Russian. They were confused. We were confused. Could this be one of the Russian soldiers, the Vlasovivs,[15] who fought on the German side?

Our bewilderment had to be kept quiet. We were liberated where we lived—on enemy territory. We were not sure if the Russians would retreat and the Germans would come back, so we decided to remain in the cellar at least that day. In the evening it was almost for us an historic decision to get out from the cellar, to get out from hiding and start walking first towards the East, just in case the Germans came back.

We realized that the Soviet armies were moving and crushing the German armies and that we were safe. But there was no enthusiasm. There were no happy, joyous outcries. We felt, perhaps, more lost than before we were liberated.

It is difficult even to recall that exact feeling. Our strong will for life was carried throughout the months of the war, but we suddenly felt all alone. We started to walk back to our hometown, where we found ourselves to be the only Jews that remained from 1,500 families, about 5,000 Jews.

I want to tell you that the experience that we had in that hometown just compelled the few of us—the 10—to leave that town and seek refuge in the bigger cities where there were a few hundred Jewish survivors. This was the unfortunate experience at the days of our liberation and immediately following it.

There were about 20 children, who were between 14 and 19, and we felt the need for families. Those of us who had no parents at all, although some of us had older brothers, reunited in February in the city of Czestochowa.[16] We felt that we wanted to be together, and by the end of February, we set out on a march to Warsaw to present our wish to the central committee that had come from Lublin and settled in Warsaw.

We wanted to tell them that it was impossible for us to live in the place where we were raised and that there was no other place for us to go other than Palestine. This was how the first kibbutz that was set up after the war in 1945 was begun. By the end of March, we had a kibbutz and the name was Al Shem Lochamei Hagetaot, In the Name of the Ghetto Fighters.

In July 1945, this group of children and four other groups of children that had formed in Poland, about 160 youngsters altogether, left Poland and arrived around August 10 in the American zone of occupied Germany. There we found to our great surprise at least a few hundred, a few thousand Jews. But what was more surprising to us was that there were already administrations. Those who had been in camps yesterday came out the next day and formed committees ready to help.

I think that if we survivors can account for the miracle of having survived, the greatest miracle is that these people, these survivors, have been able to adjust themselves so fast and so soon to normal life.

I think that if we survivors have a message to the world of what we have lived through, what the Germans and their collaborators have inflicted upon the Jewish people and upon all humanity, we also have a message to carry to the world of genuine love, love that was shown and displayed during the war and primarily after the war when we saw the survivors coming back normal people.

We the Jews—all the Jews—were assigned by the German laws to be dehumanized, starved, and liquidated under a technical description, "The Final Solution." How proud we can be that the anger from our experiences did not ultimately cause us to look at the evil but made us willing to share love with others!

When we turned to the world to take a lesson from our experiences and from what the others have done to humanity, we turn to them and ask them to study the chapter of survivors, the return to normal life and their adjustments to becoming contributing members of society.

Of course, we live with our past, but it is controlled by our deeper sense of human will to live a normal life, a life of love with the message to the world that we have seen the worst and we will try to show the free world the finest in mankind.

Yes, we live. We have children and they have children. To those fortunate ones who didn't experience the Holocaust firsthand, our strongest message is that we survivors are the examples of humans' natural will to live.

The lesson should be taken from what humanity was capable of doing to mankind, but the ultimate lesson is the greatness of humanity—life by itself.

YAFFA ELIACH

We have just heard the testimonies and the price of freedom. What did it indeed mean to be a lone survivor? What did it mean to discover that we were the only survivors of large families?

What did it mean to be a Jewish survivor? Unlike our friends from the Netherlands, from France, from Norway, we came back to a country that did not welcome us. In many instances, our neighbors wished us dead.

When I came to my hometown with my mother, father, and brother at the age of seven, we were welcomed with 15 bullets that killed my brother and nine bullets that killed my mother. It was her blood and her dead body that bought me the price of freedom, and this was after liberation.

We soon learned that the majority of the world was silent, that our journey to freedom was a costly one, and we paid a dear price for it. But only those that pay a high price for freedom value freedom more than anything else. You, us—all of us in this room—were able to transcend the bleak realities and create a new life whose motto is: "Yes, I am my brother's keeper."

During this conference, there were extraordinary experiences. The liberator of Auschwitz, General Petrenko of the Soviet delegation, is hugging people that he liberated. Gorlinsky from the Soviet Union, who liberated Terezin, recalled how he hugged and kissed American soldiers on the banks of the River Elbe. Hadassah Rosensaft discovers that in the audience is Ray Kaner, whose life she saved. Siggi Wilzig discovers that he's sitting next to one of his guardian angels.

Yes, we had moments of glory in this conference, but does it reflect reality outside? Does it reflect really what's happening? The majority of the world is the constant struggle.

The State of Israel, the haven of so many refugees and survivors of World War II, is threatened, both by foes and friend. "Zionism is racism."

Our own American liberators are here with us and together with us are trying to cope with our memories and with the price of the freedom that they offered us.

Yet, our existence is denied. "There were never camps. There was never a Holocaust. There were never liberators. There were never any of us." Never did they hear any of the stories that they just heard here.

Yes, the gates of the concentration camps, the gates to hell, were opened and hopefully closed. We are all free men. Let us have faith that the hearts and minds of men will be open to the suffering of people, to the understanding that the price that we paid for liberty was not in vain.

Let me conclude, as befitting a conference of liberators, with a quotation from an American liberator, the host country of this conference, and the state and the country that welcomed all of us around the table and offered us a home after the Holocaust. It is from Lieutenant General James M. Gavin, a liberator of Woebbelin:[17] "It had been a long and costly journey, and we overran the concentration camp and looked back with a better understanding of what we had seen. We knew it had been a journey worth every step of the way. Let's preserve inch by inch the way to freedom."

Notes

1 Most of the Norwegian merchant fleet, the world's third largest, was able to escape to Britain when Norway was overrun by Germany in April 1940. More than 3,500 Norwegian sailors died for the Allied cause during the war.

2 Piotrkow, about 25 miles south-southeast of Lodz.

3 Phylacteries: Greek for Tefillin, the two black leather cubes containing the words of the Sh'ma and attached to long leather straps. Worn during daily morning prayers except on Sabbath and holidays by observant Jewish males and some women over the age 13.

4 General Jacques Phillipe de Hauteclocque, called Leclerc, commanded Free French forces to spectacular victories in north Africa and participated in the liberation of Paris. He was made a marshal of France in 1947.

5 Term used to designate one of the major branches of the French resistance during the Nazi occupation of France. Maquis is the French word for dense thickets common in some regions in southern France, and had been used to denote bandits who would evade capture by hiding amidst the thickets. After the German defeat of France in 1940, French resistance fighters adopted the name as well.

6 Leau was the SS code name for the Buchenwald satellite camp of Bernburg.

7 Lauenburg was another satellite of Buchenwald.

8 KZ, a German acronym for Konzentrationslager, meaning concentration camp.

[9] Sosnowiec, in Upper Silisia, not far from Auschwitz, was a town with a substantial Jewish population before World War II.

[10] Plaszow is near Cracow.

[11] Miechow, about 20 miles north by northeast of Cracow.

[12] Dr. Gerhardt Riegner, the World Jewish Congress representative in Geneva, was active in making Nazi plans to exterminate the Jews known to the world. See David S. Wyman, *The Abandonment of the Jews. America and the Holocaust 1941-1945*. (New York, 1984), pp. 42 ff. and passim.

[13] The emancipation of the Jews of central Europe instituted under Napoleon was largely reversed after Napoleon's fall. Beginning in the 1830s, however, measures toward emancipation were implemented gradually in several German states. When Germany became politically unified under Bismarck's leadership between 1866 and 1871, emancipation was affirmed first in the North German Confederation and subsequently in the German Empire.

[14] The conference at Evian, France, took place in July 1938. Of the nations represented, only the Dominican Republic agreed to admit a considerable number of Jewish refugees.

[15] A reference to the troops fighting under the command of General Andrei Vlasov. A Soviet general who participated in the defense of Moscow, Vlasov fell prisoner to the Germans in 1942, whereupon he switched sides and vowed to help the Nazis defeat communism. After the war he was condemned to death and hanged for treason in the Soviet Union.

[16] Czestochowa, 65 miles northwest of Cracow.

[17] Woebbelin, a satellite of Neuengamme.

CHAPTER XI

THE UPRISINGS

Moderator: Dr. Irving Greenberg (USA): Rabbi; author and Holocaust scholar; director, National Jewish Resource Center, New York City; member, U.S. Holocaust Memorial Council.

Vladka Meed (USA): Courier in Warsaw Ghetto uprising; author of *On Both Sides of the Wall.*

Richard Glazer (Switzerland): Survivor of Treblinka.

Esther Raab (USA): Survivor of Sobibor.

Dr. Leon Wells (USA): Survivor of "Death Brigade," a group of prisoners forced by the SS to erase evidence of Nazi mass executions in Janowska.

Alexander Donat (USA): Author of *The Holocaust Kingdom* and other works on the Holocaust; survivor of the Warsaw Ghetto (now deceased).

Institutional identifications are those at the time of the Conference.

IRVING GREENBERG

This panel offers a glimpse into an incredible phenomenon within the Holocaust, that despite conditions of total oppression and overwhelming tyrannical power, human beings found the strength and the capacity to resist and to fight back.

We will focus on one aspect of the general resistance—those who were able to organize actual armed revolt within the framework of their oppression. This, of course, constitutes part of a much broader universe of moral resistance, an affirmation of dignity, but this group had the additional difficulties of organizing, obtaining weapons, and rising up.

If the numbers of survivors in each case are so pitifully small because they are one of a hundred or one of a thousand, the figures we have with us this morning are even a smaller remnant because so few of those who participated either survived the fighting or survived to this day. Therefore, it is a special privilege for them to share their testimony with us.

VLADKA MEED

The Warsaw Ghetto uprising, the symbol of Jewish resistance to the Nazis, was not an isolated event, but rather the culmination of many forms of Jewish resistance throughout the world. During the first years of the Ghetto, the nature of resistance had been to preserve our Jewish way of life against the barbaric onslaught of the Nazis. Survival, to outwit the enemy and to live and to witness the destruction—that was our goal.

It was only after July 1942, when the deportations began from the Warsaw Ghetto, that the realization slowly dawned on us that, despite the German assurances of "only resettlement" to other towns, the Final Solution meant death.

How could our people, who for generations had cherished human values, imagine the utter madness of an enemy who planned their total annihilation? How could we even conceive of the death camps perfected by German science and industry?

It took time until the ghetto Jew learned to believe the truth of the gas chambers, but finally, as the realization grew that the Nazis would spare no one, the idea of armed struggle took hold of those left in the ghettos.

In October 1942, the coordinated Jewish Fighters Organization of Warsaw—ZOB[1]—came into being and I, a member of the Jewish underground, was sent out of the Ghetto on a mission among the Poles—a Jewish girl, but I had Polish features and I was fluent in the Polish language. I was trusted to try and obtain arms for the Fighters' Organization.

The core of our Fighters' Organization consisted of illegal youth organizations—Zionists, Socialists, Bundists,[2] and Communists—who were remnants of the prewar political youth movements. Over 500 fighters were organized into 22 units. Though most of the fighters were in their teens or early twenties, they were imbued with a spirit of idealism and heroism. In the beginning, the armaments in the possession of the Jewish Fighters' Organization were one revolver.

Those who say that organized Jewish armed resistance came too late in the Ghetto would do well to remember that it came earlier than that of any other oppressed people in Europe. Every other underground movement waited with its own revolt until the Allied armies were practically at the gate of the cities, so as to assure their success. This was true of the French in Paris and later on of the Poles in Warsaw, but the Jews—the most persecuted and the ones in the most hopeless position—were the first to revolt.

It was 18 months earlier, on January 18, 1943, as soon as we got hold of a few revolvers, that the first German soldiers fell in the Warsaw Ghetto. The surprise attack induced the Germans to halt the deportation. January 18 marked the turning point for the Ghetto, for on that day the Ghetto had dared to strike back in an organized fashion by setting fire to German factories and carrying out death sentences against informers and collaborators. The Fighters' Organization won the support of the Warsaw Ghetto Jews.

Through bulletins placed on the walls of Ghetto buildings, the Jews were informed of the aims and works of the underground. A tax was put on the wealthy and on the remaining Ghetto institutions. Money and jewelry were collected. Bakers and merchants secretly supplied bread and food to the fighting units. Those who still had possessions of value had to contribute for armaments.

"Resist! Don't let yourself be taken away," was the call.

"I no longer have any authority in the Ghetto," Mark Lichtenbaum, the head of the then-appointed Jewish Council, admitted to the Nazis when he was ordered to supervise further deportations. The Fighters' Organization expressed the will and the feeling of the remaining 60,000 Warsaw Ghetto Jews.

But our biggest problem was to obtain arms. We sent out desperate pleas to the outside world begging for guns, but these pleas fell on deaf ears. Pitiful was the response from the Polish underground. Instead, the Jewish resistance organization had to find its own way.

I will never forget when Michael Klepfish, our armaments engineer, and I together tested our first homemade bomb outside the Ghetto walls, and it worked!

With mounting excitement, armaments were smuggled into the Ghetto. Primitive factories were set up in basements and attics to manufacture Molotov cocktails and grenades. By then we had learned of the German plans to make Warsaw completely Judenrein, free of Jews. The end was drawing near. Feverishly we worked preparing ourselves to face the enemy by building secret hiding places and bunkers, storing food, and practicing with small arms.

None of us expected to survive an attack on the Nazis nor did we even expect to influence in the smallest way the war. But nevertheless, a profound conviction that our cause was just drove us on.

On Passover—April 19, 1943—at two o'clock in the morning, the guards of the resistance organization noticed movements of new German troops near the Ghetto wall. The whole Ghetto was immediately alerted. Fighting groups took up their positions. Others were ordered to the prepared bunkers and hiding places, and when the first German soldiers marched into the Ghetto in the morning, they found the streets empty.

Suddenly, at certain intersections, they came under fire. From buildings, from windows, from rooftops of houses, Jews were shooting. The Germans withdrew. They set up artillery around the Ghetto walls and from there they systematically bombarded our Ghetto positions.

The Ghetto did not yield. A Jewish unit under the command of Hersh Berlinsky waited for the Germans at the entrance to the brush-making factory, where one of our few Ghetto land mines was planted. The first German ranks entered the factory; a silent signal a moment later; a loud explosion, and German corpses laid strewn on the ground amidst their own wrecked weapons. Unfortunately, it was the only one of our four mines to go off.

Such were the arms with which we fought. We were so poorly equipped. We had only a handful of grenades and revolvers against the combined might of the Wehrmacht.

Day after day, week after week passed in fighting. In the first days, the Jewish fighters tried to hold on to their positions. Then, they shifted to partisan methods. Groups would emerge from the bunkers to seek out the enemy. In these encounters, whoever saw the other first and was quickest with his weapon was the victor of the moment. Inexperienced, untrained civilians fought against a well-drilled army—a primitive Molotov cocktail against a tank, a gun against a flame-thrower, a revolver against a machine gun.

One side of the street against the other. One house against the next. Block after block, street after street, the Germans set on fire. The fire that swept the Ghetto turned night into day. The flames, the heat, and the suffocating smoke drove the Jews from their houses and bunkers. Men, women, and children jumped out of the windows and ran through the burning winds looking for places where they could breathe. But where could they go when everything was burning?

I can still see the towers of flame. I can still smell the stench of burning houses and hear the agonizing screams for help.

And in the midst of this flaming hell, the resistance went on until the entire Ghetto was a charred rubble. General Stroop, who destroyed the Warsaw Ghetto, stated in an official report that the Jewish uprising came to an end on May 16 after four weeks of struggle.[3]

We know, of course, that after that date the Ghetto was unable to continue organized resistance since the majority of our military organization had been killed. Mordecai Anilewicz, the leader of the uprising, and his entire staff at Mila 18[4] were gassed. Many others were burned to death, but for long weeks afterward, other Jews remained hidden in the still-smoldering ruins and bunkers and would not give up themselves.

For weeks shots were still heard in the Ghetto. The same General Stroop in another report informed his superiors that he blew up or gassed 631 Jewish bunkers. This means 631 Jewish points of resistance. No one knows exactly the number of Jews who perished in the bunkers. No one can tell about their last hours or their deaths.

Those final days united them all—those who had fallen with arms in hand, those who were gassed, those who suffocated in the smoking ruins, and those who were burned to their death. They were all united in one great chain of resistance against their enemy.

During the days of the uprising, the Jewish underground sent radio information to the world, to our representatives in the Polish government-in-exile in England. We pleaded for ammunition, for help, but the world sat silently by. Our people were entirely alone, abandoned. Those of us who survived can never forget the feeling of desertion we experienced. We shall never be able to find justification for having been forsaken in our last hours of struggle.

One year later, I was in the uprising of the city of Warsaw, and I remember at that time the planes flying over the city, throwing down arms and medical supplies for the fighters.

But when our Warsaw Jews were fighting, the skies over the Ghetto were empty.

In the months afterwards, we learned of other Jewish uprisings in ghettos, towns, and death camps. Later, as the Allies came closer, the other civilian uprisings took place. But the Warsaw Ghetto uprising—doomed from the start yet inspired by the highest ideals of humanity and human dignity—became the symbol of heroism and resistance for all people—and for all time.

RICHARD GLAZER

I am a survivor of the Treblinka camp and witnessed the uprising in the camp on August 2, 1943.

Let me first tell you something about the general character of the camp because it is important for the uprising. Treblinka was a very small camp. It had very small dimensions, some 300 by 500 meters, and a tremendous capacity—as many as 18,000 people a day were killed there. Except for the bottleneck on the railroads, Treblinka could have had all the six million Jews killed in the Second World War.

You must understand that these people had been persecuted for a long time even before they were deported, so they kept their last bit of property up to the last moment in the form of gold, precious metals, jewels, money, and so on which were easily transportable. Just imagine 5,000, 10,000, 15,000 people a day—a fantastic richness piled in Treblinka into a huge—what I call "mammon" and this "mammon" corrupted all the German SS, the Ukrainian guards as well the inhabitants of the whole region. The inhabitants of the whole region were very, very poor farmers with a very low level of education. They were understandably eager to enrich themselves, even though they had fear of the Nazis who would torture to the death anyone who was caught hiding a Jew, along with the Jew.

So, these were the general conditions which we had to keep in mind when preparing the uprising. It meant for us no help outside Treblinka at all. Last but not least, we shouldn't forget the traditional anti-Semitism in Poland at that time. We couldn't count on any help from the outside, and we knew that our chances for survival even in the event of a miracle that we succeeded in getting out were practically nil.

As for the preparation and organization of the uprising, we found out that out of the 450 inmates who survived after typhus and all the illnesses in the camp, during a time when the transport didn't come due to difficulties the Germans were having with the railroads, only some 40 had some military training, less than ten percent. I myself was at that time very young and had no proper military training.

Only very few had access to the SS barracks and to the ammunition stores. These were very young boys, and one of their tasks was to put a small metal chip into the lock of the ammunition stores. The Germans couldn't open the door so they called people from the locksmithy. The locksmiths were Jews so a key was made for the munitions store. The first grenades and the guns could have been smuggled out only with the help of these young boys, around 13 and 14 years old. It happened that on the day when we decided to start the uprising, the grenades that had been smuggled out were without fuses so the whole thing had to be postponed and the grenades smuggled back again.

At last, on August 2, the uprising started. We counted on some help. One kilometer from Treblinka was another camp, a slave labor camp. Probably the Nazis used this camp to hide the existence of the extermination camp. We were counting eventually on the help of the slave labor from this camp because the Germans brought those people to work outside of the camp, but that didn't happen.

The whole thing was supposed to start then at four o'clock in the afternoon with the blasting of the first grenade. But some ten minutes before, we saw that one of the traitors— there were, of course, traitors, very few, but there were traitors in Treblinka—was speaking to one of the SS, so the whole thing had to start before. We succeeded in setting Treblinka on fire and it was burned down. However, we did not succeed in attacking the watch towers or in cutting the connection to the military garrison in Malkinia.[5]

The whole uprising was half a success and half a failure. It was an act of despair in a time when we in Treblinka felt simply abandoned by the whole world. It was an act to let the world know, and not be slaves of the Nazis, and not have to burn our own people.

ESTHER RAAB

I have the distinction of being one of the 14 Sobibor survivors today in the world. I hasten to say that in spite of the fact that Sobibor is seldom mentioned, I want to say that Sobibor was exclusively an extermination center. Those who were there, like myself, were selected for sorting the clothing and valuables of the murdered, and others served in domestic chores for the SS.

The commandant of our camp was Gustav Wagner and his associate was Karl Frenzel.[6] Those two bloodthirsty hounds were only satisfied when transports for death arrived. Once there was a slowdown in the arrivals, and Wagner came into the camp, took out some young men and, before killing them, he tortured them by skinning their fingers. Frenzel was in charge of the arrivals. Once—I witnessed it—he spotted an infant among the arrivals. He grabbed it by its little feet and smashed the skull against the wall of the freight car.

Just for the record, there was a tragic competition between Sobibor and Belzec, at our expense, as to which death camp exceeded in its murderous accomplishment. On one of his spot inspections to the camp, Himmler was shown how 700 women were brought in from Majdanek. They had to undress, and their heads were shaved before they were gassed.[7]

The uprising in Sobibor came in October of 1943. The plans were made before, but the opportunity availed itself when a transport of Russian war prisoners came for extermination and a small group was selected for labor. Among them was the war prisoner Sasha Piechorski with whom the in-group began to finalize the uprising. One hour before the uprising, Sasha stood up and told us that we were all doomed to die. He did not believe that any of us would survive. However, if any one of us should make it and survive, he wanted him or her to swear to tell the story of hell as long as he or she might live.

I am fortunate to tell the story in their name.

LEON WELLS

As I'm asked here to give testimony about the uprising, I would like to emphasize that uprising or fighting in general in no way elevates my stature as a survivor or diminishes the Nazi atrocities perpetrated on the victims whom they killed because they did not fight. This statement is important to me because of the introduction of a most offensive philosophy which is called the "sheep theory,"[8] which is especially emphasized by some Jewish leaders.

In the middle of June 1943, I was the last one of my family of seven brothers and sisters and parents and grandparents. I was taken into the Death Brigade which the Germans named Sonderkommando 1005. The purpose of this Death Brigade was to erase all traces of Nazi atrocities so that no witnessing of the atrocities could take place after the war. I think it may have started in 1943 when the Nazis saw that their armies were retreating.

We dug up the graves of people that had been killed, burned their bodies, ground their bones, and took out the gold teeth or any gold we found in these ashes. We normally went through about two thousand bodies a day.

It seems that the Germans had been keeping an exact list of how many people had been shot and where they were buried since they had come into east Poland in 1941. In 1942, while at the Janowska camp, I got sick with typhus, and after three days I was taken to the "sands" in the back of the Janowska camp in Lvov to be shot. I dug my own grave, but at the last minute, after my name was called and crossed off the list, I was able to escape. However, I was presumed by the SS to be dead.

A year later in 1943, as a member of the Death Brigade, I was digging up these same graves to burn the bodies, and we could only find 182 of the 183 bodies on the list. I was the 183rd person. For three days we looked for the missing body so as not to leave any traces of these Nazi murders, but after three days we gave up.

We had been in this Death Brigade since June 15, 1943. There must have been quite a few groups before us because after two weeks these groups were shot and a new group was brought in. We started with 40 and ended up, on November 19, 1943, with 123 Jewish prisoners of war. According to some German documents I found, there were 23 such brigades, of which only three were composed of Russian prisoners of war.

During this time, we also dug up the graves of the Polish leadership that disagreed when Germany wanted to set up a Polish government. Poland was one of the few countries under Nazi occupation that did not set up their own government. Other countries, including Denmark, Holland, Hungary, Bulgaria, and Italy had cooperation governments.[9]

When these 38 people were taken and given the order to set up a government and they refused, they were all shot. It was Yom Kippur Eve, 1943. We dug up these 38 bodies, and I was one of the few witnesses left to note how these people were shot and how they were buried. They were elegantly dressed, with suits and ties, as apparently they were coming to an official dinner. This is how we found them in the graves, and we burned the bodies on Yom Kippur 1943.

In November 1943—after all the Jews were already eliminated from Lemberg and from Galicia—we decided to make an uprising. Why? It was a matter of survival among survival, but mostly we were tired. It was finished now. We were not afraid anymore that they would shoot some other people because of us.

Here is a classical example of what my predecessor said. There was a man in our group by the name of Goldberg. Goldberg was a man in his early forties, a former employee of a Polish school, an ex-fighter, and member of the Polish legionnaires.

We came to him as he was getting undressed, and we said to him, "Goldberg, don't you know we are going to attempt an escape tonight?" His answer was "What for? I lost my wife and seven children. I don't care. Good luck to you. Maybe you will survive, but for me, what does life matter any more?" He laid down to sleep, and he was shot within a few minutes later. Maybe it's because I was just 18 that my drive was a little bit different.

I couldn't have survived, probably, because only a few of us survived from this uprising, if not for a Polish family, whom I had not known before the war, who took me in with another escapee and other Jews and hid us in their basement until the liberation of 1944 when the Russians came in.

These people did not get paid. They did this on their own, sacrificing their whole family. Their name was Kalwinski— Mrs. Kalwinski died just a few months ago. Without these people, I don't believe I would have survived. Your own desire was simply not enough; some outside help was needed.

This is a short story allowed in the ten minutes about the uprising in the Death Brigade.

ALEXANDER DONAT

After the presentations of my predecessors, there is little I have to add, although there are just a few footnotes I would like to add.

I was one of the people hidden in the 631 bunkers, as we called them, or hideouts that Vladka Meed mentioned in her account. At the moment of the uprising on April 19, the majority of the Warsaw Jews were hidden in bunkers.

Before the resistance and the revolt of January 18 and April 19, we all knew that the end was coming soon and that the final liquidation of the Warsaw Ghetto was just a matter of time. Anyone who was in a position to escape from the Ghetto did so.

There were several young people who were involved in organizing the Jewish Fighting Organization and who were involved in another military organization as well as several hundred so-called "wild fighters," not affiliated with any organizations, who were armed. But the

50,000-60,000 of the Ghetto inmates were unarmed. We were all willing and ready to fight, but, of course, we had no weapons. We were the army that decided to resist the German orders to surrender.

In a few short words, I would like to relate the history of our bunker. Before the April revolt, bunkers and underground passages leading from one building to another were built in practically all the buildings of the Warsaw Ghetto. The whole Ghetto had been converted into an underground city. You could cross a whole block, which was quite a distance, without ever going out onto the street, without leaving the cellars or the attics of the buildings. In our shelter there were about 40 people—men, women, old people and only a few children. Personally, I was very lucky. Two weeks before the revolt, I had managed to give away my only child at the time, who was five, to our Christian friends who hid him. He survived the war, first under their personal care and then in a Catholic orphanage near Warsaw.

As I said, about 60,000 people were left in the Ghetto when the uprising started. There were about 10,000 people who were sheltered at the Toebbens[10] factory and other factories who were not in a position to hide. They surrendered immediately. But 50,000 decided to defy the German orders and not surrender. This was a wonderful act of defiance. The uprising in the Warsaw Ghetto was not just a revolt of the 1,000-1,500 armed units, but it was an unarmed uprising of 50,000 men, women, and children who decided it was better to be burned in the flames of the Warsaw Ghetto than to surrender and be sent to Treblinka.

There were 40 of us in our bunker, as I said, and only one man had a gun. It wasn't because we didn't want them; we just couldn't get any more. As one of the historians of this period says, the fighters in the Warsaw Ghetto were limited only by the availability of arms. If we had had 50,000 weapons, we would have had 50,000 fighters.

Eventually, this unarmed resistance forced Stroop, a combat general, to turn into an arsonist because he couldn't force the 50,000 people to leave their shelters. As he writes in his account, he decided to set every building on fire. He didn't have to fight with us. He was beyond the reach of our weapons because the ones we had were very primitive, very poor, and handmade, as Vladka pointed out—handmade Molotov cocktails, a few guns, very few rifles, and, as far as I can remember, one machine gun. What we needed was rifles and machine guns, not revolvers.

Stroop proceeded to set fire to one building after another. Our building was in a strategic position because it was located on the corner of Muranowska Street and Zamenhof Street where many of the battles took place. On the eighth day, a fierce battle took place not far from us. For the first and only time in the battle of the Warsaw Ghetto, 18 Poles appeared on Muranowska Square and participated in the actual combat. Losses were very heavy. All other acts of sympathy were just of a cosmetic nature. The alleged Polish help to the Ghetto was really of no military value and of no consequence.

On the eighth day, our time came. Buildings in Warsaw were built around a courtyard. On the far side of the courtyard were the dwelling sites. The Germans appeared in the courtyard yelling for everybody to come out. Nobody showed up. They then put gasoline on the ground floor and the wooden staircases and set fire to the building. At the same time, they threw hand grenades into the cellars where many people were hidden, and on the ground floors.

The attic was on the fourth floor under the roof, and after half an hour the flames and the smoke came up to us, and we had to leave the attic in order not to suffocate or be burned alive. We tried to escape to the roof and get to the neighboring building, but the adjacent building was already in flames. We sat on the boards on the roof and wondered what to do. We had only two alternatives: to commit suicide right there by jumping down from the fourth floor or by being burned alive, or our last hope, our last resort, was to take some cyanide which my wife, who was a pharmacist in the Warsaw Ghetto, carried with her in a little bag.

Unfortunately, or maybe fortunately, in the scramble of jumping to the burning stairs, the bag and our last hope were lost. We decided it was never too late to die, so we decided to go down through the burning staircase and surrender. There was a German officer standing there with a timer, and as we appeared with our hands up, he told us we were lucky. He had set a deadline of two seconds later for anyone who appeared to be kept alive to have the privilege of perishing in Treblinka. Anyone coming out after that time was to be shot on the spot. At that moment, people appeared from other gates and staircases, and they were shot on the spot.

I will spare you the story of our anguish as we were on a death train going to a death camp. We were very tired and emaciated after being in the shelter for nine days. But we still decided that we would jump, no matter what happened, if the train was going to Treblinka. If the train was going to Lublin, we would take our chances.

Now we come to the second chapter of what is relevant to our topic—Lublin. In Lublin we were sent Majdanek. By the way, I want to point out that of the 40 people in our shelter, 20 took poison right away when the building started burning. Of the 20 people who left the shelter, we were the only two to survive. Even the man with the gun who managed to escape to the other side was arrested, sent to Treblinka, and then sent to Lublin. It was very strange. There were two selections in Treblinka where people were chosen to be sent to other camps, to Majdanek. He was one of them, and he perished in Majdanek.

I'm going to skip the story about Majdanek, but I want to point out only one thing. Sobibor, Treblinka, and Belzec were links of the same murder train that is known as Operation Reinhard. Reinhard Heydrich was Himmler's main helper who was killed by [Czech] patriots in 1942, so they decided to honor his name by giving the name Operation Reinhard to the extermination of the Polish Jews.

The methods of gassing and the whole procedure was uniform in all three camps and, as the commandant of Treblinka said at his trial, there was a special order not to let any children survive. In other words, this was the same organization. There were three camps. Majdanek and Auschwitz were 50-50—half extermination and half concentration camps. In other words, when you arrived in Auschwitz as a Jew, you had a chance, a slight chance, but a chance to survive.

I would like to say a few words about certain conclusions concerning the subject of operating resistance. There is a problem that has bothered the researchers and the survivors for 36 years now, that is, whether uprisings saved lives or whether they just saved the honor of the Jewish people in these areas. I don't think there is an answer so far to this problem, and, of course, this is beyond the scope of our discussion here.

DISCUSSION

IRVING GREENBERG: The common theme is an expectation not to survive, in the sense that no one would help. Yet there was a sense that you had to somehow do this anyway. I just wondered to what extent people said this at the time and to what extent you felt it? What was the driving sense that you wanted to communicate in doing this nevertheless?

ESTHER RAAB: When they brought us in, we did not really know what was going on in the camps. There were rumors, but nobody believed them. I was very young—we were all young. The minute that we noticed what was going on, we decided that it was better to get shot on the barbed wire than to go to the gas chamber.

RICHARD GLAZER: And may I put it the other way? Of course, I've been asked many times what makes one survive. I don't believe that it's the physical fitness primarily. There is something which is more valuable than the physical fitness.

I think it's simply faith in life. Of course, I was very very young, but the thought that I wouldn't survive never came to me. I never gave up. Maybe it's only because I was so young, but in my view the primary thing was faith in life.

IRVING GREENBERG: Yet you did decide to draw that fire upon yourselves by trying to storm the watch towers when you could have simply run into the forest, so although there was the condition you would live, on the other hand there was a willingness to die for making the statement.

RICHARD GLAZER: Right. It's always a mixture—the fighting and, of course, the longing to survive.

ESTHER RAAB: May I add something? If the question is about organized resistance, I guess quite an important factor was the beliefs of the young people. The young people belonged to certain organizational groups in the prewar time, and this imbued them with certain beliefs in humanity and behavior and an attitude toward life that gave them the strength to be the leaders in the Resistance. The role of our youth during the Nazi occupation has not yet been recognized in our literature or history. They were the planners and the organizers of the revolts in the ghettos and in the camps.

Notes

1 ZOB is the Polish acronym for Jewish Fighting Organization: Zydowska Organizacja Bojowa.

2 Bundists were members of socialist trade unions.

3 SS Brigadier General (Brigadeführer) Jürgen Stroop. After the war he was tried in Poland and executed in 1951. Stroop's own report on the liquidation of the Warsaw Ghetto has been translated into English and published. See *The Stroop Report: the Jewish Quarter of Warsaw Is No More,* translated and annotated by Sybil Milton (New York, 1979).

4 Mila 18 was the street address of the headquarters of the Jewish uprising.

5 Malkina was about 20 miles north-northwest of Treblinka.

6 Wagner was not the commandant but a notoriously brutal SS guard, known to inmates as the "Hangman of Sobibor." For a short profile see Konnilyn Feig, *Hitler's Death Camps* (New York, 1981), p. 289. The commandants of Sobibor were Richard Thomalla, Fritz Stangl and Franz Reichleitner.

7 Survivors' accounts of a visit by Himmler to Sobibor differ as to dates and circumstances. For a discussion see Feig, 286.

8 A reference to the assertions that the Jews offered no resistance to their murderers.

9 Poland was partitioned by Germany and the Soviet Union in 1939. Germany annexed some territories while instituting occupation governments in others. After the German invasion of the Soviet Union in June 1941, all of Poland was placed under some form of direct German rule.

It should be noted that a Danish government-in-exile was set up in London in 1940, although King Christian X remained on the throne during the German occupation.

10 Walter C. Toebbens was one of several industrialists who founded enterprises in the Warsaw Ghetto in order to exploit Jewish labor.

CHAPTER XII

DISCOVERING THE 'FINAL SOLUTION'

Moderator: Marvin Kalb (USA): Television journalist.

John W. Pehle (USA): Former executive director of War Refugee Board.

Prof. Jan Karski (USA): Professor of political science, Georgetown University; courier for Polish government-in-exile during World War II.

Lt. Gen. (Ret.) Vassily Yakovlevich Petrenko (USSR): Commander of Soviet troops that liberated Auschwitz.

Robert Wolfe (USA): Archivist and historian; chief, Modern Military Branch, U.S. National Archives.

Institutional identifications are those at the time of the Conference.

MARVIN KALB

This is the concluding panel of the International Liberators Conference. It is called Discovering the Final Solution. In a way for all of us in the last two or three days, this could be regarded as a culmination point.

Late yesterday I met an American participant in this conference, neither a survivor of the camps nor a liberator. He had spent most of the day here, not all of it. It was too painful, he explained. Then after a moment he said, "It made me think back. Where was I during 1942, 1943? What did I know? What did I do?" He shook his head and again there was a look of pain, perhaps some embarrassment, that passed through his eyes. He went on, "I kept thinking that I must have known. I must have read stories in the paper, but I don't remember."

Sometimes we don't remember, those of us who were on the fringes of this mass murder. We don't remember what we cannot accept. A British journalist, on entering one of the camps, said, "It is my duty to describe something that is beyond the imagination of mankind."

When one of our panelists, Professor Jan Karski, briefed Justice Felix Frankfurter[1] in late 1942 about the massacre of Jews in Poland, the distinguished jurist said, "I can't believe you." The Polish friend with Karski told Frankfurter that Karski was telling the truth. Frankfurter answered, "I did not say this young man is lying. I said I cannot believe him. There is a difference."

It pushes the writer's ability, the speaker's eloquence, the witness' testimony, the listener's credulity, beyond what is natural, beyond the outermost limits of tolerance to absorb the enormity of the crime and, at the same time, the simplicity of the fact. Six million Jews were killed during World War II.

Senator Howard Baker,[2] during the Watergate hearings here in Washington several years ago, used to raise two basic questions about the President's knowledge of the famous break-in. What did he know, and when did he know it? If I may take the prerogative of moderator in this panel and paraphrase the Senator—What did the world know about the Holocaust, and when did it know it?

JOHN PEHLE

Discovering the Final Solution. I can only tell this audience how the enormity of this tragedy came home to me and my colleagues in the United States Treasury Department.

In 1943, I was serving as assistant to Secretary of the Treasury Henry Morgenthau and as director of the Foreign Funds Control. This agency had the responsibility of controlling the assets in the United States of persons and institutions in enemy-occupied countries. It also had the responsibility of passing on people's communications within enemy-occupied territory.

It was our policy to deny all the applications for communications with the territory. This rigid policy, I think, can be likened to the Allies' position on unconditional surrender. It was a black-and-white sort of decision. But in due course, some of the Jewish relief organizations came to us and said they needed desperately to be able to communicate with their people in occupied France who were assisting Jews who were fleeing over the mountains into Spain where they were welcomed by the Spanish people. They needed the right to communicate with their agents, and this could only be done through State Department channels. They needed a license from us to do it.

So after some soul-searching, we granted such licenses, and we discovered after a period that none of these communications was going forward.

When we asked some of our sympathetic friends in the State Department concerning the State Department policy which seemed to be blocking these communications, we were supplied with a cable recently received from the

United States legation in Switzerland, which was sent on behalf of one of the Jewish relief organizations.

This cable described the wholesale murder of Jews by the Germans. The Minister went on to say in the cable that he was sending us information despite the instructions he had received previously from the State Department not to forward such information for Jewish relief organizations except in the case of emergency, and that the reports were so grave that he felt he should send it anyway.

When Secretary Morgenthau asked the State Department for a copy of the cable that had previously been sent saying not to allow your facilities to be used for this purpose, he was furnished with a cable from which these instructions had been deleted.

Obviously, the State Department was not prepared to defend its censorship edict. These were the series of events that first brought to the attention of a group of us from the Treasury Department what was happening in Europe to the Jews and what was being kept from the American people.

When Secretary Morgenthau, Randolph Paul, who was General Counsel at the Treasury, and I met with President Roosevelt at a special meeting one Sunday afternoon, we brought these facts forcibly to the President's attention. He directed us to take immediate action in remedying the situation. The Treasury staff prepared and the President signed an Executive Order, number 9417, establishing the War Refugee Board. This Board consisted of the Secretary of State, Secretary of the Treasury, and the Secretary of War. I was made executive director. This was on January 22, 1944. It was very late to attempt to carry out the assignment we had been given.

One essential thing that the establishment of the Board and the Executive Order establishing it did, was that, overnight, it changed the policy of the United States government from one of indifference to one of affirmative action to aid the war refugees. The Executive Order stated the new policy in precise language. "It is the policy of this government to take all measures within its power to rescue the victims of enemy oppression who are in imminent danger of death and to afford such victims all possible relief and assistance consistent with the successful prosecution of the war."

The War Refugee Board was given tools to carry out its assignment. We were given money from the President's confidential funds. We fought for the right to have representatives abroad with diplomatic status, and were able to place representatives in Spain, Portugal, Turkey, Sweden, and London. I cannot say that the War Refugee Board accomplished any miracles, but it was not for lack of trying.

Our representative in Sweden, Iver Olsen, was instrumental in the appointment by the Swedish government of Raoul Wallenberg as its diplomatic representative in Hungary, and War Refugee Board funds helped finance Wallenberg's courageous and successful intervention in Hungary on behalf of Jews who had been sentenced to death.[3]

We assisted the private relief agencies in their work. We convinced most Latin American Governments not to disavow passports which their representatives in Europe had issued without authority, which resulted in a special camp being established by the Germans for people who held such passports, many of whose lives were saved. But by and large, I am afraid that the American effort to save the oppressed people of Europe was too little and too late.

With reference to what Marvin Kalb said about the difficulty of accepting the existence of the Holocaust, one experience I had highlights this difficulty. In the Spring of 1944, the War Refugee Board received two eyewitness accounts of what was happening in the German death camps. We felt that these were detailed accounts that explained exactly what was happening and how it was happening, and we felt that these documents should put to rest any remaining doubts about the execution of Hitler's program.

We duplicated these reports and released them with the War Refugee Board imprimatur with a one-week release date so that the press would have a chance to digest the reports and write their stories. I recall the next day I received a telephone call from Elmer Davis, who was director of the Office of War Information. Elmer Davis was a well-known and respected liberal journalist. He asked me to withdraw the release. I was astounded by his reaction, so I went to his office and talked to him and his staff.

They felt that no one would believe what we were saying, and that, therefore, they would tend to disbelieve other statements made by the Office of War Information relating to the war effort. They referred to the Belgian atrocity stories in World War I, some of which turned out to be false. In any event, we did not withdraw the release and the facts were printed in detail in *The New York Times* and in many national publications. I only refer to this incident to add some evidence of the reluctance of the human mind to accept the existence of the so-called Final Solution.

Finally, I tend to be an optimist. I believe that knowledge of the Holocaust can help prevent future genocides. While the War Refugee Board, despite all its struggles, was only able to bring 1,000 refugees to the United States outside immigration quotas, since then hundreds of thousands of refugees from all over the world have been welcomed to the United States.

We can only pray that the world in some ways, at least, is improving.

JAN KARSKI

I appreciate having been invited to this conference. It is my duty to participate.

The subject "Discovering the Final Solution" requires consideration of the following questions:

1) What and when did the western leaders as well as western public opinion learn about the Jewish tragedy?

2) In what way did the information reach them?

3) What was the reaction? According to evidence?

I, among many, did play a part in this story, and my usefulness to this conference lies in reporting on it for the record.

In the middle of the Summer 1942, I received a message from the delegate of the Polish government in exile for the homeland, Cyril Ratajski, that he approved of my request to be sent secretly to London as a courier for the leaders of political parties organized in the Central Political Committee, and for the delegate himself. The coming expedition was to be my fourth secret trip between Warsaw, Paris, and London.

Sometime in September 1942, the delegate informed me that the leaders of two Jewish underground organizations, the Socialist Bund and the Zionists, learned about my mission and requested permission to use my services for their own communications to their representatives in London, to the Polish government, and to the Allied authorities. The delegate was sympathetic and I agreed.

Soon after, I met the two Jewish leaders on two occasions. They met me jointly to emphasize that their communications were on behalf of all Polish Jews regardless of their political differences. They identified themselves by their functions (naturally, no names). All postwar literature identifies them as Leon Feiner (Bund leader) and Adolf Berman (Zionist). For the record, I must add that Walter Laqueur, in his recently published book, *The Terrible Secret,* suggests that the Zionist leader might have been Menachem Kirschenbaum.

The Jewish leaders sent through me various messages, instructions, and appeals to various quarters. All of them you will find in Laqueur's book as well as in a multitude of other books dealing with World War II, my own book and articles published during the war included.

Because of time limitations, I selected only those which directly pertain to the subject under discussion. Some other important ones I shall regretfully ignore.

The message given to me to relay to the Polish and Allied governments is as follows:

The unprecedented destruction of the entire Jewish population is not motivated by Germany's military requirements. Hitler and his subordinates aim at the total destruction of the Jews before the war ends and regardless of its outcome. The Polish and Allied governments cannot disregard this reality. The Jews in Poland are helpless. They have no country of their own. They have no independent voice in the Allied councils. They cannot rely on the Polish underground or population-at-large. They might save some individuals—they are unable to stop the extermination. Only the powerful Allied governments can help effectively. The Polish Jews appeal to the Polish and Allied governments to undertake measures in an attempt to stop the extermination. They place historical responsibility on the Polish and Allied governments if they fail to undertake those measures.

1. A public announcement that prevention of the physical extermination of the Jews become a part of the overall Allied war strategy, at the same time informing the German nation through radio, air-dropped leaflets, and other means about their government's crimes committed against the Jews.

2. All available data on the Jewish ghettos; concentration and extermination camps; names of the German officials directly involved in the crimes; statistics; facts and methods used should be spelled out. And public and formal demand for evidence that such a pressure has been exercised and Nazi practices directed against the Jews stopped.

3. Public and formal appeals to the German people to exercise pressure on their government to make it stop the exterminations.

4. Placing the responsibility on the German nation as a whole if they fail to respond and if the extermination continues.

5. Public and formal announcement that, in view of the unprecedented Nazi crimes against the Jews and in hope that those crimes would stop, the Allied governments were to take unprecendented steps.

These steps would include:

1. Certain areas and objects in Germany would be bombed in retaliation. The German people would be informed before and after each action that the Nazis' continued extermination of the Jews prompted the bombing.

2. Certain German war prisoners who, having been informed about their government's crimes, and who still profess solidarity with and allegiance to the Nazis, would be held responsible for the crimes committed against the Jews as long as those crimes continued.

3. Certain German nationals living in the Allied countries who, having been informed about the crimes committed against the Jews and who still profess solidarity with the Nazi government, would be held responsible for those crimes.

4. Jewish leaders in London, particularly Szmul Zygelbojm (Bund) and Dr. Ignace Szwarcbard (Zionist), are solemnly charged to make all efforts so as to make the Polish government formally forward these demands at the Allied councils.

Now I shall talk about my mission to the President of the Polish Republic (Wladyslaw Raczkiewicz). My message to him included the following comments:

Many among those who directly or indirectly contribute to the Jewish tragedy profess their Catholic faith. The Polish and other European Jews sent to Poland feel entitled on humanitarian and spiritual grounds to expect protection of the Vatican. Religious sanctions, excommunication included, are within the Pope's jurisdiction. Such sanctions, publicly proclaimed, might have an impact on the German people. They might even make Hitler, a baptized Catholic, reflect.

Because of the nature of this message and the source it came from, as well as because of diplomatic protocol requirements, I was instructed to deliver the message to the President of the Republic only. They wanted him to use his conscience and wisdom in approaching the Pope. I was explicitly forbidden to discuss that subject with the Jewish leaders. Their possible maladroit intervention might be counterproductive.

The message to the Prime Minister and Commander in Chief (General Wladyslaw Sikorski), Minister of Interior (Stanislaw Mikolajczyk), Zygelbojm, and Szwarcbard was as follows:

Although the Polish people at large sympathize or try to help the Jews, many Polish criminals blackmail, rob, denounce, or murder the Jews in hiding. The underground authorities must apply punitive sanctions against them, executions included. In the last case, the identity of the guilty ones and the nature of their crimes should be publicized in the underground press.

Zygelbojm and Szwarcbard must use all their pressure so that pertinent instructions would be issued.

In order to avoid any risk of anti-Polish propaganda, I was explicitly forbidden to discuss that subject with any non-Polish Jewish leaders. I was to inform Zygelbojm and Szwarcbard about that part of my instructions.

The message to the Allied individual government/civic leaders as well as to international Jewish leaders was as follows:

There is a possibility to save some Jews if money were available. The Gestapo is corrupted not only on the low level, but also on the medium and even high level. They would cooperate for gold or hard currency. The Jewish leaders are able to make appropriate contacts.

Some Jews might be allowed to leave Poland semiofficially in exchange for gold, dollars, or delivery of certain goods.

Some Jews would be allowed to leave Poland provided they have original foreign passports. Origins of those passports are unimportant. As large a supply of such passports as possible should be sent. They must be blank. Forged names, identification, data, etc., would be overlooked by the German authorities – for money, of course.

Provisions must be made that those Jews who do succeed in leaving Poland would be accepted by the Allied or neutral countries.

Some Jews of non-Semitic appearance could leave the ghettos, obtain false German documents, and live among other Poles under assumed names.

Money to bribe the ghetto's guards and various officials as well as subsistence funds are needed.

Many Christian families would agree to hide the Jews in their homes. But they risk instant execution if discovered by the Germans. All of them are in dire need themselves. Money is needed, at least for subsistence.

Money, medicines, food, and clothing are most urgently needed by the survivors in the ghettos. Subsidies obtained from the delegate of the Polish government as well as other funds sent through various channels by the Jewish international organizations are totally insufficient. More hard currency, sent without any delay, is a question of life or death for thousands of Jews.

In addition to all the messages I was to carry, both Jewish leaders solemnly committed me to do my utmost in arousing the public opinion in the free world on behalf of the Jews. I solemnly swore that, should I arrive safely in London, I would not fail them.

At the end of the second meeting, the Bund leader confronted me with the following. He knew the English people. My report might seem incredible. My mission would be enhanced if I were able to say that I witnessed the Jewish tragedy. The Jewish underground does have some contacts, even with Gestapo. They are able to smuggle me to the Warsaw Ghetto. They are even able to smuggle me—in disguise—to the Belzec camp. In the Ghetto, he himself, would be my guide. In Belzec a Nazi official would take care of my expedition. Both trips are dangerous, but they are feasible. He has no right to ask me to undertake them. But, he said, "Witold" (my pseudonym at the time), I know much about you and your work. Who knows—perhaps you will volunteer to help our Jewish cause." I agreed.

I visited the Jewish Ghetto twice in the middle of October 1942. A few days later, I visited Belzec. All three trips proved successful. These trips became the last items in collecting data, messages, instructions, and complaints of various political leaders in the underground. Two or three days later, I embarked on my secret journey to London.

Again, my trip was successful. This fourth secret mission between Paris, London, and Warsaw lasted 21 days: Warsaw-Berlin-Brussels-Paris-Lyon-Perpignan-Pyrenees Mountains on foot-Barcelona-Madrid-Algeciras-Gibralter. In Gibralter I had a ceremonious dinner with the Governor and a good night's sleep. The next day a plane was waiting.

In the last week of November 1942, I already began reporting in London. Now one must realize that my Jewish reports were only a part of my overall mission. In addition, I was supposed to go back to Poland—on my fifth mission. The Polish Prime Minister's office, which organized all of my contacts, asked every individual I had been sent to not to identify me publicly.

As to my Jewish materials, I was not the only informant. Since 1941, secret radio contacts with London functioned. Coded data on the Jewish ghettos, deportations, and extermination had been regularly transmitted from Poland to London for information and public distribution. Most of the messages, however, were considered as lacking credibility. The head of the secret radio service, throughout the entire war, was Stefan Korbonski, who was eventually the last head of the Polish underground state.

To whom did I report the Jewish material in England during the period November 1942–June 1943? Because of time constraints, I give here only the most important personalities.

1) The Poles: All government and political leaders; Liaison to Cardinal Hlond (at the time residing in the Vatican): Monsignor Kacynski; Jewish leaders: Zygelbojm (Bund); Szwarcbard (Zionists); Grosfeld (Socialist).

2) The English: four members of the War Cabinet: Anthony Eden, Foreign Secretary; Arthur Greenwood, Labor Party; Lord Cranborne, Conservative Party; Hugh Dalton, President of the Board of Trade.

I also talked with Lord Selbourne, War Office, European underground resistance; Miss Ellen Wilkinson, Labor, Member of Parliament; William Henderson, Labor Party leader, Member of Parliament; Owen O'Malley, British ambassador to the Polish government; Anthony D. Biddle, American ambassador to the Polish government; and Sir Cecil Hurst, chairman of the United Nations War Crime Commission.

I pressed for and did contact several nongovernment English personalities: H.G. Wells, world-known author; Arthur Koestler, world-known author; Victor Gollancz, Penguin publishing firm; Allen Lane, Penguin; Kingsley Martin, editor-in-chief, *New Statesman* and *Nation;* Ronald Hyde, editor, *Evening Standard;* and Gerard Berry, editor, *News Chronicle.*

Actions resulting from my mission and, no doubt, other reports are as follows:

1) On December 7, 1942, two weeks after I began reporting, the Polish National Council passed a resolution dealing with the Jewish extermination and committing the government to act without any delay.

2) Three days later, on December 10, 1942, the Polish government issued a formal appeal to the Allied governments concerning the extermination of the Jews in Poland.

3) On December 17, 1942, the Allied Council (which included representatives of all Allied governments) unanimously passed a public Appeal of the Allied Nations on behalf of the Jews.

4) Two days later, on December 19, 1942, the President of the Polish Republic sent a note to Pope Pius XII asking for inter-

vention on behalf of the Jews.

5) Then, one month later, on January 18, 1943, the Polish Foreign Minister, Edward Raczynski, presented his government's demands on behalf of the Polish Jews at the Allied Nations' Council. They asked for the bombing of Germany as reprisals for the continued extermination of the Jews, the forwarding of demands to Berlin to let the Jews out of the German-dominated countries, and action as to make the Allied as well as neutral countries accept the Jews who succeeded or would succeed in leaving the German-dominated countries.

He did not advance demands for reprisals against German war prisoners and German nationals living in the Allied countries, considering them contrary to the acceptable practices of international relations.

British Foreign Secretary, Anthony Eden, in the name of His Majesty's government, rejected all demands, offering vague promises to intervene in some neutral countries.

Beginning in March 1943, secret executions of the Polish hoodlums who acted against the Jews were carried out. The names of the criminals and the nature of their crimes were publicized in the underground press.

The Directorate of the Civil Resistance which organized Underground courts had been established already in 1942. It was headed again by Korbonski. Last April—36 years after the war ended—he was decorated by the Israeli ambassador with a Yad Vashem Medal for the Righteous Among the Nations.

In early 1943, numerous articles based on my information appeared in the British press. Public demonstrations had been organized. In May 1943, a pamphlet was published, authored by a prominent Soviet writer, Alexey Tolstoy; German writer Thomas Mann; and myself (described as a "Polish Underground Worker"). The pamphlet was entitled "The Fate of the Jews."

With regard to my mission in the USA, in June 1943, at the suggestion of American Ambassador Biddle, I was sent to Washington, still secretly, under a false name—Jan Karski. I stayed there until August 1943, living on the premises of the [Polish] embassy. The Polish Ambassador, Jan Ciechanowski, supervised my activities and organized my contacts.

I reported to the following individuals (only the most important will be mentioned): Franklin Delano Roosevelt, President of the United States; Cordell Hull, Secretary of State; Henry Stimson, Secretary of War; Francis Biddle, Attorney General; Colonel Donovan, Chief, Office of Strategic Services (OSS); Apostolic Delegate, Cardinal Ameleto, Giovanni Cicognani; Archbishop Mooney; Archbishop Spellman; Archbishop Strich; Dr. Nahum Goldman, President, American Jewish Congress; Rabbi Stephen Wise, President, World Jewish Congress; Waldman, American Jewish Congress; Felix Frankfurter, Justice of the Supreme Court; and Mr. Backer, Joint Distribution Committee.

Among the prominent journalists with whom I spoke were: Mrs. Ogden Reed, publisher, *New York Herald Tribune;* Walter Lippmann; George Sokolsky; Leon Dennen, editor, *The American Mercury;* Eugene Lyons; Dorothy Thompson; William Prescott, *The New York Times;* Frederick Kuh, *Chicago Sun;* and George Creel, former chief, Office of War Information.

Upon my return to London, Prime Minister Mikolajczyk informed me that he would not send me to Poland for the duration of the war. I had seen too many people in the United States and I had become too well-known. The German radio had mentioned my activities in America, describing me, by the way, as a "Bolshevik agent on the payroll of American Jews." Oh, Washingtonians love to gossip! My additional shortcoming—as he explained—were recognizable scars on my wrists. In June 1940, on my third secret expedition, I had been captured by the Gestapo in Preshov, Slovakia. Unable to withstand torture, I tried to commit suicide, cutting my veins with a concealed blade. It did not work.

Transported to Poland for further interrogation, I had been rescued by the underground. But, even after a cosmetic operation, the scars remained. The Gestapo certainly had my files and I had become a public figure, Mikolajczyk argued.

Two months later, in October 1943, I was sent to the United States—for the second time but this time openly and again as Karski—to speak, to write, to report, to inform the public-at-large—openly.

From October 1943 until the end of the war, I delivered some 200 lectures in the United States from coast to coast, from Rhode Island to Florida. In all of them I spoke about the Jewish tragedy. Every lecture was reviewed in the local press.

Then came my articles on what the Jews demanded, on what I saw in the Warsaw Ghetto and Belzec. These were published in *Colliers; New York Times; American Mercury; La France Libre; The Jewish Forum; Common Cause; Herald Tribune; New Europe;* and *Harper's Bazaar*. Many of them were illustrated—several under my personal supervision: "No phony inspiration! Paint as I am telling you." Various exhibitions were organized.

Then, in 1944, still during the war, I published a book, *Story of a Secret State*. Its central theme was my visits to the Warsaw Ghetto and Belzec. The book became a Book-of-the Month Club Selection. It was published simultaneously also in Great Britain, Sweden, Switzerland, France.

Many of you at this conference gave testimony on the Jewish Gehenna.[4] Respect is due to you. The Lord assigned me a role to speak and write during the war, when—as it seemed to me—it might help. It did not.

For me today, October 28, 1981, the curtain is down. The theater is empty.

Furthermore, when the war came to its end, I learned that the governments, the leaders, the scholars, the writers did not know what had been happening to the Jews. They were taken by surprise. The murder of six million innocents was a secret, a "terrible secret" as Laqueur reports.

Then, I became a Jew like the family of my wife, who is sitting in this audience—all of them perished in the ghettos, in the concentration camps, in the gas chambers—so all murdered Jews became my family.

But I am a Christian Jew. I am a practicing Catholic. And, although not a heretic, still my faith tells me: the second Original Sin had been committed by humanity: through commission, or omission, or self-imposed ignorance, or insensitivity, or self-interest, or hypocrisy, or heartless rationalization.

This sin will haunt humanity to the end of time.

It does haunt me. And I want it to be so.

*VASSILY YAKOVLEVICH PETRENKO**

I am here as one of the participants of the Second World War during which the anti-Hitler coalition defeated the armies of the aggressors and saved mankind from fascist slavery. Hitler's troops, in the destruction of which my country—the Soviet Union—made a decisive contribution, were the strongest, the most atrocious and bloodthirsty of all our common enemies.

I am addressing you as one of the soldiers whose fate it was to storm fascist concentration camps to liberate the inmates, citizens of many countries and many nationalities. After all these years, 36 years, the memories have not been erased and the horror of horrible crimes is still there. The bleeding wounds of millions of those who have suffered at the hands of fascist butchers are still open. Another evidence of it is the present confer-

*Gen. Petrenko made his remarks in Russian. This is the simultaneous translation.

ence, which we conduct in a spirit of goodwill and which will help the world.

In January of 1945, the Soviet armed forces continued to liberate enslaved European nations from Hitler's invaders. At that time, the 60th Army, which my division was part of, was fighting on the territory of Poland, fulfilling missions which were part of the Vistula and Oder offensive drive of the First Ukrainian Front. Advancing along the banks of the Vistula River, the 60th Army, apart from other military missions, had the task of capturing Oswiecim [Auschwitz] to liberate the inmates of the fascist concentration camp in that vicinity.

Our soldiers defeated the enemy troops and on January 27 liberated the concentration camp and the area. The advance of Soviet troops was so rapid and decisive that the fascists had failed to kill all the inmates and to conceal the traces of their crimes.

However, many of the inmates liberated by the Soviet Army in Oswiecim were moved to other places and to other parts of Europe. It was not very pleasant. From among those liberated there are some present here at this conference. I wish them good health and personal happiness.

Much has been written about the captives, and the delegates have mentioned it here at this conference. Perhaps it would not seem necessary to talk about the horrors of Oswiecim, but I will say my words. I would like to speak to the young people who are not well informed about the deeds of the Nazis and perhaps do not quite understand what the former inmates have been through.

But there are those who would like to forget the past, to refute these horrible barbaric plans to destroy nations and peoples, and the monstrous means that were used in concentration camps—the way it was planned and the cruelty, how to destroy people in Oswiecim. Oswiecim is one of the first, unparalleled.

A long, long path had to be followed by Soviet soldiers to reach Oswiecim. Over 300 days and bloody battles were necessary to free their country and the countries occupied by Hitler's troops in Europe.

In the battle of Oswiecim, the 60th Army joined other troops, and when they freed the camp, hundreds of Soviet soldiers and officers lost their lives. Therefore, those who visit that museum which exists where that horrible camp was, shake their heads about the mass grave where Soviet soldiers are buried who gave their lives to free the inmates of that camp.

I would like to say to those who are present from socialist countries, and those who came from other countries who freed other camps, that the most horrible concentration camp, the most brutal one, was the Oswiecim concentration camp. Even in the historical past, occupying forces never behaved in the way the so-called civilized fascists did—poisoning, murder, torture, mobile extermination, incinerations in crematoria designed for it, and medical experiments on adults and children. Everything was done by the fascists on men and women who were innocent.

They not only destroyed four million people in Oswiecim, that is, 40 percent of those destroyed in all camps, but they used the dead bodies. Gold teeth were extracted. Human hair and skin were removed to make lamp shades, wallets, and gloves. Fat was used for soap. Bones were ground and used with ashes for fertilizer. There are documents indicating this.

For us, the soldiers who participated in the liberation of inmates of fascist concentration camps, it is very painful to know that many of the fascist war criminals have not yet been punished for their crimes and are living quietly among honest people in many countries. Moreover, they continue fascist propaganda. They praise Hitler and his former assistant murderers, and henchmen are dreaming of revenge and dreaming of new wars.

It is our common duty to the memory of the victims to fight jointly against all forms of fascism and fascist groups, terrorism, and fascist dictatorial regimes to ensure man's basic right to live in peace. The point of departure of the Soviet Union, the Communist Party, the government, and our people is that there is nothing more important to any nation in the world than to secure the right to life.

Present-day means of warfare, as you well know, are horrible indeed. While it took fascist murderers five years to kill four million people in the Oswiecim concentration camp, during World War II over 40 million people lost their lives; if there is a nuclear conflict, all mankind will die in a very short time. For the sake of the memory of the victims of fascism and for the living and coming generations, it is imperative to prevent the horrible threat of self-destruction that is facing us now. We have to destroy nuclear weapons before they destroy the human race on earth.

There is only one way to resolve this situation. That is immediate, honest, equal, and effective negotiations. This is precisely what our country proposes—concrete measures to curb, reduce, and finally destroy nuclear missiles. Mankind must do and should be able to do it. Participants of this conference, inmates of concentration camps, and the liberators: this is a noble cause that we are pursuing.

*ROBERT WOLFE**

Preceding speakers have described their roles as key participants in the discovery of the Holocaust, and in the failed attempt to achieve timely public disclosure and preventative action. Although I served as an infantry officer in the Second World War and in the US Military Government thereafter, I make no claim to a significant role. My discovery of the Holocaust has been through the records of the Nazi perpetrators: the Third Reich paperwork of "the Final Solution of the Jewish question" found among the captured German and Nuremberg trial records in the National Archives.

For the discovery of the Holocaust, the Nuremberg trials were both a boon and a bane. No mere historical research could have mustered the costly five-year effort in staff and resources that were commanded by the proclaimed Allied policy of punishing war criminals. Documents were thus quickly uncovered that we might otherwise still be hunting 35 years later. But documents were also often irretrievably torn from their context, carelessly excerpted, poorly translated, duplicated under various unrelated designations, and incorrectly assembled in artificial folders in a manner that muddles their meaning and taints their authenticity.

The Nuremberg trials are of unquestioned value to history as well as law (in another context, I described them as "existential" justice). Nevertheless, dislocation and distortion of key documentation was inevitable in such a mammoth operation, given the deadline pressures of impatient victor-government paymasters. Subsequent careless use of sources, to say nothing of that genre of fiction which battens on the lurid attraction of jackbooted murder *cum* sex, have added to Holocaust historians' difficulties by giving neo-Nazi revisionists too many opportunities to question the authenticity of specific documents, and therewith the actuality of the Holocaust itself.

Just a few examples: One of the best known Nuremberg trial documents[5] is the partial transcript of the day-long meeting chaired by Hermann Göring on November 12, 1938, just three days after the Kristallnacht, which prepared the total aryanization of the German economy, beginning with the notorious decree fining the victims one billion Reichsmarks to compensate the Nazi perpetrators for the property damage done. To me, the real significance of this document is that it reveals that during extensive discussions, the conferees not only devised the legal measures for the aryanization of the German economy, but unintentionally canvassed the steps and phases which eventually

*The notes to Mr. Wolfe's paper were supplied by the author.

evolved into the so-called Final Solution of the Jewish Question: social, cultural, and personal discrimination, culminating in a Jewish badge of identification and ghettoization; a Central Office for Jewish Emigration (including a preview of the abortive Madagascar project of 1940)[6] which would coordinate expropriation, denaturalization, and expulsion; and finally what Göring referred to cryptically as "a great settlement of accounts" with Jewry should the German Reich "come into foreign policy conflict." Heydrich, at least, clearly anticipated how the insane logic of Nazi anti-Semitism must inexorably end, but Göring and the other conferees, even the venomous Goebbels, seemed unwilling to admit, perhaps even to themselves, that their unbridled racism was leading to mass murder.

This document is of such basic evidentiary value in deciding the disputed issue of whether Nazi leaders premeditated the Holocaust, that it would be preferable if its origin were unblurred. Unfortunately, the paperwork context is complicated. Dr. Fritz Dörr, one of the Reichstag stenographers who recorded the discussion of November 12, 1938, had then submitted his transcript, but retained his stenographic notes. On finding these in the summer of 1945, he again transcribed them, and a copy quickly reached U.S. Military Government Headquarters in Berlin-Zehlendorf. When brought in to identify his transcript, Dörr surrendered his shorthand notes and the ribbon copy.[7]

Now, the vulnerability of this documentary source stems from the fact that the transcripts, ribbon,[8] and carbon, are of early postwar occupation-era vintage, while the 1938 transcripts have disappeared and may well have been destroyed. The best contemporary source, of course, would be Dörr's stenographic notebooks, which came into American Military Government hands, but are not in the Nuremberg file with the postwar transcript. I have been vainly hunting those notes for many years, but am encouraged by a cryptic notation in the Nuremberg file to hope that they may turn up among Office of Strategic Services records scheduled for eventual accession by the National Archives.

The fact that this is only a partial transcript, which some revisionists find suspicious, I find reassuring. What "disinformation" expert would manufacture a partial postwar document when he might just as well manufacture a complete contemporary document? But, as is customary whenever stenographers record extensive discussion, they work in short stints or shifts. This is borne out by Dörr's designation of his odd-numbered stints as "turns 1,3,5, and 7 [Turnus is his German word]." Apparently neither notes nor transcripts of his colleague's "turns" survived.

Another example: the Wannsee Protocols, the minutes of the January 20, 1942 Third Reich interagency meeting to coordinate the so-called Final Solution of the Jewish question, are recognized by anyone familiar with the Holocaust, due perhaps to the dramatically licensed presentation in the Gerald Green TV docudrama. But because the Protocols were offered in evidence as an isolated document in subsequent Nuremberg trials[9]— it had not yet been discovered when the International Military Tribunal pronounced its verdict on Göring and other Nazi leaders—few are aware that it was part and parcel of a series of interrelated documents that render its authenticity incontrovertable.

The only known extant copy of the Wannsee minutes, the 16th of 30 numbered copies, was and is deposited in a two-folder German Foreign Office file bearing the title, "Final Solution of the Jewish Question," which contains documentation pertaining to that subject filed in reverse, approximate chronological sequence from January 25, 1939, through November 30, 1943.[10] This file includes not only the minutes of the Wannsee meeting, but of two other such interagency meetings held in Eichmann's office at Kurfürstenstrasse 116 on March 6 and October 27, 1942.[11] In fact, copy 16 of the minutes of the January meeting was forwarded to the Foreign Office with a covering note announcing the March meeting.[12] Not only do repeated subsequent references document and detail the fact of the Wannsee meeting, but this Foreign Office file contains an initial Heydrich invitation to Undersecretary Luther to a "conference followed by a luncheon on Dec. 9, 1941."[13] On January 8, Heydrich reissued the invitation for January 20, 1942, because of a last minute postponement when "sudden . . . events . . . required the attention of part of the invitees,"[14] an obvious reference to Pearl Harbor. At least two signed copies of both invitations exist; the other sequence addressed to SS Gruppenführer Otto Hofmann was extracted from files of the Race and Resettlement Head Office for Nuremberg use.[15] The fact that copies were found in two entirely separate Nazi agency files, of course, would be hard to manufacture.

If further corroboration of the authenticity of the Wannsee Protocols were required, it may be found in the official diaries of Hans Frank as head of the so-called General Government, that remainder of Poland not formally annexed by Germany. (I was privileged during a 1979 visit to my esteemed colleague, Dr. Pilichowski, in Warsaw, to hold volumes of the Frank diary in my hand, if you want to attest to its authenticity.) In a pre-Christmas 1941 speech to a cabinet session in his headquarters in the Wawel castle in Cracow, Hans Frank said: "I will therefore think of the Jews only in the basic expectation that they disappear . . . in January a great discussion of this question is to take place . . . in the Reich Security Main Office of SS Obergruppenführer Heydrich."[16]

Had we been more careful, at Nuremberg and since, to stress the records, context as well as the content of the Wannsee Protocols, no neo-Nazi revisionist could venture to dispute either.

Yet another example: during a visit to Auschwitz in 1979, I asked one of the archivists whether many used cans of Zyklon-B had been found after the SS evacuation and the Soviet liberation, and whether there were still any on hand. (I did not state my reason for inquiring, which was that I had hitherto seen but one can, a Nuremberg trial exhibit taken from manufacturers' stock, which bore the printed label: "Attention, without warning odor." Kurt Gerstein reported,[17] and Rudolf Hoess, at both the Nuremberg and Auschwitz trials testified, that the trace chemical incorporated into the Zyklon-B pesticide formula to protect its human users, much as is done with natural gas, had to be omitted when it was converted for use on human beings—on Jews to be specific—because it prematurely warned the victims and because it caused violent retching rather than the quiet sleep of carbon monoxide.) The archivist took me to a backroom workshop, where an exhibit specialist showed us several empty Zyklon-B cans of various sizes. I gingerly picked one up; its printed label bore no indication that the warning odor had been deleted, but rubber-stamped thereon was the statement: "Attention, without warning odor."

It is a universal practice of all bureaucracies to use up supplies of outmoded printed labels, by amending them with a hand stamp, before new labels are printed.

A last example: the public interest roused by the 1978 television Holocaust docudrama prompted U.S. government analysts to search still-classified Allied World War II aerial photography for photographic evidence of the Auschwitz-Birkenau gas chambers in operation. When their technically masterful classified study was ready, I was generously given a private presentation by its two authors. I suggested on two counts that publication be withheld pending revision: 1) that the original photographs used by Allied photo analysts in 1944–45, as they still were in 1978 and still are in the cartographic holdings of the National Archives,[18] be published side-by-side with the enlarged, cropped, and captioned versions the authors had derived from them in 1978; 2) that pertinent Allied air force textual records[19] be searched to determine what priorities the hard-worked wartime analysts were given, what their immediate reports disclosed, and what the detailed subsequent reports by the Strategic

Bombing Survey[20] elaborated. The 1978 analysis was based exclusively on postwar eyewitness testimony, trial evidence such as that of Rudolf Hoess, and other ground corroboration not available to Allied analysts in 1944. Nor had any use been made of the best contemporary ground corroboration, records of the SS Concentration Camp Administration,[21] which to be sure were also not available until after the war.

I also expressed two paramount concerns if my caveats were not heeded: first, that the media would seize on the most spectacular 1978 enlargements and captions, and that the general public would assume that labels such as "GROUP ON WAY TO GAS CHAMBER," had been put there in 1944, rather than in 1978. In fairness to the two authors, they agreed to my proposal, but it was too late. Public relations was in the saddle, and a series of high-level lateral passes broke the story.[22] In the event, my fears were justified, and we shall never be able to reverse that first mistaken impression. From this emerged the unsophisticated conclusion that the Allied governments had the photographs, knew the facts, but would not act; a conclusion as damaging as it is simplistic.

My other concern was for a long-range insidious danger. After the initial furor subsided, neo-Nazi revisionists would take advantage of the inevitable reaction of American and other Allied citizens to the implication of indifference or worse on the part of Allied governments and citizenry, and raise doubts about the authenticity of the Allied aerial photography of Auschwitz-Birkenau itself. Soon, the revisionists may be suggesting that it was a convenient coincidence that only after the Holocaust had become a popular media subject, did CIA photo analysts, of all people, surface aerial photographs of Auschwitz gas chambers.

We can, of course, counter with the irrefutable argument that it would have been more convenient to American policy to publish these photographs at the Nuremberg trials, during the early punitive phase of the occupation of Germany, and not when the Federal Republic of Germany had meanwhile become one of our closer allies. If anything, the inopportune political timing speaks for authenticity as does the concatenation of Allied aerial photography and related textual records with seized German records; not only the SS textual records I have already noted, but a sequence of two seized German aerial photographs[23] of Auschwitz-Birkenau taken on December 27, 1944, perhaps to determine what the frantic dismantling and evacuation looked like to Allied air observers, and three frames taken on February 19, 1945, probably to discover what damaging evidence the Soviet liberators were unearthing on the ground. There could be no better corroboration of the authenticity of the Allied photographs than the near-identicality of photographs of Auschwitz-Birkenau taken, analyzed, and filed within a few days of each other by opposing air forces, with nearly a half-year of bitter total warfare ahead before the victor powers would unknowingly hold all the evidence in one hand. That it lay unknown and unused for one-third of a century after war's end may yet be of advantage to history.

If the problem before and during the Holocaust was that no one could and would believe what would happen, and was happening, in the middle of the "civilized" 20th century, as Messers Karski and Pehle have borne witness from this platform today, the problem now and in the future is that most of us cannot grasp that there are many people who claim or believe that the Holocaust *never happened*. One day, when all the eyewitnesses—survivors, liberators, bystanders, and even perpetrators—are gone, each succeeding generation will have to discover anew the truth of the Holocaust. Their only unassailable source will be the contemporary record. The duty of our generation is to avoid any further muddling of that record, lest we provide the means for future revisionists to mislead the innocent, and seduce the depraved into genocidal disaster.

To that paramount purpose, I take the

liberty to suggest that the U.S. Holocaust Memorial Council inscribe the following on its cornerstone: "To overstate the horror of the Holocaust is impossible. To embellish the truth of the Holocaust is unnecessary. To exploit the agony of its martyrs is unworthy."

DISCUSSION

MARVIN KALB: We started this particular panel by asking two questions—What did the world know? And when did it know it?—and the questions, like almost everything else that tries to address this issue, tend to oversimplify the problem.

On the basis of the testimony of our four panelists today, there clearly was information. It was clearly made available to important people early on, in time to have affected some of the outcome. Yet from the record it is also clear that not all that much was actually done to affect the outcome, so we are left, it seems to me, with the very large moral question of why did that happen.

I really would like to address the question to Mr. Pehle first because in your speech you did talk about a cable, for example, that was sent by the State Department representative in which he made reference to yet another cable asking him not to allow the facilities of the Department to be used in transmitting this information. That is very puzzling, and I would like to ask you why. You must have asked the question yourself. What kind of answers did you get from the US government at that time?

JOHN PEHLE: It's hard to look into someone else's mind. There were those who felt that knowledge of the Holocaust spread in the United States would cause such a fervor emanating from the Jewish groups that somehow it would impede the war effort.

There was some element of anti-Semitism. There was the thing we have referred to—you have referred to it and I have too—the reluctance of all of us to comprehend something as tragic as this was going on, that people in the western world that we thought were civilized were engaged in an uncivilized wholesale murder. You tie all those things together and nothing much happened.

MARVIN KALB: When was the cable that you made reference to sent? The one not to use the facilities of the department.

JOHN PEHLE: In the latter part of 1943.

MARVIN KALB: Was this with the knowledge of the Secretary of State?

JOHN PEHLE: As you know, State Department cables very often are sent—and it may have Hull's name at the end of it, but that doesn't mean that Mr. Hull signed it. I don't know. But I think it was consistent with State Department policy at the time.

MARVIN KALB: Do you feel that the policy at the time had the sanction of the White House?

JOHN PEHLE: I don't know.

MARVIN KALB: When the issue was raised before President Roosevelt, and he asked you to take immediate action—and that was in 1944—did you have the impression that the President at that time was shocked by the information brought to him?

JOHN PEHLE: Yes. I think he was particularly shocked by the fact that there was this attempt to suppress the information. Also, we had been misled by the State Department. In other words, when we asked for a copy of the cable, we got an expurgated copy that didn't contain the instructions that had been sent out. Therefore, you had one department of the United States government misleading the Secretary of the Treasury.

So I think the President decided that this whole issue should be taken out, and it was effectively taken out. The staff of the War Refugee Board was largely Treasury people, and we had quite free ability to operate.

MARVIN KALB: Mr. Wolfe, may I address a question to you? Do you have a copy of that cable that we are talking about?

ROBERT WOLFE: The cable would be in the Diplomatic Branch of the National Archives. I have not seen it myself, and the expertise has to be segregated, so I would rather have you consult the experts in the Diplomatic Branch.

MARVIN KALB: I'm just curious whether that particular cable was unique. Was it the only one of its kind or were there a series of cables like that?

ROBERT WOLFE: I would be breaking my own rules if I testified without having looked at the documents. I think that is the kind of thing that needs exploration.

I'm far away from saying that documents don't lie. But if one applies the proper, and I would say old-fashioned, historical canons to documents, one can extract approximate truth or near truth from them. The more people who work at that honestly, the more truth we will get. That's a good research project which I would recommend: Trace that cable down.

MARVIN KALB: General Petrenko, we have heard a great deal about information provided at very top levels of the U.S. government and what American officials did not do once they had that information. I would like to ask you, on the basis of whatever knowledge you may have, was this kind of information known to Soviet staff officers towards the end of the war, early on in the war?

VASSILY YAKOVLEVICH PETRENKO: The Soviet people and the armed forces from the first few months of the war were well-informed about the barbarism of fascism in the occupied areas of the Soviet Union—the hundreds of camps where they immediately started to exterminate people that they captured.

We soldiers who were fighting the war received our information about the barbarism of the fascists against prisoners, war prisoners, and civilians in Oswiecim before our troops attacked it. The personnel knew through the political leadership of the front and the army that along the path of our attack we would encounter concentration camps and certain places where Hitlerites were killing people, including the camp Oswiecim.

Of course, we had such details because our task as commanders was not only to destroy opposing Hitlerite forces, but also to free Polish villages and towns, including a concentration camp around Oswiecim. We didn't have coordinates because that covered a large territory, but we had orders that commanders of units who would attack in that direction should prepare their sanitation and medical battalions to bring immediate help to victims who would be freed from these camps.

In my case, we had our orders. My battalion had these orders on January 27 when we freed that particular camp.

MARVIN KALB: Could you tell us whether you had some sense in advance of what you found at Auschwitz?

VASSILY YAKOVLEVICH PETRENKO: No. No. No such ideas. Nothing of what we saw. No, we could not imagine it. But on the way to it, we could see the bestiality, people buried in the ground, and we knew that living people were buried, buried alive. People shot in the neck or the head, through the back—piled up in trenches, in holes—men, women, children.

So, of course, we expected to see such bestial facts there. But there it was much more horrible than anything that we saw before.

MARVIN KALB: Let me be clear about one thing. Did you have specific orders to get into Auschwitz as quickly as you could?

VASSILY YAKOVLEVICH PETRENKO: In my speech I mentioned it and will mention it again. When the task was given to the military units, the commanders of the 60th Army knew that in that area there were some barracks, some buildings. We, as commanders on the divisional level, didn't have any particular detailed information. We knew the camp was there. The commander stressed first of all to destroy the enemy as quickly as possible, because there was frontal attack and there was some on the flanks, to cut off the retreating Germans so that they could not escape to the West.

MARVIN KALB: I want to ask this to clear the record. There are some stories to the effect that the Soviet army held back before going on to Auschwitz. You seem to be saying that that is not the case at all, and I just want the record to be clear on that point.

VASSILY YAKOVLEVICH PETRENKO: Only criminals who hated Soviet troops could have said that. Soviet troops never, never had such an order. No, no, never. Soviet troops did everything possible, made all efforts to reach it as quickly as possible. We received our orders in Sandomierz at the staging area, that was 150 kilometers from Oswiecim. We knew what was there, and in 20 days we covered over 250 kilometers. What delay? There were no delays because we were attacking for 27 days and we didn't stop for one minute. Oswiecim was liberated during the night, and then the following day we just cleaned up that area.

ROBERT WOLFE: I would like to support that. Military historians of World War II will tell you that one of the most rapid advances made was the one through Cracow, which rescued it from destruction at the hands of the retreating Germans. The survival of a good deal of the records of the German occupation of Poland, almost intact and well ordered, including those pertaining to the Holocaust, which is a fair percentage, is due to the rapid Soviet advance in that area and in southern Poland.

MARVIN KALB: Mr. Wolfe, let me ask you a question relating to the documentation again. One of the issues that comes up all the time concerns the railroad lines leading into Auschwitz, and I include this question and I address it as well to the Soviet side. On the basis of the records, why weren't those railroad lines bombed?

ROBERT WOLFE: Well, the argument we're talking about—Allied records now—was that the one place to hit it would have been very difficult for aerial bombardment—and I'm not an expert on aerial warfare—and that railroad lines were reconstructed so very rapidly. I hesitate to talk about railroad operations with Raul Hilberg sitting in the room. I always defer to greater authority.

MARVIN KALB: Mr. Pehle, do you have any elaboration you could give us on why the railroad lines were not hit?

JOHN PEHLE: I think that what was just said was correct—that we, the War Refugee Board, were asked to arrange with the War Department for the bombing of railroad lines.

When we went into the question, we were told—and I think correctly—that railroad lines can be restored overnight. This would be a self-defeating thing.

MARVIN KALB: Given your own sense of semidisillusionment with what you were told by other US government officials at that time on this subject, did you take that with any degree of skepticism?

JOHN PEHLE: No. However, as many people here know, the issue became more critical when it was finally decided that we should consider asking the War Department to bomb Auschwitz itself.

I wrote a strong letter to Mr. McCloy,[24] who was our liaison with Secretary Stimson,[25] and we were advised that this was not militarily feasible because the bombers would have to come from England, and the fighter escorts didn't have the capacity to go that far; therefore, they would be exposed to attack.

Later, it turned out, at the time we were being told this, the Allies were bombing all around Auschwitz from Italy, but we had no knowledge of that at the time.

MARVIN KALB: Mr. Karski, yours was perhaps one of the most extraordinary statements I've listened to in a long time, all based upon your personal experience. You did not tell us because you did not have the time, sir, about your meeting with Roosevelt. Could you share that with us now?

JAN KARSKI: As an individual, I was a little man, young and unknown. The mission was important. Its structure was such that I was not supposed to ask questions. I was only to answer questions if they were directed at me. In very many instances, very powerful people did not ask any questions concerning the Jewish problem, by the way. They were interested in the Polish issues—the boundaries, the politics, etcetera.

Now, with President Roosevelt, yes, I did speak about this horrible thing happening to the Jews, but not with much detail, as there was no time. During most of the session, his main area of interest was what aid Poland would be needing after the Second World War.

Secondly, he said that direct stipulations of Polish eastern boundaries would take place, and the Poles would have to understand that Poland would be recompensed with the German territories.

At the end of the meeting, when the Secretary opened the door, meaning that I had to go, and the President made a gesture of good-bye, I stood up, and I told the President that I was going back to Poland. I told him that every Polish leader, all of those who sent me from Poland, will ask me, "You saw President Roosevelt. What did the President tell you in answer to your report?"

The President limited himself, and certain things one never forgets, of course—you remember every gesture—"You will tell your leaders that we shall win this war. You will tell your leaders that the guilty ones will be punished for their crimes. Justice, democracy, peace will be restored. Your country will emerge more prosperous than ever in the past. You will tell them that they have a friend in this house, that the American people admire your country. This is what you will tell them."

MARVIN KALB: You also had a conversation, by your own account, with Secretary of State Hull. Did the question of the massacre of Jews in Poland come up with him?

JAN KARSKI: Forty years have passed, so I must be careful, you know, and not too blunt. Whatever I remember, Cordell Hull made an impression on me and all the men. I had some doubts if he even understood my foreign accent. He was interested exclusively in Polish political matters, and so was Henry Stimson.

MARVIN KALB: Were you yourself at the time surprised by that?

JAN KARSKI: Mr. Kalb, I know you so well from television and I am your admirer. You are a wise man so you will understand that at that time during the war I was not surprised by anything. I had no human feelings. Now, I have human feelings, and sometimes I cannot take it.

At that time, I was a recording machine. I was a tape recorder. If I had any human feelings—surprise, shock—I would have gone crazy a long time ago. I had no feelings at all. So, don't ask me was I surprised or not. I was not surprised about anything.

MARVIN KALB: I think you have answered my question very eloquently, sir.

Notes

[1] Felix Frankfurter served as a US Supreme Court Justice from 1939 to 1962. For many years prior to his appointment to the Court he had been a leading legal scholar and teacher at Harvard Law School.

[2] Senator Howard Baker, Republican from Tennessee.

[3] Raoul Wallenberg disappeared after the war. He is widely presumed to have been placed in a Soviet prison camp. The government of the Soviet Union, however, has steadfastly denied any knowledge of Wallenberg's fate or whereabouts.

[4] Gehenna: The valley of Hinnom, near Jerusalem, where propitiatory sacrifices were made to Moloch. (See II Kings 23:10.) More generally it refers to any place of extreme suffering and torment.

[5] International Military Tribunal (IMT) document 1816-PS, Exhibit No. US-621, National Archives Record Group 238: Records of War Crimes Tribunals.

[6] The idea of deporting the Jews of Europe to Madagascar, a French island colony in the Indian Ocean, had been proposed as early as the 1920s by a Dutch anti-Semite. Officials in the German Foreign Ministry and the SS began to plan the creation of such a reservation for Jews in 1940, when it appeared as though Germany's defeat of France would place Madagascar at the disposal of the Nazis. The plan was never carried through for a variety of reasons. It was never enthusiastically received in the highest levels of the Nazi hierarchy. Moreover, Germany failed to achieve a major military precondition for the realization of the project, namely the defeat of Great Britain. With the additional prospect of dealing with five million Soviet Jews after Germany's expected conquest of the Soviet Union, Nazi leaders concluded that a mass deportation to Madagascar would be impossible.

[7] See Dörr's sworn affidavit of March 25, 1948, subsequent Nuremberg trial document NG–5090. The IMT certification of September 14, 1945, had erroneously attributed the transcript to Dörr's former supervisor, Peter Jacob Vossen, who had passed on to U.S. Military Government officials the carbon copy he received from Dörr.

[8] The 1945 ribbon copy, given by Dörr to Dr. Fischer, former head of the Reichstag library, was also turned in to US Military Government headquarters in Berlin.

[9] Nuremberg document NG–2586, entered in evidence on October 22, 1947, as Prosecution Exhibit No. 1544, Case XI.

[10] National Archives Microfilm Publication T120, Roll 780, frames 371885–2223.

[11] Ibid., frames 371942–8 and 371961–70.

[12] Ibid., frame 372023.

[13] Ibid., frames 372043–4.

[14] Ibid., frame 372309.

[15] IMT document 709–PS, Prosecution Exhibit No. 2506, Case XI.

[16] IMT document 2233–D–PS, 1941, p. 77.

[17] IMT document 1553–PS.

[18] National Archives Record Group 373: Records of the Defense Intelligence Agency.

[19] Mediterranean Allied Air Force records, part of Allied Forces Headquarters, Mediterranean, deposited in National Archives Record Group 331: Records of Allied Operational and Occupational Headquarters, World War II.

[20] National Archives Record Group 243: Records of the U.S. Strategic Bombing Survey.

[21] Pertinent items can be found among both National Archives Records Group 238: Records of War and Crimes Tribunals, and Record Group 242: Collection of Foreign Records Seized 1941–.

[22] Dino A. Brugioni and Robert G. Poirier, "The Holocaust Revisited: A Retrospective Analysis of the Auschwitz-Birkenau Complex," Washington, D.C.: Central Intelligence Agency, 1979.

[23] National Archives Record Group 373: Records of the Defense Intelligence Agency, GX series of captured German aerial photographs.

[24] John J. McCloy was appointed American Military Governor for Germany in May 1949. In the following month his title was changed to American High Commissioner for Germany. McCloy remained in this position until August 1952. Prior to his assignment in Germany, McCloy had been Assistant Secretary of War and the President of the International Bank for Reconstruction and Development.

[25] Henry Stimson, at age 73, was appointed Secretary of War by President Roosevelt in 1940, and remained in that office throughout the war. Stimson had served previously as Secretary of War from 1911 to 1913, and had been Secretary of State from 1929 to 1933.

CHAPTER XIII
CONCLUSION

Chairman: Miles Lerman (USA): Businessman; Holocaust survivor; chairman, International Relations Committee, U. S. Holocaust Memorial Council.

Eli Zborowski (USA): Businessman; Holocaust survivor; honorary president, American Federation of Jewish Fighters, Camp Inmates and Nazi Victims; member, Executive Committee, Yad Vashem; member, U.S. Holocaust Memorial Council.

Mark E. Talisman (USA): director, Washington Action Program, Council of Jewish Federations; Vice Chairman, U.S. Holocaust Memorial Council.

Dr. Leo Eitinger (Norway): Professor of Psychiatry, University of Oslo; survivor of Auschwitz.

Elie Wiesel (USA): Author; Andrew W. Mellon Professor in the Humanities, Boston University; Chairman, U. S. Holocaust Memorial Council.

Institutional identifications are those at the time of the Conference.

MILES LERMAN

Thirty-six years ago, you and your comrades-in-arms liberated the world from the greatest evil that mankind has ever designed. Today, before we formally proceed with honoring you, the living liberators, we must take a moment to pay tribute to those who died on the battlefields against this terrible oppression. We recall and honor the brave soldiers and officers of all Allied nations who fell in the battle from the shores of Normandy to the snows of Stalingrad. In their struggle to drive the invaders from their homelands, they died courageously so their children could grow up and live as free men. We honor their memory.

We remember with sadness the unfortunate prisoners of war who were subjected to the most cruel hardships, starvation, and infectious diseases. Their German captors, in total defiance of all international military understanding and laws, treated them as slaves and not as prisoners of war, and killed them by the hundreds and hundreds of thousands. We remember them in sadness.

We render special honor to the valiant heroes and heroines of the partisan units who with meager weapons but with enormous courage stood up to the mighty enemy, disrupted their supply lines, and caused them heavy losses in every possible way. Their bravery and heroism is the great inspiring legend for generations to come.

With deep respect and reverence, we recall the national patriots, political opponents, and spiritual leaders whose undaunted patriotism and love for their national freedom secured their eternal place in the memory of their respective nations. Many of them were torn away from their families never to return; they were beaten and brutally tortured by their Gestapo interrogators, but they chose to die rather than to betray their comrades. They went to the gallows with patriotic songs on their lips. It was their struggle that gave the power of endurance to their people. These acts of courage will long be remembered.

We will forever remember the Righteous Gentiles who at the risk of their own lives reached out with brotherly hands to offer desperately needed food and shelter to some of their Jewish neighbors and friends. Their noble behavior served as a beacon of light in the world of total darkness. By their actions, those Righteous Gentiles preserved the sense of godliness in a world bereft of human compassion. Their acts of mercy will be hallowed in the annals of history of mankind.

With an abiding sense of loss, we mourn the innocent victims of the Holocaust—the six million men, women, and children who were systematically annihilated not for what they had done or intended to do, but for one reason only—because they were born Jews. These we will remember and vow never to forget. May the memory of their tragic deaths serve as a lesson and warning to us and the generations that will follow.

ELI ZBOROWSKI

We, the survivors of the Holocaust, are grateful to the soldiers of the Allied forces who liberated us from Nazi tyranny. We owe our entire lives to you.

As members of the United States Holocaust Memorial Council, we are privileged to greet you as our guests at this historic meeting of the liberators together with the survivors. We welcome you, who have come from near and far, to share with us a few days of recollection.

We, who witnessed man's inhumanity to man, also bear witness to the finest in man. We have seen both faces of humanity. We witnessed the German atrocities committed against innocent civilians, the murder of six million Jews, the destruction of hundreds of villages and the complete destruction of the Jewish communities and their culture in Europe.

We then lived to see the other face of humanity, the entire world united in dedication to a common aim of the defeat of Nazism.

We have seen the courageous soldiers who displayed heroism in saving us, the remnants of European Jewry. The Allied armies crushed the Nazi beast and restored peace and freedom to a suffering, occupied Europe.

We heard our Chairman, the renowned author Elie Wiesel, recall in a way only possible to Wiesel a glimpse of the survivors' feelings at the moment of liberation.

We heard a most moving eyewitness account of Colonel Dr. Chilczuk, who recalled what he had seen when he and his Polish unit as part of the Soviet army liberated the concentration camp of Sachsenhausen.

We heard Rabbi Herschel Schacter, who as a young chaplain of the American army was confronted with the indescribable reality of the concentration camp of Buchenwald. Rabbi Schacter moved to tears the generals and other participants when he described the eyes of the skeletons looking at him in disbelief when he said to them in Yiddish, "Jews, Jews, you are free. I am an American, an American Jew. You are free, Jews."

We toast the brave and heroic armies of the East and the West, the sons of those countries who laid down their lives in their fight against Nazism and who gave us life once more.

We, Jews, the only people destined by the Nazis for a "Final Solution," were saved and fascism was defeated thanks to the Allied forces. Thanks to your bravery.

We are alive, yes, we are here, although only remnants of the once-flourishing European Jewish communities, and we are here thanks to you, our liberators.

The happy moments of liberation are beyond description and are cherished by all survivors. I recall January 17, 1945, as the day when I was liberated by the Soviet forces led by General Petrenko, who came from Moscow to participate in this conference, and whose soldiers entered the death camp of Auschwitz.

There were other heroic people during the Holocaust. We recall the partisans and organized resistance throughout Europe that fought the Germans behind the front lines. We remember the lonely battle of the Warsaw Ghetto and the uprisings in other ghettos. We recall the brave soldiers of the Jewish Brigade. And we remember with special gratitude and recognition those Righteous Gentiles who risked their lives to save Jews.

My family was saved by such heroic individuals in western Poland, and my wife, a child of 13 all alone, was saved by a Polish woman in eastern Poland. We recall with overflowing joy the liberation, but unfortunately liberation came too late for many suffering people, too late for my father. So was the liberation too late for six million Jews and millions of other victims.

Our meetings at the State Department are symbolic. Today, they are our hosts, while during the years of the Holocaust, we were denied entry visas to the free world.

Today, we are grateful to all those countries who received us after the war and gave us a place to live so that we could rebuild our lives and our families and become, once more, contributing members of society and, in countless instances, leaders and influential citizens. We, former camp inmates and Nazi victims, together with you, our liberators, have a duty to bear witness, to leave a legacy behind for mankind that transcends all political, social, or economic boundaries, so that the lives of our dear ones and the lives of all those soldiers fallen in action will not have been in vain.

You, who opened the gates of the death camps and the concentration camps as our liberators, have an obligation to remind the world of what you saw there.

We, as survivors, who saw both faces of humanity, the darkest hour of human history, and the most noble deeds of man, want the generations to come to draw a lesson from our experiences as to what racism, anti-Semitism, and hatred can lead to.

And we want our children to retell it to their children that after all our sufferings, we have not lost our faith in humanity. Just the opposite. While we call on all decent people never to forget and not to let the world forget the horrors of the past, we want to stress our belief in humanity and our hope that a world of friendship, freedom, and coexistence can be built, must be built.

MARK E. TALISMAN

As these days' events have amply demonstrated to all of us and to the world, it is vital to remember, even when remembering is excruciatingly painful; even as our minds are willingly dulled to the levels of pain and suffering which can be consciously inflicted upon humankind in the name of government and law; even when morality is suborned in the name of so-called civilization to eradicate a people from this earth and raise the horrors of war efficiently to break, maim, and murder millions of others, assuming such infamous, incomparably despicable behavior would go unchallenged and undaunted.

You, the liberators, have taken the enormous step to be present together these days individually and collectively to recount, to jog memory of nearly four decades of debris, ashes, and what must be unwittingly natural acts of suppression, and by so doing, you have served your children and their children so very well. It is your eyes and your acts and those whom you represent, who brought this unprecedented period of the darkest history to a close.

Yet it is with your presence here together and individually that you continue to bear witness to the future of humankind which must never allow such calumny again to occur. Your voices and your words must be indelibly etched in the moral memory of each generation, far into the future, long past your last breath, your last ounce of strength, and your physical presence.

Uniquely, you each have served magnificently, nearly 40 years ago. You have again been asked and have willingly, once again, acted affirmatively to serve at this conference, and you must continue, as long as you can, to be an eyewitness.

I was four years old at the time. My wife, Jill, was two. We face the challenging tasks of bringing up two very small children, Jessica and Raphael. We are deeply grateful to you. For with your help it is conceivable that the leadership of this planet will remember and its citizens will not forget. With your help, and that of millions of others, such remembering will not be denigrated in any way but instead will be seized upon as the ultimate challenge and opportunity which you surely have provided in your original deeds and in these days of witness to our children and theirs, who will be able to remember through your eyes.

DR. LEO EITINGER

It is an unexpected and undeserved privilege, and, may I say, one of the greatest honors ever bestowed upon me, to be allowed on behalf of all delegates present, to address this unique meeting. Please forgive me for feeling overwhelmed, not only by the memories of the past that were recalled in so many ways during our meetings of the last days, but also—or rather first of all—by my feelings of gratitude which I share with all the delegates who have been invited to be at this conference.

Our thanks go first of all to the creators of the conference. It took the imagination and ingenuity of Elie Wiesel to conceive an idea that seems so simple and obvious: that we the the survivors, scattered throughout the world, should at least once in our lifetimes meet with some of the men to whom we owe our liberation. We all know that the most obvious things are very often the most difficult to realize. But it also required the resources of the United States to establish a Holocaust Memorial Council, and the resources of the United States Department of State to organize and convene such a conference, providing resources, but first and foremost, moral and humanitarian support.

Our thanks go to the liberators. Not only did they free us by liberating the concentration camps while hurrying through Europe to victory. No, while the decisive battles were taking place, they used manpower and material with an organizing effort and effectiveness we never experienced before to rescue human beings, the weak and the sick, the seemingly hopeless cases.

The English Dr. Collins, who came to Bergen-Belsen together with his troops immediately after the liberation, wrote an extremely dramatic account of his experience, and he himself called the description a gross understatement. He concluded his article in the following way: "The problem of what to do with these forsaken, almost lost souls is immense, but one which if not tackled and solved will make all our efforts a mere waste of time, for then it were kinder to let them die than to have brought them back to mere existence and more sufferings in a hostile world, where they no longer have even a hope of being able to compete in the struggle of the survival of the fittest—and must inevitably go down."

Well, the American troops surely did not tarry in trying to tackle and solve the problem. Never shall I forget my admiration and my incredulity when seeing in Buchenwald, US soldiers carrying with their own hands sick and helpless prisoners. They transported them from the desolate barracks, to so-called sick bays, a travesty of language, to hospitals established by the US army immediately after its arrival. In this very practical and prosaic way, hundreds of human beings were saved.

What could give me more satisfaction than having the opportunity to say finally—and here in Washington: Thank you for what you have done for my comrades and for us all in rescuing them and us from certain death, because, unlike the other Norwegian prisoners, the remnants of the deported Norwegian Jews, numbering 22, were not rescued by the Swedish Red Cross before the end of the war.

But, first of all, thank you for having restored our belief in humanity and mankind. Because what Dr. Collins did not know, and did not take into consideration, was the fact that many concentration camp inmates made the most heroic efforts to remain human beings in spite of everything, in spite of all the Nazis' efforts to kill them psychologically before the final somatic annihilation.

It has been stated that identification with the aggressor was the most general coping mechanism in the camps. In reality it was seldom the case and nearly always led to the destruction of those involved. It was also true, as Collins correctly surmised, that the suffering in the camps would lead to disastrous lifelong consequences. Much work—medical, psychiatric, and social—was needed to alleviate these pathological states and to reintroduce a more or less normal life to the traumatized victims.

On the other hand, those people inside the camps who were able to liberate themselves internally from the yoke of slavery; who retained their humanity, their self-respect, their human values; people who, like the young Elie Wiesel, were ready to undergo additional suffering voluntarily in order to spare others from being humiliated—people who were concerned not only with themselves, but with the fate of others, were those who were able to survive with less psychological damage than people who abandoned themselves and their innermost values, people who were completely overwhelmed by the notion that they had nobody and nothing to struggle or live for. The inner liberation from slavery and from the ideology of fascism proved to be of importance not because it gave one a capacity for immediate physical survival, but also it enabled one to survive without too many psychological disturbances, and with one's personality intact—as far as this was possible at all.

So my final thanks to all of you who have shown not by words, but by deeds, not under luxurious circumstances, but under the most extreme restrictions, that human values are real values. Our thanks go to you who are bearers of the torch which brings light and hope to thousands and hundreds of thousands of human beings working for a better life in a better world without persecution of any minorities, where minority groups are allowed to live in peace, a world with less suffering.

Our thanks go to you who have honored us as delegates and have invited us to be together with you; it makes us proud and at the same time very humble indeed, and brings all of us a deep debt of gratitude to all of you.

ELIE WIESEL

May I tell you a story? I wrote a book many, many years ago, and that book was my first. It was a memoir about the war, the only autobiographical work that I have written. It's about suffering, evil, inhumanity. Here and there are a few sparks of humanity. One of those moments, one of those sparks, tries to describe a scene in the hospital in Buna which is Auschwitz.[1]

I was very young, and suddenly my left foot was injured. I was taken to the hospital. My father was still alive, and I felt the end had come for me. In the hospital, I found one of the most beautiful human beings in the world; in the camp, inside the kingdom of darkness and night, there was a man who was total humanity in his expressions, in his words, in his caring, in the way he looked at people. After surgery, I remember, when I came to, I was in terrible pain. This doctor stood near my bed, and he began consoling me, and he began speaking to me about good things that will happen, because they are bound to happen one day. He told me one day I would walk again and one day man would be free again, and one day maybe God would listen again, and one day we would smile again. Do you know who that man is? [The reference is to the previous speaker, Dr. Leo Eitinger.]

In a way, we have gathered here under the sign and the seal of gratitude. I cannot begin to tell you the depths of gratitude that I feel now for you, not only because of the past, but now because of what happened in the last three days.

I hope you will believe me that I was afraid. We did not know. My colleagues and I worked for months, and months, and months, but yet deep down there was a fear in me. What if it failed? It would have been a catastrophe. After all, we come from different countries, from different systems, from different places. We are Jews and non-Jews; religious Jews and less-religious Jews, and good Christians, and liberators, and victims, and children of the survivors.

Yet, in spite of the fears, we pulled it off. I was a journalist once upon a time, and I have covered a lot of conferences and I do not remember a conference where there has been such a harmony. Why? I was wondering why. Because we all felt this should not fail. This is a historic event, which has metaphysical implications. The Holocaust has metaphysical implications. It brings out either the worst in the bad—as it was with the killers—or the best in the good—as it was with the liberators, the partisans, the victims. It is either way. Anyone who is in touch with that period, with that pain, with that event, suddenly feels that he or she lives on a different planet.

So for the last three days we lived a moment in time which was outside time. On one hand, you have the feeling that we've just begun, and on the other, you have the feeling it lasted so long, so long. I do not really believe that I heard one dissonant sound. After all, you represent different systems and countries and governments, ideologies. There are tensions. There must be. It's not normal not to have tensions. But there were none here. None. Somehow we all spoke the same language. We became what we are—a fraternity, a human community dedicated to the ideal that after all there must be more in man to be admired than to be despised. In spite of everything, we must go on believing in that and in each other.

There was another fear in me. It may become morbid. After all, you have seen and we have lived in the darkest, the ugliest chapter in history. It was not only the death; it was the ugly face of death. My God, do you know what was difficult for us after the war? Not to adjust to life, but to adjust to death, to the fact that death is something individual, that death is not a normal phenomenon, that death is a scandal, and death is an injustice, and that we cannot accept death as a day-to-day phenomenon. But then it was. People disappeared, they vanished. My God, when you looked at those people whom the killers have degraded, in their rags, when you look at those children—I always remember the children. I could live my entire life and only speak of those children, of those million Jewish children. Yet, how could we go on? How could we laugh?

I remember two books. One of them was written by a man named Yankel Wiernik, a carpenter. He participated in the uprising of Treblinka, and he wrote a book in 1944. He said, among other things, Will I be able to laugh again one day? And I saw this as the end. Nothing could be more tragic. But then I read two diaries written by members of the Sonderkommando. I'm sure you spoke about it at the uprising session. They had written for history, and the documents were buried under the ashes, and they were discovered years later. In one of these books is a sentence which breaks me up. The author asks, Will I ever be able to cry again? So I was afraid maybe we will cry.

My friends, the liberators, to whom we owe so much, look whom you liberated. Look at us. We are not bitter, and we are not vengeful. We are not even morbid, and maybe this is the greatest anomaly in the world. Normally, my friends, we should have all gone into an asylum. After having gone through what we have gone through, and after having seen what you have seen, we should have ended up in a lunatic asylum, depressed forever. But we have not. There are temptations. For me, to be Jewish is to be human. Just as for you to be human is to be Russian or to be French, and that is my expression of humanity. There are so many reasons in the world. The cynicism of so many, the forgetfulness of so many, the materialism of so many, and the viciousness of so many.

I was in Cambodia two years ago. I saw what was happening there. The incredible murder, and the world didn't say anything. Then I saw the boat people. Before that there were so many wars in the world. How is it possible to have wars in the world?

That is why we speak. That is the reason why. It is not easy. It is not. It took me 10 years to write my first book. I did not want to write, because suffering is something so personal, so private, that often parents do not even talk to their children about it. We only accept our suffering in our nightmares. But then if we had not decided to break out and to share with you, I am afraid we would have caused humanity to be ashamed now, even more, for what it had let be done then. Therefore, we go on bearing witness for all men, in spite of everything.

We must prevent more violence. We must prevent more wars. We must unmask hatred. Unless we do that, mankind has no chance of survival.

Of course, we speak on behalf of suffering. That gives us a certain authority, but I do not believe, I never have, that suffering confers any privilege. It is what you do with suffering that matters. If you use suffering to cause more suffering, then you betray your suffering. But if you live your suffering and you accept it to prevent other suffering, you have the moral authority to speak.

Therefore, we met here, and I am utterly convinced that these are the ideas and thoughts that moved you as they moved me for the last two and three days. We had privileged moments here, such as my meetings with General Petrenko and General Gudz, with an officer who liberated me in Buchenwald, and the meetings that I had with friends I had not seen for 40 years. I am sure it happened to you as well. There were privileged moments when we heard certain addresses, when we heard you, Mr. Hausner, speak so eloquently about the failure of education in the Nazi system, or about the death marches that Yehuda Bauer spoke of, or Karski's speech. I would take his speech and print it in *The New York Times,* at our expense—since they don't want to publish anything else—I would buy two pages and print the entire speech of Karski.

In conclusion, the French minister urged us a few times not to be only bent to the past, but to look to the future. We are looking for the future. If it were not for our children, we would not do it. It is too painful. But we are thinking of tomorrow's generation, and we do want to set an example. It is possible for man and woman to be together and not to hate each other. It is possible for men and women of all creeds, of all ages, to be together and declare together that there is something about human dignity which we must cherish. There is something about human respect which we must espouse. There is something about freedom, and something about the future, and something about beauty – I use the word advisedly – that bind us together. Therefore, we are looking to the future, Monsieur Laurain, as we spoke before.

You may know already, we have decided to try and keep our group, our community, together, which means whatever happened here should not be the end of an anecdote. It has to be part of history. And it will be. Therefore, we shall meet again. The chairmen of all the delegations will meet in a few weeks, or a few months—I think that we shall prevail upon Monsieur Laurain to speak to Monsieur Mitterand about perhaps meeting in France in May—and from time to time simply to meet to reassure ourselves that we can make a difference. If we speak with enough conviction and humanity, people will listen. They have to.

My friends, we have met once 40 years ago. We meet again now. We gave each other something. We gave each other a lesson in gratitude. The words that came back in every speaker's words were gratitude. I am sure our group will confirm that there was one word that was, I think, officially stricken from the SS vocabulary. Do you know that? The SS had no right to use the expression "thank you," because they thought everything was coming to them, that they could take everything. We who survived and those who saw the survivors know that there is in the world and in life and in man a reason to justify gratitude.

For us survivors, everything is an offering, everything is grace, every minute is grace. I could have remained there. By luck we came out. That is why we are trying to use every minute that we have and every word at our disposal to do something with our lives. Yes, occasionally we are accused of being prisoners of our memories. True. But we are prisoners who want to set other people free. That is our task. I thank you and wish you farewell until we meet again.

Notes

[1] In 1941, the giant German chemical cartel, I.G. Farben, established a synthetic rubber (Buna) factory at Monowitz, near Auschwitz. The factory was to exploit slave laborers interned at Auschwitz. Farben later set up its own concentration camp at Monowitz for easier access to the labor.

The term Buna is a contraction of the German words Butadien and Natrium (butadiene and sodium), two essential ingredients in the synthetic rubber formula.

OFFICIAL DELEGATIONS

INTERNATIONAL LIBERATORS CONFERENCE

UNITED STATES OF AMERICA

Dr. Leon Bass, Pennsylvania
Congressman James Blanchard, Michigan
Senator Rudy Boschwitz, Minnesota
Brigadier General James L. Collins, Washington, D.C.
Senator John Danforth, Missouri
Senator Robert Dole, Kansas
Father Edward Doyle, Rhode Island
The Honorable John S.D. Eisenhower, Pennsylvania
Mrs. Marie Ellifritz, Buckroe Beach, Virginia
Adrian S. Fisher, Esquire, Washington, D.C.
Mr. Fred W. Friendly, New York
Congressman S. William Green, New York
Professor Raul Hilberg, Vermont
Dr. Douglas Kelling, Illinois
Brigadier General (Retired) Samuel Koster, Maryland
Congressman William Lehman, Florida
The Honorable Clare Boothe Luce, Hawaii
Secretary of the Army John O. Marsh, Jr., Virginia
Rabbi Judah Nadich, New York
John Pehle, Esquire, Washington
Senator Claiborne Pell, Rhode Island
Lt. General (Retired) William W. Quinn, Washington, D.C.
Congressman Stephen J. Solarz, New York
Mr. Robert Wolfe, Washington, D.C.
Reverend George B. Wood, Alabama
Congressman Sidney R. Yates, Illinois

BELGIUM

The Honorable André Mernier, Embassy of Belgium, Washington, D.C.

CANADA

The Honorable Charles Mills Drury, Brigadier (Retired) Chairman of the National Capitol Commission
Mr. Andrew Armit
Captain George Blackburn (Retired)
Brigadier T. G. Gibson
Mr. Brereton Greenhous
Mr. Norval Lee
Mr. John Leeson
Mr. Keith MacLellan
Professor David Pollack
Mr. Alan Rose
Mr. Lawrence A. Snell
Mr. Philip Stuchen

CZECHOSLOVAKIA

The Honorable Eduard Kukan, Minister Counselor, Embassy of the Czechoslovak Socialist Republic, Washington, D.C.
Major Jan Vasicek

DENMARK

The Honorable Frode Jakobsen, Leader of the Freedom Council, Denmark
His Excellency Otto R. Borch, Ambassador to the United States
Dr. Jorgen Haestrup
Dr. Svenn Seehusen
Dr. Mogens Staffeldt

FRANCE

The Honorable Jean Laurain, Minister of Veterans Affairs
Madame Renée Aubry
Mr. Georges Bonnet
Mr. Delphin Debenest
Mr. Charles Dubost
Mr. Guy Fassina
Mr. Gilbert Faure
Colonel Guy Hinterlang
General Henri Raguet de Brancion de Liman
Mr. Gilles Vaubourg

JEWISH BRIGADE (WORLD WAR II)

Lieutenant Colonel Arieh Pinchuk, Chairman of the War Veterans League
Lieutenant Colonel (Reserve) Dan Dagen
Lieutenant Colonel (Reserve) David Gineo
Captain (Reserve) Menashe Hauser
Colonel (Reserve) Dan Hiram
Lieutenant Colonel (Reserve) Johanan Peltz
Efraim Weichselfisch

THE NETHERLANDS

Professor Dr. L. deJong
The Honorable Andries Ekker
Mrs. A. S. Fels-Kupferschmidt
Ms. M. A. van Drunen Littel
Dr. A. H. Paape
Dr. C. J. F. Stuldreher
Mr. A. F. van Velsen

NEW ZEALAND

Captain L. J. Tempero, Royal New Zealand Navy Deputy of the Defense Staff, Embassy of New Zealand, Washington, D.C.
Major M. E. Rumble

NORWAY

The Honorable Trygve Bratelli, former Prime Minister and Member of Parliament
Dr. Leo Eitinger
Lieutenant General Kjell Bjoerge-Hansen
The Honorable Per Haugustead
His Excellency Knute Hedemann
Lieutenant General Wilhelm Mohr

POLISH PEOPLE'S REPUBLIC

Brigadier General (Retired) Franciszek Skibinski
Dr. Michal Chilczuk
Dr. Czeslaw Pilichowski

SOCIALIST FEDERAL REPUBLIC OF YUGOSLAVIA

His Excellency Budimir Loncar, Ambassador to the United States
Captain (Reserve) Branko Lakic
Colonel Branko Pavlovic

UNION OF SOVIET SOCIALIST REPUBLICS

Lieutenant General Pavel Danilovich Gudz
Mr. Adolf Leonidovich Fedetov
Colonel (Retired) Henry Borisovich Gofman
Major General (Reserve) Alexei Kirillovich Gorlinsky
Colonel (Retired) Nikolai Mikhailovich Kotlyar
Lieutenant General (Reserve) Vassily Yakovlevich Petrenko

UNITED KINGDOM

Major General Michael S. Gray, Military Attaché, British Embassy, Washington, D.C.
Professor Colonel G.I.A.D. Draper
The Honorable Alan F. Goulty
Colonel J. C. Hardy

GLOSSERY OF TERMS, NAMES, AND CAMPS

BY ALAN E. STEINWEISS

Anschluss
Literally "connection" or "union" in German, used to describe the annexation of Austria to Germany on March 13, 1938.

Aryan
In Nazi racial theory, a person of pure German "blood." The term "non-Aryan" was used to designate Jews, part-Jews, and others of supposedly inferior racial stock.

Auschwitz-Birkenau
Polish name: Oswiecim. Nazi extermination camp in southwestern Poland. Originally erected in 1940 as a camp for Polish prisoners. Converted in 1942 into a modern facility for the mass annihilation of human beings with poison gas. Approximately one million Jews from all over Nazi-occupied Europe, as well as large numbers of non-Jews, including thousands of Gypsies, were murdered there between 1942 and late 1944. Liberated by Soviet troops in January 1945, although by this time the Nazis had largely dismantled the killing facilities and forced most of the remaining inmates on a "death march" towards the West.

Belzec
Nazi extermination camp in eastern Poland. Erected 1942. Approximately 550,000 Jews were murdered there in 1942 and 1943. The Nazis dismantled the camp in the fall of 1943.

Bergen-Belsen
Nazi concentration camp in northwestern Germany. Erected 1943. Thousands of Jews, political prisoners, and POWs were killed there. Liberated by British troops in April 1945, although many of the remaining prisoners died of typhus after liberation.

Bradley, Omar
Commander of U.S. First Army at time of Normandy invasion. Later commander of U.S. 12th Army Group, the largest battlefield force ever commanded by a U.S. general. It included the 9th Army under William H. Simpson, 1st Army under Courtney H. Hodges, 3rd Army under George S. Patton, and 15th Army under Leonard T. Gerow.

Brecht, Bertolt
Anti-fascist German poet and playwright, author of among other works, *The Three Penny Opera, The Rise and Fall of the Town Mahagonny, The Caucasian Chalk Circle, Mother Courage and Her Children, The Good Person of Setzuan, Terror and Misery of the Third Reich,* and *The Life of Galileo*. Brecht spent the Nazi years in exile (Denmark, Sweden, Finland, and the USA).

Buchenwald
Nazi concentration camp in central Germany. Erected 1937 for internment of German political prisoners. During the war thousand of Jews, POWs, and political prisoners were killed there. Liberated in April 1945 by its own inmates a few hours prior to the arrival of American troops.

Chelmno
Known also as Kulmhof. Nazi extermination camp in western Poland. Established 1941. The first of the Nazi extermination camps. Approximately 150,000 Jews were murdered there between late 1941 and 1944, although not continuously. In comparison to the other extermination camps, especially Auschwitz, Chelmno was technologically primitive, employing carbon monoxide gas vans as the main method of killing. The Nazis dismantled the camp in late 1944 and early 1945.

Dachau
Nazi concentration camp in southern Germany. Erected in 1933, this was the first Nazi concentration camp. Used mainly to incarcerate German political prisoners until late 1938, whereupon large numbers of Jews, Gypsies, Jehovah's Witnesses, homosexuals, and other supposed enemies of the state and anti-social elements were sent as well. Nazi doctors and scientists used many prisoners at Dachau as guinea pigs for experiments. During the war construction began on a gas chamber, but it never became operational. Dachau was liberated by American troops in April 1945.

DP
Displaced Person. The upheavals of war left millions of soldiers and civilians far from home. Millions of these DPs had been eastern European slave laborers for the Nazis. The tens of thousands of Jewish survivors of Nazi camps either could not or did not want to return to their former homes in Germany or eastern Europe, and many lived in special DP camps while awaiting migration to America or Palestine.

Eichmann, Adolf
Gestapo official who coordinated the deportation of Jews from their homes in Nazi-occupied Europe to ghettos and extermination camps in eastern Europe. After the war he escaped to South America, where he lived incognito until 1960, when Israeli agents captured him in Argentina. Eichmann was tried in Jerusalem in 1961, condemned to death, and hanged in 1962.

Einsatzgruppen
Literally, Special Task Groups. Units composed of SD and Gestapo personnel, organized in May 1941 prior to the German attack on the Soviet Union. Their mission was to follow German troops into Russia and liquidate Jews, Gypsies, and Communist Party officials. There were four Einsatzgruppen, designated A, B, C, and D, which were further subdivided into units called Einsatzkommandos. It has been estimated that in 1941 and 1942 the Einsatzgruppen murdered about one million Jews. The Nazis phased out use of the Einsatzgruppen when the extermination camps went into operation.

Eisenhower, Dwight D.
As Supreme Commander of the Allied Expeditionary Forces, General Eisenhower commanded all Allied forces in Europe beginning in 1942.

"Final Solution" of the Jewish Question
A Nazi euphemism for the plan to exterminate the Jews of Europe.

Flossenbürg
Nazi concentration camp in central Germany. Erected 1938. Prior to liberation by American troops in April 1945, the Nazis had forced the vast majority of the 15,000–20,000 remaining prisoners on a "death march" away from the camp. The liberating troops found only 2,000 inmates when they entered the camp.

Gestapo
Acronym for Geheime Staatspolizei, meaning Secret State Police. Prior to the outbreak of war, the Gestapo used brutal methods to investigate and suppress resistance to Nazi rule within Germany. After 1939 the Gestapo expanded its operations into Nazi-occupied Europe.

Great Patriotic War
The official designation by the Soviet Union of its war against Nazi Germany.

Heydrich, Reinhard
As Chief of the RSHA, Heydrich was entrusted in 1941 with implementing the "Final Solution" of the Jewish Question. He presided over the conference at Wannsee in Berlin on January 20, 1942, at which representatives of numerous German agencies discussed plans for the liquidation of Europe's Jews. Czech partisans assassinated Heydrich in Prague in 1942.

Himmler, Heinrich
As head of the SS and the secret police apparatus, Himmler had control over the vast network of Nazi concentration and extermination camps, the Einsatzgruppen, and the Gestapo. Reinhard Heydrich, Ernst Kaltenbrunner, and many other key officials in the implementation of Nazi anti-Jewish measures were subordinate to Himmler. Himmler committed suicide in 1945 after his arrest.

Hoess, Rudolf
Commandant of Auschwitz. After the war he was tried and executed in Poland. Hoess' memoir, *Commandant of Auschwitz* (London, 1959) provides a chilling account of the killing operations at the most notorious of the Nazi camps.

Hull, Cordell
American Secretary of State during most of World War II. Resigned in November 1944.

International Military Tribunal (IMT)
Popularly known as the Nuremberg Trial. Twenty-four so-called "major war criminals" were tried before a joint American, British, French, and Soviet tribunal in Nuremberg in 1945–46. The IMT should not be confused with a series of trials conducted by an American tribunal in Nuremberg in subsequent years, or with the host of other trials of Nazi war criminals conducted by numerous countries since 1945.

Kaltenbrunner, Ernst
Succeeded Reinhard Heydrich as Chief of RSHA. Played major role in implementation of the "Final Solution." Tried at Nuremberg and executed in 1946.

Kommando
German term for a satellite camp. Most of the major concentration camps were ringed with numerous smaller prison and labor camps, or Kommandos.

Kristallnacht
Literally, "crystal night" in German, also described as the "night of broken glass," refers to the state-inspired pogrom of November 9, 1938, against the Jews in Germany during which Nazi hooligans attacked synagogues and Jewish businesses and beat up Jewish citizens.

Luftwaffe
The German air force.

Majdanek
Also known as Lublin. Nazi extermination camp in eastern Poland. Established 1941. Approximately 50,000 Jews were murdered by gassing there in 1942 and 1943. Soviet troops occupied the camp after a hasty evacuation by the Nazis in 1944.

Marshall, George C.
Chief of Staff of the U.S. Army. President Roosevelt's chief military adviser. Widely regarded by American historians as the "Architect of Victory."

Mauthausen
Nazi concentration camp in northern Austria. Erected August 1938. Several thousand in-

mates were killed by gassing and other methods between 1942 and 1945. Liberated by American troops in May 1945.

Mengele, Josef
SS physician at Auschwitz. Notorious for cruelty to prisoners, the cold-blooded Mengele often made the "selection" of which Jews would die in the gas chambers and which would be used for slave labor. Conducted numerous perverse medical experiments on inmates. Escaped to South America after the war. Now widely presumed dead on the basis of medical analysis of the skeleton found in Brazil in 1985.

Mischling
"Mixed breed" or "mongrel." The Nazi racial classification for people of mixed Jewish and Aryan "blood."

National Socialism
Nazism (Nationalsozialismus.) A diverse mixture of political philosophies, National Socialism had anti-Semitism, racism, and German expansionism at its core. The official name of the Nazi party was the National Socialist German Workers' Party (Nationalsozialistische Deutsche Arbeiter Partei).

Neuengamme
Nazi concentration camp in northern Germany. Erected June 1940. Neuengamme and its satellites were important centers of slave labor for industries in northern Germany. It has been estimated that of the 90,000 prisoners incarcerated in Neuengamme between 1940 and 1945, 40,000 died. Liberated by British troops in May 1945.

Nordhausen
Also known as Dora. Nazi concentration camp in central Germany. Established 1943. German industry used its prisoners as slave labor in the production of V–1 flying bombs and V–2 rockets. Liberated by American troops in April 1945.

Ohrdruf
Nazi concentration camp in western Germany. Established in late 1944 as a satellite of Buchenwald. Liberated by American troops in April 1945. The first Nazi concentration camp liberated on the western front.

Oranienburg
Nazi concentration camp in northern Germany. Established in 1933 to incarcerate political prisoners. Ceased operation 1935, but was reestablished in 1943 as a satellite of Sachsenhausen. Liberated by Soviet troops and units of the Polish Peoples Army in April 1945.

OSS
Office of Strategic Services. American agency created in 1942 to collect intelligence on enemy powers and to conduct espionage operations behind enemy lines. Dissolved in 1945. The Central Intelligence Agency, created in 1947, is considered to be the successor of the OSS.

Panzer
German for armor. A Panzerwagen, usually shortened simply to Panzer, was a tank.

Patton, George S.
Commander of U.S. 3rd Army. Celebrated for his flamboyant personality and both military tactics.

Ravensbrück
Nazi concentration camp in northern Ger-

many. It was established in 1939 as a camp exclusively for female prisoners. Liberated by Soviet troops in April 1945.

RSHA
Abbreviation for Reichssicherheitshauptamt, or Reich Security Main Office. This agency was established in the SS in 1939 to coordinate administration of security and police agencies, including the Gestapo and the SD. First chief of RSHA was Reinhard Heydrich, who was succeeded by Ernst Kaltenbrunner.

Sachsenhausen
Nazi concentration camp in northern Germany. Established 1936. Liberated by Soviet troops in April 1945.

SD
Abbreviation for Sicherheitsdienst, or Security Service. An agency in the SS involved in many anti-Jewish measures in Germany prior to the outbreak of war. Many of the personnel of the Einsatzgruppen were drawn from the SD.

SHAEF
Acronym for Supreme Headquarters, Allied Expeditionary Forces, the designation for the office of General Eisenhower, the Supreme Commander.

Sobibor
Nazi extermination camp in eastern Poland. Established 1942. Approximately 200,000 Jews were murdered there in 1942 and 1943. The Nazis dismantled the camp in the Fall of 1943.

SS
Abbreviation for Schutzstaffel, or Protection Forces. Originated as bodyguard for Hitler before 1933, the SS grew into a massive organization by 1944 with control over the police and security apparatus, the concentration and death camp system, diverse industrial enterprises, and armed divisions known as Waffen (armed or military) SS. The blackshirted members of the SS often thought of themselves as the elite cadre of Nazi Germany. Reich Leader of the SS was Heinrich Himmler.

Stalag
Acronym for Stammlager, or branch camp. Stalag, with an accompanying number (e.g. Stalag 17) was a method of designating prisoner-of-war camps.

Stutthof
Nazi concentration camp in northern Poland. Established in 1939 immediately after German invasion of Poland. Liberated by Soviet troops in May 1945.

Terezin
Called Theresienstadt in German. Nazi concentration camp in northwestern Czechoslovakia. Established 1941, it served for a while as a Nazi show camp for visiting Red Cross inspectors. Liberated by Soviet troops in May 1945.

Treblinka
Nazi extermination camp in central Poland. Established 1942. Approximately 750,000 Jews were murdered there in 1942 and 1943. The Nazis dismantled the camp in the fall of 1943.

Warsaw Ghetto
Jewish ghetto created by Nazis in 1940. At the beginning of 1942, almost half-a-million

Jews lived in the ghetto under miserable conditions. In July 1942, the Nazis began to deport Jews from the ghetto for extermination, mainly at Treblinka. By October, only about 70,000 remained in the ghetto. At this point representatives of a number of Jewish organizations in the ghetto formed the Jewish Fighting Organization to resist further deportations. In April 1943 a force of about 3,000 Waffen SS troops, German and Polish police, and a battalion of Ukrainians collaborating with the Nazis attempted to liquidate what was left of the ghetto. Short of weapons, and outnumbered two-to-one, the Jewish fighters were nonetheless able to hold out for approximately one month.

Wehrmacht
The German armed forces, consisting of the army, navy, and air force. The term is often used to refer only to the army.

Zhukov, Georgi Konstantinovich
The most important Soviet general of World War II. Armies under his command defended Moscow and Leningrad, pushed the Germans from Soviet territory back into Poland and then Germany, and captured Berlin.

INDEX